CHRISTIAN PUBLISHING
HOUSE CLASSICS

HOW TO STUDY

Study the Bible for the Greatest Profit

DO YOUR BEST TO PRESENT YOURSELF TO GOD AS ONE
APPROVED, A WORKMAN WHO DOES NOT NEED TO BE ASHAMED,
RIGHTLY HANDLING THE WORD OF TRUTH. (2 TIM. 2:15)

R. A. TORREY AND EDWARD D. ANDREWS
UPDATED AND EXPANDED EDITION

HOW TO STUDY

Study the Bible for the Greatest Profit

Updated and Expanded

R. A. Torrey and Edward D. Andrews

Christian Publishing House

Cambridge, Ohio

Christian Publishing House

Professional Conservative Christian
Publishing of the Good News!

CPH Since 2005

Unless otherwise stated, Scripture quotations are from the Updated American Standard Version (UASV) Copyright © 2016 by Christian Publishing House

HOW TO STUDY: Study the Bible for the Greatest Profit [Updated and Expanded]

Authored by R. A. Torrey and Edward D. Andrews

ISBN-13: **978-1-945757-11-2**

ISBN-10: **1-945757-11-6**

Preface

This book has been written for two reasons: first, because it seemed to be needed; second, to save the authors time and labor. Messages are always coming in from all quarters asking how to study the Bible. It is impossible to refuse to answer a question so important as that, but it takes much time to answer it at all as it should be answered. This book is written as an answer to those who have asked the question, and to those who may wish to ask it. Nothing is more important for our own mental, moral and spiritual development or for our increase in usefulness than Bible study. However, not all Bible study is equally profitable. Some Bible study is absolutely profitless. "How to study the Bible so as to get the largest profit from it," is a question of immeasurable importance. The answer to the question, found in this book, has been for the most part given in addresses by the author, at the Chicago Bible Institute, before the summer gatherings of college students, at ministerial conferences and the like. Many, especially elders, pastors, and ministers, who have heard these addresses have asked that they might be put into a permanent shape. I have promised for two years to comply with this request but have never found time to do so until now.—**R. A. Torrey**

INTRODUCTION

There is a great and constantly growing interest in the study of the English Bible in these days. However, very much of the so-called study of the English Bible is unintelligent and not fitted to produce the most satisfactory results. The authors of this book already have a book entitled "HOW TO STUDY: Study the Bible for the Greatest Profit," but that book is intended for those who are willing to buy out the time to put into thorough Bible study.

The present book is intended, first of all, to impress men and women[1] with the Importance and Value of Bible Study; secondly, to show busy men and women how to get the most out of their Bible Study; thirdly, to set forth the fundamental principles of correct Biblical Interpretation.—**R. A. TORREY.**

The Bible is unlike any other book—it contains loving instruction from God. (1 Thess. 2:13) If we apply what the Bible teaches, we will benefit greatly. We will increase your love for God and will draw close to him, the Giver of "every good gift and every perfect present." (Jam. 1:17) We will come to know how to approach him in prayer. During times of trouble, we can experience God's help. If we harmonize our life with the standards set out in the Bible, God will give us everlasting life.—Romans 6:2

The Bible contains truths that give enlightenment. Those who gain Bible knowledge are liberated from the misconceptions that dominate the lives of millions. For example, knowing the truth about what happens after we die frees us from fear that the dead can harm us or that our dead relatives and friends are suffering. (Ezekiel 18:4) The Bible's teaching of the resurrection gives comfort to those who have lost loved ones in death. (John 11:25) Knowing the truth about wicked angels alerts us to the dangers of Spiritism and helps us to understand why there is so much trouble on earth.

The godly principles in the Bible show us how to live in a way that brings physical benefits. For example, being "moderate in habits" contributes to good health. (1 Tim. 3:2) By 'cleansing ourselves of every defilement of flesh and spirit,' we avoid damaging our health. (2 Cor. 7:1)

---

[1] In this book, the masculine pronoun will be used. However, this information is applicable to both boys and girls, teenage boys and girls, men and women. The Bible does the same. Although the uses the masculine gender, this in no way suggests a lack of concern for girls and women.

Applying God's counsel found in the Bible also promotes happiness in marriage and self-respect.—1 Corinthians 6:18.

Hundreds of millions of Christians around the world are lacking the basic knowledge of the Bible's teachings. Moreover, they are, therefore, unable to take advantage of the full happiness of partaking in the joint worship of God; they need to have their powers of discernment trained by constant practice to distinguish good from evil, they need to leave the elementary doctrine of Christ and move on to maturity. This book has been penned for that very purpose, to help all Christians to increase and expand their understanding of God's Word and to apply it more fully in their lives. Be aware that this book will ask questions that are designed, to help us investigate our inner-self.

God has chosen to convey an extremely important message to the human family, one that is a matter of life and death. In the Bible of 66 smaller books, we find God's **will and purpose** for us and what role we need to play to receive the gift of life. Sir Matthew Hale, lord chief justice of England, once said: "The Bible is the only source of all Christian truth;—the only rule for the Christian life;—the only book that unfolds to us the realities of eternity."

If we are to know God, it only stands to reason; we must know his Word—The Bible. Jesus Christ makes this all too clear for us when he said in prayer to his Father: "This is eternal life, that they may know you, the only true God, and the one whom you sent, Jesus Christ." (John 17:3) Therefore, here we see that "eternal life" is closely related to our knowing (having a personal relationship with) God and his Son, Jesus Christ. It is the apostle John who answers the why: "The world is passing away, and its lusts; but the **one who does the will of God remains forever**."—1 John 2:17.

To know "**the will of God**," we must recognize that the Bible is our only guide in this matter. Paul wrote, "For this reason also, since the day we heard of it, we have not ceased to pray for you and to ask that you may be filled with the accurate knowledge[2] of his will in all spiritual wisdom and understanding, so as to walk in a manner worthy of the Lord, fully pleasing to him bearing fruit in every good work and increasing in the accurate knowledge of God. (Col. 1:9-10) Is it possible to "**walk worthily**" of God without fully knowing his **will**? Is it possible to know his **will** without first understanding the Bible?

---

[2] *Epignosis* is a strengthened or intensified form of *gnosis* (*epi*, meaning "additional"), meaning, "true," "real," "full," "complete" or "accurate," depending upon the context. Paul and Peter alone use *epignosis*.

3

Psalm 119:165 Updated American Standard Version

[165] Abundant peace belongs to those loving your law,
And for them there is no stumbling block.

At times it must be difficult for us even to contemplate the idea of finding any measure of peace in the world we now know. However, it is our love for God's Word and the application of that Word, which will give us a righteous standing before our Creator (being justified in his eyes) and a measure of peace and happiness now. Thus, the incentive to know our Bible is far greater than one might have thought—approval in God's eyes as well as peace and happiness and the hope of a future eternal life.— **EDWARD D. ANDREWS**

Part I The Methods of the Most Profitable Bible Study

CHAPTER 1 Introductory Chapter to Methods of Bible Study

We shall consider the most profitable Methods of Bible Study before we consider the Fundamental Conditions of Profitable Bible study. Many readers of this book will probably be frightened, at first, at the seeming ambitiousness and difficulty of some of the methods of study suggested. However, they are not as difficult as they appear. Their practicability and fruitfulness have been tested in the classroom, and not with classes made up altogether of college graduates, but largely composed of persons of very moderate education; in some cases of almost no education. They do require time and hard work.[3] It must be remembered, however, that the Bible contains gold, and almost anyone is willing to dig for gold, especially if it is certain that he will find it. It is certain that one will find gold in the Bible if he digs. As one uses the methods here recommended, he will find his ability to do the work rapidly increasing by exercise, until he can soon do more in fifteen minutes than at the outset he could do in an hour.

The first method of study suggested will be found to be an exceptionally good mental training. When one has pursued this method of study for a time, his powers of observation will have been so accelerated, that he will see at a glance what, at first, he only saw upon much study and reflection. This method of study will also train the logical powers, cultivating habits of order, system and classification in one's intellectual processes. The power of clear, concise and strong expression will also be developed. No other book affords the opportunity for intellectual development by its study that is to be found in the Bible. No other book, and no other subject, will, so abundantly repay close and deep study. The Bible is much read, but comparatively little studied. It will probably be noticed by some that the first method of study suggested is practically the method now pursued in the study of any scientific field; first, careful analysis and ascertainment of facts; second, classification of facts. However, the facts of revelation far transcend those of science in excellence, suggestiveness, helpfulness and practical utility. They are also far more accessible. We cannot all be profound students of science; we can all be profound students of Scripture. Many an otherwise illiterate person has a marvelous grasp of Bible truth. It was acquired by study. There are persons who have studied little else, who have studied the Scriptures, by the hour, daily, and their consequent wisdom is the astonishment and sometimes the dismay of scholars and theologians.

---

[3] Buy out the time; use it to praise God (Ephesians 5:15-20)

CHAPTER 2 The Study of Individual Books

The first method of Bible study that we shall consider is the study of the Bible by individual books. This method of study is the most thorough, the most challenging, and the one that yields the largest and most permanent results. We take it up first because in the author's opinion it should occupy the greater portion of our time.

Select the Book to be Studied

This is a crucial matter. If one makes an unfortunate selection, he may become discouraged and give up a method of study that might have been most fruitful.

A Few Helpful Points

1. *For our first book-study, choose a short book.* The choice of a long book, to begin with, will lead to discouragement in anyone but a person of rare perseverance. It will be so much time before the final results, which far more than pay for all the labor expended, are reached, that the ordinary student will give it up.

2. *Choose a comparatively easy book.* Some books of the Bible present grave difficulties not to be found in other books. One will wish to meet and overcome these later, but it is not the work for a beginner to set for himself. When his powers have become trained because of use, then he can do this successfully and satisfactorily, but if he attempts it, as so many rashly do, at the outset, he will soon find himself floundering. The First Epistle of Peter is an exceedingly precious book, but a few of the most difficult passages in the Bible are in it. If it were not for these difficult passages, it would be a good book to recommend to the beginner, but given these difficulties, it is not wise to undertake to make it a subject of exhaustive study until later.

3. *Choose a book that is rich enough in its teaching to illustrate the advantages of this method of study and thus give a keen appetite for further studies of the same kind.* When one has gone through one reasonably large and full book by the method of study about to be described, he will have an eagerness for it that will make it sure, that he will somehow find time for further studies of the same sort.

A book that meets all the conditions stated is the First Epistle of Paul to the Thessalonians. It is quite short, it has no significant difficulties of interpretation, meaning or doctrine, and it is exceedingly rich in its teaching. It has the further advantage of being the first in point of time of the Pauline Epistles. The First Epistle of John is not in most respects a difficult book, and it is one of the richest books in the Bible.

Master the General Contents of the Book

The method of doing this is very simple. It consists of merely reading the book through without stopping and then reading it through again, and then again. It is suggested that we start with a least a dozen times in all, at a single sitting. To one who has never tried it, it does not seem as if that would amount to much, but any thoughtful man who has ever tried it will tell us quite differently. It is simply incredible how a book takes on new meaning and beauty upon this sort of an acquaintance. It begins to open up. New relations between different parts of the book start to disclose themselves. Fascinating lines of thought running through the book appear. The book is grasped as a whole, and the relation of the various parts to one another apprehended, and a foundation laid for an intelligent study of those parts in detail.

James M. Gray of Boston, a great lover of the Bible and prominent teacher of it, says that for many years of his ministry he had "an inadequate and unsatisfactory knowledge of the English Bible." "The first practical idea which he received in the study of the English Bible was from a layman. The brother possessed an unusual serenity and joy in his Christian experience, which he attributed to his reading of the Epistle to the Ephesians. Mr. Gray asked him how he had read it, and he said he had taken a pocket copy of the Epistle into the woods one Sunday afternoon, and read it through in a single sitting, repeating the process as many as a dozen times before stopping. When he arose he had gotten possession of the Epistle, or rather its wondrous truths had taken possession of him. This was the secret, simple as it was, for which Mr. Gray had been waiting and praying." From this time on Mr. Gray studied his Bible through in this way, and it became to him a new book.

Prepare an Introduction to the Book

Write down at the top of separate sheets of paper or cards[4] the following questions: **(1)** Who wrote this book? **(2)** To whom did he

---

[4] If one must, they can use a Word document; However, the old fashioned way of writing things out seems to implant it in our longterm memory.

write? **(3)** Where did he write it? **(4)** When did he write it? **(5)** What was the occasion of his writing? **(6)** What was the purpose for which he wrote? **(7)** What were the circumstances of the author when he wrote? **(8)** What were the circumstances of those to whom he wrote? **(9)** What glimpses does the book give into the life and character of the author? **(10)** What are the leading ideas of the book? **(11)** What is the central truth of the book? **(12)** What are the characteristics of the book? **(13)** Under what circumstances did the author write the book? **(14)** What was noteworthy about historical setting of Paul's day?

We will want to do all of this without having consulted a Bible commentary or a Bible handbook. Yes, we cannot answer all of these questions without those tools, but we can get several of them. Having prepared our sheets of paper with these questions in the head, lay them side by side on our study table before us, and go through the book slowly, and, as we come to an answer to any one of these questions, write it down on the appropriate sheet of paper. It may be necessary to go through the book several times to do the work thoroughly and satisfactorily, but we will be amply repaid. When we have finished our own work in this line, and not until then, it will be well, if possible, to compare our results with those reached by others. [5]

Once we have as many answers as we can, it is time to consult a couple of Bible commentaries and a Bible handbook. We are seeing if we were correct in our analysis, or if we agree with the findings of the commentary author. We are adding the answers to the questions we did not find to our list as well. The introduction one prepares for himself with the answers to these questions will be worth many times more to him than any that he can procure from others. The work itself is a rare education of the faculties of perception, comparison, and reasoning.

The answers to our questions will sometimes be found in some related book. For example, if we are studying one of the Pauline Epistles, the answer to our questions may be found in the Acts of the Apostles, or in the Epistle written to the place from which the one studied was written. Of course, not all the questions given will apply to every book in the Bible. Moreover, do not be frustrated because we cannot know the Bible background and historical setting of these books because that is found in a deeper study of secular sources, which our Bible background authors like John H. Walton, Victor H. Matthews and Mark W. Chavalas in their IVP Bible Background Commentary Volume Old Testament will

---

[5] After we have gotten the answers to these questions on our own, we can check them by using the Holman Illustrated Bible Dictionary; or by using the Holman Bible Handbook.

have spent years investigating. Then, there is Craig S. Keener in The IVP Bible Background Commentary New Testament.

After we have read First Thessalonians through a dozen times and have found as many answers to the above questions as we can, our next step is to have these background commentaries. We also need at least one good commentary volume to First Thessalonians and a Bible handbook. The Holman Old Testament and New Testament Commentary volumes are best for the beginner to intermediate student, as well as the Holman Bible Handbook. We also will want to invest in two other books: *The Big Book of Bible Difficulties: Clear and Concise Answers from Genesis to Revelation* (2008) by Norman L. Geisler and Thomas Howe; and we will want *New International Encyclopedia of Bible Difficulties* (Zondervan's Understand the Bible Reference Series) (2011) by Gleason L. Archer Jr. These are the premiere tools in our quest to study the Bible book by book.

There are literally thousands of Bible difficulties from the Book of Genesis to Revelation. Bible difficulties are not contradictions, errors, or mistakes. Rather, they are difficult readings because we are coming at them wrong in our interpretation, we are thousands of years removed from their historical setting, and we speak a modern day language while they were written in biblical Hebrew or Greek. These tools address thousands of these difficulties. These two books answer such questions as Did God approve of Rahab's lie? Why are many of the Old Testament quotes in the New Testament not literal? Does the Bible class abortion with murder? Where did Adam and Eve's sons get their wives? Does 1 Corinthians 7:10–16 authorize divorce for desertion? Now that we have answered as many of the above fourteen questions, we should do the following in our next study session.

- Take up the Holman Bible Handbook, and read the entire chapter on 1 Thessalonians. This is a very small section of pages but it will address most of our above questions, giving us some basic Bible background and historical information.

- Next, take up the Holman New Testament Commentary volume on 1 Thessalonians, and read that entire chapter. It will give us an introduction, a verse-by-verse explanation of the Bible book, an overview of the principles and applications from the book, a life application of the book, and a historical, geographical, and grammatical enrichment of the Bible book.

- After that, take up the IVP Bible Background Commentary New Testament and read the section on 1 Thessalonians. It will give us an understanding of the cultural background to the Bible book.

- Then, take up The Big Book of Bible Difficulties and read the section on 1 Thessalonians. It will answer the question of 1 Thessalonians 4:13, Did Paul teach the doctrine of soul-sleep? 1 Thessalonians 4:15, Did Paul teach that he would be alive when Christ returned? There only two difficulties that Geisler and Howe deal with here in 1 Thessalonians. It varies in each book. At times, like in Genesis we might have to deal with over forty questions. However a book that size, we would break it a part in sections.

- Finally, we check New International Encyclopedia of Bible Difficulties, and find for 1 Thessalonians, there are no Bible difficulties. One thing about Archer over Geisler and Howe, at times he will get very deep, spending many pages to answer just one Bible difficulty.

Why are we covering the Bible information to such a level? Are Christians are to be evangelists, apologist, proclaimers, and teachers of God's Word whether we are doing it locally or as a missionary. "If **evangelism** is planting seeds of the Gospel, then **pre-evangelism** is tilling the soil of people's minds and hearts to help them be more willing to listen to the truth (1 Corinthians 3: 6). Tilling the soil is important because sometimes the ground is too hard, making it more difficult to plant the seeds of the Gospel in people's hearts (1 Corinthians 2: 14)."[6] A **proclaimer** is one who makes known God's Word. **Christian apologetics** [Greek: apologia, "verbal defense, speech in defense"] is a field of Christian theology which endeavors to offer a reasonable and sensible basis for the Christian faith , defending the faith against objections. It is reasoning from the Scriptures, explaining and proving, as one instructs in sound doctrine, many times having to overturn false reasoning before he can plant the seeds of truth. It can also be earnestly contending for the faith and saving one from losing their faith, as they have begun to doubt. Moreover, it can involve rebuking those who contradict the truth. It is being prepared to make a defense to anyone who asks the Christian evangelist for a reason for the hope that is in him or her. (Jude 1.3, 21-23; 1 Pet 3.15; Acts 17:2-3; Titus 1:9) A Christian

---

[6] Geisler, David; Geisler, Norman. Conversational Evangelism (Kindle Locations 417-420). Harvest House Publishers. Kindle Edition.

teacher is one who conveys information or skill to their Bible students by word or by example. An effective and efficient teacher regularly provides logical, sound, rational his listeners to accept and remember what they have heard. The Christian uses his Bible knowledge in three primary ways.

- **These are tools** for the Christian to publicly presenting biblical truths: proclaiming, teaching, and making disciples.—Matthew 24:14; 28:19-20; Acts 1:8.

- **These are tools** to prepare every churchgoer in publicly defending the faith and biblical truths.—1 Peter 3:15.

- **These are tools** for Christians in publicly laying the foundation and background to defending the faith, reasoning from the Scriptures, explaining and proving, instructing in sound doctrine, overturning false reasoning, and saving those who have begun to doubt.—Jude 1:3, 22-23.

If one is not willing to give the time and labor necessary, this introductory work can be omitted, but only at a great sacrifice. Single passages in an epistle can never be correctly understood unless we know to whom they were written. Much false interpretation of the Bible arises from taking some direction manifestly intended for local application to be of universal authority. Therefore, also, oftentimes, false interpretation arises from applying to believers today what was intended for the apostles or even the first-century Christian congregation alone.

Noting the occasion of writing will clear up the meaning of a passage that would be otherwise obscure. Bearing in mind the circumstances of the author when he wrote, will frequently give new force to his words. When we remember that the jubilant epistle to the Philippians, with its oft-repeated "rejoice in the Lord" and its "In nothing be anxious; but in everything by prayer and supplication with thanksgiving let your requests be made known to God," (Phil. 4:6) was written by a prisoner awaiting possible sentence of death, how much more meaningful it becomes. Bearing in mind the main purpose of which a book was written, would help to interpret its incidental exhortations in their proper relations. In fact, the answers to all the questions will be valuable in all the work that follows, as well as valuable in themselves.

Divide the Book into its Proper Sections

This work is not indispensable, but still, it is valuable. Go through the book and notice the principal divisions in the thought, and mark these. Then go through these divisions and find if there are any natural subdivisions and mark these. In this work of dividing the epistle, the English Standard Version, which is not chopped up by a purely mechanical and irrational verse division, but divided according to a logical plan, will be of great help.

Having discovered the divisions of the book, proceed to give to each section an appropriate caption. Make this caption as precise a statement of the general contents of the section as possible. Make it also as concise and striking as possible, so that it will fix itself in the mind. As far as possible let the captions of the subdivisions connect themselves with the general caption of the division. Do not attempt to elaborate a division at first. The following division of first Peter will be given as a basic outline, an intermediate outline, and an advanced outline.

BASIC OUTLINE OF FIRST PETER

I. Greetings (1:1–2)

II. The Method and Nature of Salvation (1:3–12)

III. A Demand for Holiness (1:12–2:3)

IV. A Description of the People of God (2:4–10)

V. The Christian Witness in the World (2:11–3:12)

VI. Appeals and Promises to the Persecuted (3:13–4:19)

VII. Assurances for Faithful Servants (5:1–9)

VIII. Praises to God and Greetings to the Church (5:10–14)[7]

INTERMEDIATE OUTLINE OF FIRST PETER

I. Opening (1:1–2)

II. Called to Salvation as Exiles (1:3–2:10)

    1.   Praise for Salvation (1:3–12)

        (1) A Promised Inheritance (1:3–5)

        (2) Result: Joy in Suffering (1:6–9)

        (3) The Privilege of Revelation (1:10–12)

---

[7] David S. Dockery et al., *Holman Bible Handbook* (Nashville, TN: Holman Bible Publishers, 1992), 763.

V. Concluding Words (5:12-14)[8]

ADVANCED OUTLINE OF FIRST PETER

SECTION OUTLINE ONE (1 PETER 1)

Peter opens his first letter with an overview of some glorious facts concerning salvation.

I.   The Source of Our Salvation (1:1-2)

A.   **We have been chosen by the Father (1:1-2a).**

B.   **We have been made holy by the Spirit (1:2b).**

C.   **We are cleansed by the blood of the Son** (1:2c).

II.   The Guarantee of Our Salvation (1:3-5)

A.   **The proof (1:3): It is guaranteed by the resurrection of Christ.**

B.   **The permanence (1:4): It is kept in heaven for us.**

C.   **The power (1:5): God's mighty power assures us that we will safely arrive in heaven.**

III.   The Joy of Our Salvation (1:6-9)

A.   **The promise (1:6): This joy can be ours even in the midst of trials.**

B.   **The products (1:7-9): Our trials produce a twofold fruit.**

1.   *They increase our faith in God* (1:7).

2.   *They increase our love for God* (1:8-9).

IV.   The Old Testament Prophets and Our Salvation (1:10-12a)

A.   **What they did not understand (1:10-11): They could not fully comprehend all their prophecies concerning the future work of the Messiah.**

1.   *In regard to his grief* (1:10-11a)

---

[8] Thomas R. Schreiner, *1, 2 Peter, Jude*, vol. 37, The New American Commentary (Nashville: Broadman & Holman Publishers, 2003), 48.

15

2. *In regard to his glory* (1:11b)

B. **What they did understand (1:12a): They knew that their prophecies would not be fulfilled until after their deaths.**

V. The Angels and Our Salvation (1:12b): They long to know more about this wonderful subject.

VI. The Response to Our Salvation (1:13–17)

A. **In regard to ourselves (1:13): We are to be self-controlled.**

B. **In regard to our Savior (1:14–17)**

1. *We are to be holy before God* (1:14–16).

2. *We are to be respectful toward God* (1:17).

VII. The Cost of Our Salvation (1:18–21)

A. **The price (1:18–19)**

1. *Negative* (1:18): It was not purchased with silver or gold.

2. *Positive* (1:19): It was bought by the precious blood of Jesus.

B. **The planning (1:20–21): Christ was chosen before the foundation of the world to do this.**

VIII. The Vehicle of Our Salvation (1:22–25)

A. **The new birth (1:22–23a): One must experience regeneration to be saved.**

B. **The old book (1:23b–25): It is God's Word that brings this about.**

SECTION OUTLINE TWO (1 PETER 2)

Peter speaks of renouncing, relationships, respect, and a role model.

I. The Renouncing (2:1–3, 11)

A. **What we are to renounce (2:1, 11b): We are to rid ourselves of deceit, hypocrisy, envy, slander, and worldliness.**

B. **What we are to receive (2:2–3): We are to crave pure spiritual milk.**

II. The Relationships (2:4–12)

A.   **What Christians are (2:5, 9a, 10–11a)**

1.   *We are living stones (2:5a).*

2.   *We are royal priests (2:5b).*

3.   *We are a chosen people (2:9a, 10).*

4.   *We are strangers on earth (2:11a).*

B.   **What Christ is (2:4, 6–8, 9b, 12)**

1.   *He is the living foundation (2:4a).*

a.   He is a precious foundation for believers (2:4b, 7a).

b.   He is a stumbling block for unbelievers (2:8).

2.   *He is the cornerstone (2:6, 7b).*

3.   *He is the chosen one (2:4c).*

4.   *He is the judge (2:12).*

5.   *He is the light (2:9b).*

III.   The Respect (2:13–20): For the Lord's sake, we are to show respect (and submission) to the following parties:

A.   **Civil authorities (2:13–16)**

B.   **Employers (2:18–20)**

C.   **Everyone (2:17)**

IV.   The Role Model (2:21–25)

A.   **Who he is** (2:21–22): He is our sinless Savior, Jesus Christ.

B.   **What he did (2:23–24a): He died on Calvary's cross.**

C.   **Why he did it** (2:24b–25)

1.   *That his wounds might heal ours (2:24b)*

2.   *That we might turn to the Shepherd (2:25)*

SECTION OUTLINE THREE (1 PETER 3)

Peter talks about appropriate conduct for believers in light of what Christ has done for us.

I.   The Conduct of Believers (3:1–17)

A. **Responsibilities of wives (3:1–6)**

1. *Peter's exhortation (3:1–5)*

a. Concerning their behavior (3:1–2): Wives should depend upon their lives more than their lips in witnessing to unsaved husbands.

b. Concerning their beauty (3:3–5): Inner beauty is far more important than outer beauty.

2. *Peter's example* (3:6): He uses Sarah of the Old Testament as a role model.

B. **Responsibilities of husbands (3:7)**

1. *What they are to do* (3:7a): Husbands must be considerate of their wives and respect them.

2. *Why they are to do it* (3:7b): If they fail here, their prayers will not be answered.

C. **Responsibilities of all** (3:8–17)

1. *Live in loving harmony* (3:8).

2. *Reward both good and evil with good* (3:9–14).

3. *Worship Christ as Lord, and always be ready to explain your faith* (3:15).

4. *Be ready to defend your faith* (3:16–17).

II. The Christ of Believers (3:18–22): Peter describes a fourfold ministry accomplished by the Savior.

A. **His death** (3:18)

1. *The permanence* (3:18a): He died for our sins once and for all.

2. *The purpose* (3:18b): He died to reconcile sinners to God.

B. **His journey to the spirit world** (3:19–20)

1. *The transgression* (3:19): Jesus preached against the sins of these evil spirits.

2. *The time* (3:20): They committed their wickedness in the days of Noah.

C. **His resurrection (3:21)**

1. *The salvation* (3:21a): Jesus' resurrection guarantees our redemption.

2. *The symbol* (3:21b): Water baptism.

D. **His ascension and exaltation (3:22)**

SECTION OUTLINE FOUR (1 PETER 4)

Peter writes about suffering.

I. The Purpose of Suffering (4:1–11, 15, 17–18)

A. **To cleanse and purify the spiritual believer (4:1–11)**

1. *The triumph* (4:1–3): Suffering causes sin to lose its power.

2. *The testimony* (4:4–6): The unsaved friends of a new Christian marvel that he does not desire to share their wicked lifestyle as he once did.

3. *The tenderness* (4:7–9): Suffering should develop our love for other believers.

4. *The talents* (4:10–11): We should faithfully employ all of our God-given spiritual gifts.

B. **To chasten and punish the carnal believer (4:15, 17–18): God will judge his people.**

II. The Privilege of Suffering (4:12–14, 16)

A. **It is to be expected (4:12): All believers will be allowed to suffer.**

B. **It is to be esteemed (4:13–14, 16)**

1. *To suffer for Christ means to share his past grief* (4:13a, 14a, 16a).

2. *To suffer for Christ means to share his future glory* (4:13b, 14b, 16b).

III. The Patience in Suffering (4:19): We are to do two things in the hour of pain.

A. **We are to commit ourselves to God (4:19b).**

B. **We are to continue to do good** (4:19a).

SECTION OUTLINE FIVE (1 PETER 5)

Peter gives advice for elders and other church members and sends his final greetings.

I.   The Appeal by Peter (5:1–11)

A.   He writes to the elders in the church (5:1–4).

1.   *The role model* (5:1): Peter himself is an elder in his church.

2.   *The responsibilities* (5:2–3)

a.   Feed the flock of God (5:2).

b.   Lead the flock of God (5:3).

3.   *The reward* (5:4): To receive a crown of glory from the head Shepherd himself.

B.   He writes to the other members of the church (5:5–11).

1.   *Live as a servant* (5:5–7).

a.   Be in subjection to your superiors (5:5).

b.   Be in subjection to your Savior (5:6–7).

2.   *Live as a soldier* (5:8–9).

a.   Recognize the enemy (5:8).

b.   Resist the enemy (5:9).

3.   *Live as a sufferer* (5:10–11).

a.   The duration (5:10): It only lasts for a short time.

b.   The dynamics (5:11): It makes one strong, firm, and steadfast.

II.   The Assistance to Peter (5:12–14): Silas, whom Peter considers a faithful brother, has helped Peter write this letter.[9]

---

[9] H. L. Willmington, *The Outline Bible* (Wheaton, IL: Tyndale House Publishers, 1999), 1 Pe 1–5:14.

Take up Each Verse in Order and Study It

The first thing to be done in this verse by verse study of the book is to get the exact meaning of the verse. How is this to be done? There are three steps that lead into the meaning of a verse.

Exact Meaning of the Word(s) Used

There will be found two classes of words: those whose meaning is entirely apparent, those whose meaning is doubtful. It is entirely possible to find the precise meaning of these uncertain words. This is not done by consulting a dictionary like Webster or Oxford. (The following discussion is drawn from Mounce's Complete Expository Dictionary of Old & New Testament Words)[10]

Words have a "semantic range." "Semantic" refers to a word's meaning; "semantic range" refers to the range of possible meanings a word possesses. Think of all the ways we use the word "run."

I scored six runs today.

Could you run that by me again?

My computer runs faster than yours!

He runs off at the mouth.

I left the water running all night.

He ran to the store.

The car ran out of gas.

The clock ran down.

Duane ran for Senate.

Her nose ran.

I ran up the bill.

Languages are not codes. There is not a one-to-one correspondence between languages, and this is particularly true of vocabulary. Rarely if ever can we find one word in one language that corresponds exactly to another word in another language, especially in its semantic range. English

---

[10] William D. Mounce, Mounce's Complete Expository Dictionary of Old & New Testament Words (Grand Rapids, MI: Zondervan, 2006), xv–xxi.

has no single word that matches the range of meanings for en. The semantic range of a Greek and English word may overlap, but they are not identical.

So how do we translate the Bible when we do not have English words that correspond exactly to the Greek? We have to interpret, which is why all translation is interpretive; no Bible translation is neutral. For example, in 1 Tim. 6:13–14 Paul writes,

In the presence of God who gives life to all things, and of Christ Jesus who in his testimony before Pontius Pilate made the good confession, I charge you to keep the commandment unstained and free from reproach until the appearing of our Lord Jesus Christ. (RSV)

The Greek word behind "charge" is *parangello*, which means, "to command, insist, instruct, urge." Quite a wide range of meanings for which there is no single counterpart in English. The translator must decide whether Paul is "commanding" Timothy (who is a member of his inner circle, fully trusted, and probably his best friend) or "urging" him. This is an interpretive decision that must be made by the translator. The RSV chose "charge," the NLT "command," and the NKJV rightly (in my opinion) selected "urge."

However, let us say that we want to know what Paul means when he "charges" Timothy to keep the commandment unstained. It doesn't do any good to look up the English word "charge," because "charge" can't mean "urge" (and "urge" can't mean "charge"). If we really want to decide for ourselves what Paul is saying, we have to know the Greek word behind the English, learn its semantic range, and see the decision faced by the translators.

How do we do this? There are four steps. **(A)** Decide what English word to study.[11] **(B)** Identify the Greek word.[12] (C) Discover its semantic

---

[11] We are choosing those words that we are certain we do not know what they mean. On the other hand, we may be looking to do further research on the word that is the key term in the entire passage.

[12] We need to identify the Greek word that is behind our English word. If we were in the Old Testament, it would be the Hebrew word behind our English word. We can use an interlinear, which is a book with the Greek text, and underneath is the corresponding English term. Other options would be Bible software, a concordance, or a lexicon.

range.[13] (D) Look for something in the context that helps determine what the biblical author meant by this word in this particular verse.[14]

Look at the Context

The second step in ascertaining the meaning of a verse is to carefully notice the context (what goes before and what comes after). Many verses, if they stood alone, might be capable of several interpretations, but when what goes before and what comes after is considered, all the interpretations but one are seen to be impossible. Take for example,

John 14:18 Updated American Standard Version (UASV)

[18] "I will not leave you as orphans; I will come to you.

To what does Jesus refer when he says, "I come to you"? One commentator says that Jesus is referring to his reappearance to his disciples after his resurrection to comfort them. Another says that Jesus is referring to his second coming, as it is commonly called. Another says Jesus is referring to his coming through the Holy Spirit's work to manifest himself to his disciples and make his abode with them. Which does Jesus mean? When those with Ph.D.'s in biblical studies disagree, how is the churchgoer to decide? Yes, it would seem impossible for the churchgoer to ascertain the real meaning if someone with eight years of higher education in theology and biblical studies is unable to arrive at the correct understanding.[15] However, that is not really the case. If anyone will

---

[13] The semantic range is all the different meanings the Greek word can have, according to the New Testament usage, as well as the common usage of the time period.

[14] Simply read the section before our section, and the one thereafter, and determine which corresponding English word from the lexicon or concordance best fits the context of our word.

[15] **Ephesians 4:30** Updated American Standard Version (UASV)

[30] And do not **grieve the Holy Spirit** of God, by[15] whom you were sealed for the day of redemption.

How do we grieve the Holy Spirit? We do that by acting contrary to its leading through deception, human weaknesses, imperfections, setting our figurative heart on something other than the leading.

Ephesians 1:18 Updated American Standard Version (UASV)

[18] having the **eyes of your heart** enlightened, that you may know what is the hope to which he has called you, what are the riches of the glory of his inheritance in the holy ones,

"Eyes of your heart" is a Hebrew Scripture expression, meaning spiritual insight, to grasp the truth of God's Word. So we could pray for the guidance of God's Spirit, and at the

carefully note what Jesus is talking about in the verses immediately preceding (verses 15–17) and in the verses immediately following (verses 19–26), he will have no doubt as to what coming Jesus refers to in this passage. You can see this by trying it for yourself.

John 14:15-17 Updated American Standard Version (UASV

¹⁵ "If you love me, you will keep my commandments. ¹⁶ And I will ask the Father, and he will give you another Helper, that he may be with you forever; ¹⁷ the Spirit of truth, whom the world cannot receive, because it does not see him or know him, but you know him because he remains with you and will be in you.

John 14:[18]-26 Updated American Standard Version (UASV

¹⁸ "I will not leave you as orphans; I will come to you. ¹⁹ Yet a little while and the world will see me no more, but you will see me; because I live, you will live also. ²⁰ In that day you will know that I am in my Father, and you in me, and I in you. ²¹ The one who has my commandments and

---

same time, we can explain why there are so many different understandings (many wrong answers), some of which contradict each other. This is because of human imperfection that is diluting some of those interpreters, causing them to lose the Spirit's guidance.

A person sits down to study and prays earnestly for the guidance of Holy Spirit, that his mental disposition be in harmony with God's Word [or simply that his heart be in harmony with . . .], and sets out to study a chapter, an article, something biblical. In the process of that study, he allows himself to be moved, not by a mental disposition in harmony with the Spirit, but by human imperfection, by way of his wrong worldview, his biases, his preunderstanding.[15] A fundamental of grammatical-historical interpretation is that that we are to look for the simple meaning, the essential meaning, the obvious meaning. However, when this one comes to a text that does not say what he wants it to say, he rationalizes until he has the text in harmony with his preunderstanding. In other words, he reads his presuppositions into the text,[15] as opposed to discovering the meaning that was in the text. Even though his Christian conscience was tweaked at the correct meaning, he ignored it, as well as his mental disposition that could have been in harmony with the Spirit, to get the outcome he wanted.

In another example, it may be that the text does mean what he wants, but this is only because the translation he is using is full of theological bias, which is **violating** grammar and syntax, or maybe textual criticism rules and principles that arrive at the correct reading. Therefore, when this student takes a deeper look, he discovers that it could very well read another way, and likely should because of the context. He buries that evidence beneath his conscience, and never mentions it when this text comes up in a Bible discussion. In other words, he is grieving the Holy Spirit and loses it on this particular occasion.

Human imperfection, human weakness, theological bias, preunderstanding, and many other things could dilute the Spirit, or even grieve the Spirit. So that while one may be praying for assistance, he is not getting it or has lost it, because one, some, or all of these things he is doing has grieved the Spirit.

keeps them, that one is the one who loves me; and the one who loves me will be loved by my Father, and I will love him and will reveal myself to him." 22 Judas (not Iscariot) said to him, "Lord, what has happened that you will reveal yourself to us, and not to the world?" 23 Jesus answered and said to him, "If anyone loves me, he will keep my word; and my Father will love him, and we will come to him and make our abode with him. 24 The one who does not love me does not keep my words; and the word that you hear is not mine, but the Father's who sent me.

25 "These things I have spoken to you while remaining with you. 26 But the Helper,16 the Holy Spirit, whom the Father will send in my name, that one will teach you all things and bring to your remembrance all that I have said to you.

A very large proportion of the debated questions of Biblical interpretation can be settled by this very simple method of noticing what goes before and what comes after. Many of the sermons one hears, become very absurd when one takes the trouble to notice the setting of the preacher's text and how utterly foreign the thought of the sermon is to the thought of the text, regarded in the light of the context. Therefore, what did Jesus mean by the promise at the end of verse 18: **I will come to you**? In the context of these verses, it surely means the coming of the Holy Spirit at Pentecost. Nevertheless, some interpreters still go astray as to the context in the same area of verses right here. So, let us deal with that before going to the next point. Some authors say,

> Jesus **lives in us** [bold and underline mine] through the person and power of the Holy Spirit.

> The Holy Spirit **lives in us** [bold and underline mine]to identify his children. The doctrine of the indwelling Holy Spirit does not rest completely on this passage, but verse 17 is of great significance. Of this important verse Gromacki writes:

>> First, the spirit was dwelling "with" the apostles in the Gospel era. In Greek the words "with you" literally mean "beside you." In that sense, the Holy Spirit had a companion ministry to the apostles. He was beside them, but not inside them.

---

16 Or, *Advocate*. Or, *Comforter*. Gr., *ho ... parakletos*, masc.

Second, Christ predicted that the Spirit would be in them. After the death, resurrection, and ascension of Christ, the same Spirit who was beside them would be inside them. Christ also changed verbal tenses to show the difference in the two relationships of the Spirit to the apostles. The verb *menei* ("dwells") is in the present tense, whereas the verb *estai* ("will be") is in the future tense (Gromacki, p. 136).

Not only that, but **this indwelling** [bold and underline mine] will be endless—the new Counselor will **be with you forever.** No orphans in the family of God, no abandoned people with no place to turn. The Holy Spirit will be a constant presence of Jesus with all believers.[17]

EXCURSION: How Are We to Understand the Indwelling of the Holy Spirit?

> **1 Corinthians 3:16** Updated American Standard Version (UASV)
>
> [16] Do you not know that you are a temple of God and that the Spirit of God dwells in you?
>
> Before delving into the phrase, "indwelling of the Holy Spirit, let us consider another **mistaken view** of New Testament scholars Simon J. Kistemaker and William Hendriksen, who wrote,
>
> > The Spirit of God lives within you." The church is holy because God's Spirit dwells in the hearts and lives of the believers. In 6:19 Paul indicates that the Holy Spirit lives in the physical bodies of the believers. But now he tells the Corinthians that the presence of the Spirit is within them and they are the temple of God.
> >
> > The Corinthians should know that they have received the gift of God's Spirit. Paul had already called attention to the fact that they had not received the spirit of the world but the Spirit

---

[17] Kenneth O. Gangel, *John*, vol. 4, Holman New Testament Commentary (Nashville, TN: Broadman & Holman Publishers, 2000), 268.

of God (2:12). He teaches that Christians are controlled not by sinful human nature but by the Spirit of God, who is dwelling within them (Rom. 8:9).

The behavior—strife, jealousy, immorality, and permissiveness—of the Christians in Corinth was reprehensible. By their conduct the Corinthians were desecrating God's temple and, as Paul writes in another epistle, were grieving the Holy Spirit (Eph. 4:30; compare 1 Thess. 5:19).[18]

First, it must be told that I am almost amazed at how so many Bible scholars say nonsensical things, contradictory things when it comes to the Holy Spirit. Bible Commentators use many verses to say that the Holy Spirit literally,

(1) **dwells in** the individual Christian believers,

(2) having **control over** them,

(3) **enabling them** to live a righteous and faithful life,[19]

(4) with the believer **still being able to sin**, even to the point of grieving the Holy Spirit (Eph. 4:30).

Let us walk through this again, and please take it slow, ponder whether it makes sense, is reasonable, logical, even Scriptural. The Holy Spirit literally dwells in individual believers, controlling them so they can live a righteous and faithful life, yet they can still freely sin, even to the point of grieving the Holy Spirit. Does this mean that the Holy Spirit is not powerful enough to prevent their sinful nature from affecting them? The commentators say the Holy Spirit now controls the Christian, not their sinful nature. If that were true, it must mean the Holy Spirit is ineffectual and less powerful than their sinful nature of the Christian, because the Christian can still reject the Holy Spirit and sin to the point of grieving the Holy Spirit. If the Holy Spirit is controlling the individual Christian, how is it possible that he still possesses free will?

Let us return to the phrase of "indwelling of the Holy Spirit." Just how often do we find "indwelling" in the Bible? I have looked at over fifty English translations and found it once in the King James Version ad

---

[18] Simon J. Kistemaker and William Hendriksen, *Exposition of the First Epistle to the Corinthians*, vol. 18, New Testament Commentary (Grand Rapids: Baker Book House, 1953–2001), 117

[19] Millard J. Erickson, *Introducing Christian Doctrine* (Grand Rapids: Baker Book House, 1992), 265–270

two in an earlier version of the New American Standard Bible. One reference is to sin dwelling within us, and the other reference is to the Holy Spirit dwelling within us.

The Updated American Standard Version removed such usage. We may be asking ourselves since "indwelling" is almost nonexistent in the Scriptures, why the commentaries, Bible encyclopedias, Hebrew and Greek word dictionaries, Bible dictionaries, pastors and Christians using it to such an extent, especially in reference to the Holy Spirit? I say in reference to the Holy Spirit because some scholars refer to the indwelling of Christ and the Word of God.

Before addressing those questions, we must take a look at the Greek word behind 1 Corinthians 3:16 "the Spirit of God **dwells [οἰκέω]** in you." The transliteration of our Greek word is *oikeo*. It means "'to dwell' (from *oikos*, 'a house'), 'to inhabit as one's abode,' is derived from the Sanskrit, *vic*, 'a dwelling place' (the Eng. termination —'wick' is connected). It is used (a) of God as 'dwelling' in light, 1 Tim. 6:16; (b) of the 'indwelling' of the Spirit of God in the believer, Rom. 8:9, 11, or in a church, 1 Cor. 3:16; (c) of the 'indwelling' of sin, Rom. 7:20; (d) of the absence of any good thing in the flesh of the believer, Rom. 7:18; (e) of the 'dwelling' together of those who are married, 1 Cor. 7:12-13."[20]

Thus, for our text, means the Holy Spirit dwelling in true Christians. The TDNT tells us, "Jn.'s μένειν [*menein*] corresponds to Paul's οἰκεῖν [*oikein*], cf. Jn. 1:33: καταβαῖνον καὶ μένον ἐπ' αὐτόν [descending and remaining upon him]. The new possession of the Spirit is more than ecstatic."[21] What does TDNT mean? It means that John is using *meno* ("to remain," "to stay" or "to abide") in the same way that Paul is using *oikeo* ('to dwell').

When we are considering the Father or the Son alone, and even the Father and the Son together, we are able to have a straightforward conversation. However, when we get to the Holy Spirit we tend to get off into mysterious and mystical thinking. When we think of humans and the words *dwell* and *abide*, both have the sense of where we 'live or reside in a place.'

However, there is another sense of 'where we might stand on something,' 'our position on something.' Thus, in English dwell and abide

---

[20] W. E. Vine, Merrill F. Unger, and William White Jr., *Vine's Complete Expository Dictionary of Old and New Testament Words* (Nashville, TN: T. Nelson, 1996), 180.

[21] Gerhard Kittel, Geoffrey W. Bromiley, and Gerhard Friedrich, eds., *Theological Dictionary of the New Testament* (Grand Rapids, MI: Eerdmans, 1964–)

can be used interchangeably, similarly, just as Paul and John use *meno* "abide" or "remain" and *oikeo* "dwell" similarly. Let us look at the apostle John's use of meno,

1 John 4:16 Updated American Standard Version (UASV)

¹⁶ We have come to know and have believed the love which God has for us. God is love, and the one who remains [*meno*] in love remains in God, and God remains [*meno*] in him.

Here we notice that God is the embodiment of "love" and if we **abide in** or **remain in** that love, God then **abides in** or **remain in** us. We do not attach any mysterious or mystical sense to this verse, such as God literally being in us and us being in God. If we suggest that this verse, i.e., God being in us, means his taking control of our lives, does our being in God, also mean we control his life? We would think to suggest such a thing is unreasonable, illogical, nonsensical, and such. Commentator Max Anders in the *Holman New Testament Commentary* says, "This is the test of true Christianity in the letters of John. We must recognize the basic character of God, rooted in love. We must experience that love in our own relationship with God. Others must experience this God kind of love in their relationships with us." (Walls and Anders 1999, 211) Our love for God and man is the motivating factor in what we do and not do as Christians. John is saying that we need to remain in that love if we are to remain in God and God is to remain in us. We may be thinking, well, is it not true that God guides and direct us? Yes, however, this is because we have given our lives over to him.

1 John 2:14 Updated American Standard Version (UASV)

¹⁴ I have written to you, fathers, because you know Him who has been from the beginning. I have written to you, young men, because you are strong, and the word of God remains [*meno*] in you, and you have overcome the evil one.

Here we see that the Word of God abides or remains in us. Does this mean that the Word of God is literally within our body, controlling us? No, this means that our love for God and our love for his Word is a motivating factor in our walk with God. We are one with the Father as Jesus was and is one with the Father and he is one with us. Listen to the words of Paul in the book of Hebrews,

Hebrews 4:12 Updated American Standard Version (UASV)

¹² For the word of God is living and active and sharper than any two-edged sword, and piercing as far as the division of soul and spirit, of

both joints and marrow, and able to judge the thoughts and intentions of the heart.

Is the Word of God literally living, and an animate thing? No, it is an inanimate object. Is our Bible literally sharper than a two-edged sword? No, if we decide to stab someone with it, it would look quite silly. Is the Word of God literally able to pierce our joints and marrow? No, again, this would seem ridiculous. If we literally hold the Bible up to our head, is it able to discern our thinking, what we are intending to do? What did Paul mean? The Word of God does these things by our being able to evaluate ourselves by looking into the light of the Scriptures, which helps us to identify the intentions of our heart, i.e., inner person. When we meditatively read God's Word daily and ponder what the author meant, we are taking into our mind, God's thoughts and intentions. When we accept the Bible as the inspired, inerrant Word of God, take its counsel and apply its principles in our lives, it will have an impact on our conscience. The conscience is the moral code that God gave Adam and Eve, our mental power or ability that enables us to reason between what is good and what is bad. (Rom. 9:1) Then, the inner voice within us is not entirely ours, but is also God's Word, empowering us to avoid choosing the wrong path.

1 John 2:24 Updated American Standard Version (UASV)

²⁴ As for you, let that remain [*meno*] in you which you heard from the beginning. If what you heard from the beginning remains [*meno*] in you, you also will remain [*meno*] in the Son and in the Father.

Those who had followed Jesus **from the beginning** of his three and half ministry cleaved to what they had heard about the Father and the Son. Therefore, if the same truths are within our heart, inner person, our mental power or ability, we too can **abide** or **remain [*meno*]** in the Son and the Father. (John 17:3) It is as James said, if we draw close to God, through his Word the Bible, he will draw close to us. (Jam. 4:8) In other words, God becomes a part of us and we a part of him through the Word of God that is "living and active, sharper than any two-edged sword, piercing to the division of soul and of spirit, of joints and of marrow, and discerning the thoughts and intentions of the heart."

In John chapter 14, we see this two-way relationship more closely. Jesus said, "Believe me that I am in the Father and the Father is in me, or else believe on account of the works themselves." **(14:11)** He also said, "In that day you will know that I am in my Father, and you in me, and I in you." **(14:20)** We see that the Father and Son have a close relationship, a relationship that we are invited to join.

All through the above discussion of the Father and the Son, we likely had no problem following the line of thought. However, once we interject the Holy Spirit, it is as though our common sense is thrown out. Christians know that the Father and the Son reside in heaven. They also understand that when we speak of the Word of God, the Father and the Son dwelling in us, it is in reference to our being one with them, our unified relationship, by way of the Word of God. However, when we contemplate the Holy Spirit, it is as though our mental powers shut down, and we enter the realms of the mysterious and mysticism. However, we just understood John **14:11** and **14:20**, i.e., how Jesus is in the Father, the Father in Jesus, and their being in us. So, let us now consider the verses that lie between verse **11** and **20**.

Jesus Promises the Holy Spirit

John 14:16-17 English Standard Version (ESV)

¹⁶ And I will ask the Father, and he will give you another Helper, to be with you forever, ¹⁷ even the Spirit of truth, whom the world cannot receive, because it neither sees him nor knows him. You know him, for he dwells [*meno*] with you and will be in you.

John 14:16-17 Updated American Standard Version (UASV)

¹⁶ And I will ask the Father, and he will give you another Helper, that he may be with you forever; ¹⁷ the Spirit of truth, whom the world cannot receive, because it does not see him or know him, but you know him because he remains [*meno*] with you and will be in you.

Do we not find it a bit disconcerting that, all along when looking at John's writings as to the Son and the Father abiding [*meno*] in one another, in us, and us in them. In those places, the translation rendered *meno* as abiding, but now that the Holy Spirit is mentioned, they render *meno* as "dwell."

Do these verses call for us to; drive off the path of reason, into the realms of mysteriousness and mysticism talk? No, these verses are very similar to our 1 John 2:24 that we dealt with above, but will quote again, "Let what you heard from the beginning **abide [meno]** in you. If what you heard from the beginning **abides [meno]** in you, then you too will **abide [meno]** in the Son and in the Father." In 1 John 2:24, we are told that if the Word of God that we heard from the beginning of being a Christian, **abides [meno]** in us, we will **abide [meno]** in the Son and the

Father. In John 14:15-17, if we keep Jesus' commands, the Holy Spirit will **dwell**, actually **abide [meno]** in us. In all of this, the common denominator has been the spirit inspired, fully inerrant Word of God. It is what we are to take into our mind and heart, which will affect change in our person, and enable us to abide or remain in the Father and the Son, and they in us, as well as the Holy Spirit abiding or remaining in us.

The Holy Spirit, through the Spirit inspired, inerrant Word of God is the motivating factor for our taking off the old person and putting on the new person. (Eph. 4:20-24; Col. 3:8-9) It is also the tool used by God so that we can "be transformed by the renewal of your mind, so that you may approve what is the good and well-pleasing and perfect will of God." (Rom. 12:2; See 8:9) *The Theological Dictionary of the New Testament* compares this line of thinking with Paul's reference, at Romans 7:20, to the "sin that dwells within me."

The dwelling of sin in man denotes its dominion over him, its lasting connection with his flesh, and yet also a certain distinction from it. The sin which dwells in me (ἡ οἰκοῦσα ἐν ἐμοὶ ἁμαρτία) is no passing guest, but by its continuous presence becomes the master of the house (cf. Str.-B., III, 239).[22] Paul can speak in just the same way, however, of the lordship of the Spirit. The community knows (οὐκ οἴδατε, a reference to catechetical instruction, 1 C. 3:16) that the Spirit of God dwells in the new man (ἐν ὑμῖν οἰκεῖ, 1 C. 3:16; R. 8:9, 11). This "dwelling" is more than ecstatic rapture or impulsion by a superior power.[23]

How does the Holy Spirit control a Christian? Certainly, some mysterious or mystical feeling does not control him.

Paul told the Christians in Rome,

Romans 12:2 Updated American Standard Version (UASV)

² And do not be conformed to this world, but be transformed by the **renewing of your mind**, so that you may prove what the will of God is, that which is good and acceptable and perfect.

Just how do we **renew our mind**? This is done by taking in an accurate knowledge of Biblical truth, which enables us to meet God's

---

[22] Str.-B. H. L. Strack and P. Billerbeck, *Kommentar zum NT aus Talmud und Midrasch*, 1922 ff.

[23] Gerhard Kittel, Geoffrey W. Bromiley, and Gerhard Friedrich, eds., *Theological Dictionary of the New Testament* (Grand Rapids, MI: Eerdmans, 1964–), 135

current standards of righteousness. (Titus 1:1) This Bible knowledge, if applied, will allow us to move our mind in a different direction, by filling the void, after having removed our former sinful practices, with the principles of God's Word, principles that guide our actions, especially ones that guide moral behavior.

Psalm 119:105 Updated American Standard Version (UASV)

[105] Your word is a lamp to my feet
and a light to my path.

The Biblical truths that lay in between Genesis 1:1 and Revelation 22:21 will transform our way of thinking, which will in return affect our mood and actions and our inner person. It will be as the apostle Paul said to the Ephesians. We need to "to put off your old self, which belongs to your former manner of life and is corrupt through deceitful desires, and to be renewed in the spirit of your minds, and to put on the new self, created after the likeness of God in true righteousness and holiness ..." (Eph. 4:22-24) This force that contributes to our acting or behaving in a certain way, for our best interest is internal.

Paul told the Christians in Colossae,

Colossians 3:9-11 Updated American Standard Version (UASV)

[9] Do not lie to one another, seeing that you have put off the old man[24] with its practices [10] and have put on the new man[25] who is being **renewed through accurate knowledge**[26] according to the image of the one who created him, [11] where there is not Greek and Jew, circumcised and uncircumcised, barbarian, Scythian, slave, free; but Christ is all, and in all.

Science has indeed taken us a long way in our understanding of how the mind works, but it is only a grain of sand on the beach of sand in comparison to what we do not know. We have enough in these basics to understand some fundamental processes. When we open our eyes to the light of a new morning, it is altered into and electrical charge by the time it arrives at the gray matter of our brain's cerebral cortex. As the sound of the morning birds reaches our gray matter, it comes as electrical impulses. The rest of our senses (smell, taste, and touch) arrive as electrical currents

---

[24] Or *old person*

[25] Or *new person*

[26] See Romans 3:20 ftn.

in the brain's cortex as well. The white matter of our brain lies within the cortex of gray matter, used as a tool to send electrical messages to other cells in other parts of the gray matter. Thus, when anyone of our five senses detects danger, at the speed of light, a message is sent to the motor section, to prepare us for the needed action of either fight or flight.

Here lies the key to altering our way of thinking. Every single thought, whether it is conscious or subconscious makes an electrical path through the white matter of our brain, with a record of the thought and event. This holds true with our actions as well. If it is a repeated way of thinking or acting, it has no need to form a new path; it only digs a deeper, ingrained, established path.

This would explain how a factory worker who has been on the job for some time, gives little thought as he performs his repetitive functions each day; it becomes unthinking, automatic, mechanical. These repeated actions become habitual. There is yet another facet to be considered; the habits, repeated thoughts and actions become simple and effortless to repeat. Any new thoughts and actions are harder to perform, as there needs to be new pathways opened up.

The human baby starts with a blank slate, with a minimal amount of stable paths built in to survive those first few crucial years. As the boy grows into childhood, there is a flood of pathways established, more than all of the internet connections worldwide.

Our five senses are continuously adding to the maze. Ps. 139:14: "I will give thanks to you, for I am fearfully and wonderfully made. . . ." (NASB) So, it could never be overstated as to the importance of the foundational thinking and behavior that should be established in our children from infancy forward.

Paul told the Christians in Ephesus,

Ephesians 4:20-24 Updated American Standard Version (UASV)

20 But you did not learn Christ in this way, **21** if indeed you have heard him and have been taught in him, just as truth is in Jesus, **22** that you take off, according to your former way of life, the old man, who is being destroyed according to deceitful desires, **23** and to be **renewed in the spirit of your minds**, **24** and put on the new man,[27] the one created according to the likeness of God in righteousness and loyalty

---

[27] An interpretive translation would have, "put on the new person," because it does mean male or female.

of the truth.

How are we to understand being **renewed in the spirit of our minds**? Christian living is carried out through the study and application of God's Word, in which, our spirit (mental disposition), is in harmony with God's Spirit. Our day-to-day decisions are made with a biblical mind, a biblically guided conscience, and a heart that is motivated by love of God and neighbor. Because we have,

- Received the Word of God,

- treasured up the Word of God,

- have been attentive to the Word of God,

- inclining our heart to understanding the Word of God,

- calling out for insight into the Word of God,

- raising our voice for understanding of the Word of God,

- sought the Word of God like silver,

- have searched for the Word of God like gold,

- we have come to understand the fear of God, and have

- found the very knowledge of God, which now

- leads and directs us daily in our Christian walk.

Proverbs 23:7 New King James Version (NKJV)

⁷ For as he thinks in his heart, so is he. "Eat and drink!" he says to you, But his heart is not with you. [Our thinking affects our emotions, which in turn affects our behavior.]

Irrational thinking produces irrational feelings, which will produce wrong moods, leading to wrong behavior. It may be difficult for each of us to wrap our mind around it, but we are very good at telling ourselves outright lies and half-truths, repeatedly throughout each day. In fact, some of us are so good at it that it has become our reality and leads to mental distress and bad behaviors.

When we couple our leaning toward wrongdoing with the fact that Satan the devil, who is "the god of this world," (2 Co 4:4) has worked to entice these leanings, the desires of the fallen flesh; we are even further removed from our relationship with our loving heavenly Father. During these 'last days, grievous times' has fallen on us as Satan is working all the more to prevent God's once perfect creation to achieve a righteous standing with God and entertaining the hope of eternal life. – 2 Timothy 3:1-5.

When we enter the pathway of walking with our God, we will certainly come across resistance from three different areas (Our sinful nature, Satan and demons, and the world that caters to our flesh). **Our greatest obstacle** is **ourselves**, because we have inherited imperfection from our first parents Adam and Eve. The Scriptures make it quite clear that we are **mentally bent toward bad**, not good. (Gen 6:5; 8:21, AT) In other words, our natural desire is toward wrong. Prior to sinning, Adam and Eve were perfect, and they had the natural desire of doing good, and to go against that was to go against the grain of their inner person. Scripture also tells us of our inner person, our heart.

Jeremiah 17:9 Updated American Standard Version (UASV)

9 The **heart is more deceitful** than all else,
and desperately sick;
who can understand it?

Jeremiah's words should serve as a wake-up call, if we are to be pleasing in the eyes of our heavenly Father, we must focus on our inner person. Maybe we have been a Christian for many years; maybe we have a deep knowledge of Scripture, perhaps we feel that we are spiritually strong, and nothing will stumble us. Nevertheless, our heart can be enticed by secret desires, where he fails to dismiss them; he eventually commits a serious sin.

Our conscious thinking (aware) and subconscious thinking (present in our mind without our being aware of it) originates in the mind. For good, or for bad, our mind follows certain rules of action, which if entertained one will move even further in that direction until they are eventually consumed for good or for bad. In our imperfect state, our bent thinking will lean toward wrong, especially with Satan using his world, with so many forms of entertainment that simply feeds the flesh.

James 1:14-15 Updated American Standard Version (UASV)

14 But each one is tempted when he is carried away and enticed by his own desire.[28] **15** Then the desire when it has conceived gives birth to sin, and sin when it is fully grown brings forth death.

1 John 2:16 Updated American Standard Version (UASV)

16 For all that is in the world, the lust of the flesh and the lust of the

---

[28] Or "own *lust*"

eyes and the boastful pride of life, is not from the Father, but is from the world.

Matthew 5:28 Updated American Standard Version (UASV)

28 but I say to you that everyone who looks at a woman with lust[29] for her has already committed adultery with her in his heart.

1 Peter 1:14 Updated American Standard Version (UASV)

14 As children of obedience,[30] do not be conformed according to the desires you formerly had in your ignorance,

If we do not want to be affected by the world of humankind around us, which is alienated from God, we must again consider the words of the Apostle Paul's. He writes (Rom 12:2) "Do not be conformed to this world, but be transformed by the renewal of your mind that by testing you may discern what is the will of God, what is good and acceptable and perfect." Just how do we do that? This is done by taking in an accurate knowledge of Biblical truth, which enables us to meet God's current standards of righteousness. (Titus 1:1) This Bible knowledge, if applied, will enable us to move our mind in a different direction, by filling the void with the principles of God's Word, principles that guide our actions, especially ones that guide moral behavior.

Psalm 119:105 Updated American Standard Version (UASV)

105 Your word is a lamp to my feet
and a light to my path.

We have said this before but it bears repeating. The Biblical truths that lay in between Genesis 1:1 and Revelation 22:21 will transform our way of thinking, which will in return affect our mood and actions and our inner person. It will be as the apostle Paul set it out to the Ephesians. We need to "to put off your old self, which belongs to your former manner of life and is corrupt through deceitful desires, and to be renewed in the spirit of your minds, and to put on the new self, created after the likeness of God in true righteousness and holiness ..." (Eph. 4:22-24) This force that contributes to our acting or behaving in a certain way, for our best interest is internal.

---

29 ἐπιθυμία [Epithumia] to strongly desire to have what belongs to someone else and/or to engage in an activity which is morally wrong—'to covet, to lust, evil desires, lust, desire.'– GELNTBSD

30 I.e., *obedient children*

Bringing This Transformation About

The mind is the mental ability that we use in a conscious way to garner information and to consider ideas and come to conclusions. Therefore, if we perceive our realities based on the information, which surrounds us, generally speaking, most are inundated in a world that reeks of Satan's influence. This means that our perception, our attitude, thoughts, speech, and conduct are in opposition to God and his Word. Most are in true ignorance to the changing power of God's Word. The apostle Paul helps us to appreciate the depths of those who reflect this world's disposition. He writes,

Ephesians 4:17-19 Updated American Standard Version (UASV)

[17] This, therefore, I say and bear witness to in the Lord, that you no longer walk as the Gentiles [unbelievers] also walk, in the futility of their mind [emptiness, idleness, slugishness, vanity, foolishness, purposelessness], [18] being darkened in their understanding [mind being the center of human perception], alienated from the life of God, because of the ignorance that is in them, because of the hardness of their heart [hardening as if by calluses, unfeeling]; [19] who being past feeling gave themselves up to shameless conduct,[31] for the practice of every uncleanness with greediness.

Hebrews 4:12 Updated American Standard Version (UASV)

[12] For the word of God is living and active and sharper than any two-edged sword, and piercing as far as the division of soul and spirit, of both joints and marrow, and able to judge the thoughts and intentions of the heart.

By taking in this knowledge of God's Word, we will be altering our way of thinking, which will affect our emotions and behavior, as well as our lives now and for eternity. This Word will influence our minds, making corrections in the way we think. If we are to have the Holy Spirit controlling our lives, we must 'renew our mind' (Rom. 12:2) "which is being renewed in knowledge" (Col. 3:10) of God and his will and purposes. (Matt 7:21-23; See Pro 2:1-6) All of this boils down to each individual Christian digging into the Scriptures in a meditative way, so he can 'discover the knowledge of God, receiving wisdom; from God's

---

[31] Or "loose conduct," "sensuality," "licentiousness" "promiscuity" Greek, *aselgeia*. This phrase refers to acts of conduct that are serious sins. It reveals a shameless condescending arrogance; i.e., disregard or even disdain for authority, laws, and standards.

mouth, as well as knowledge and understanding.' (Pro. 2:5-6) As he acquires the mind that is inundated with the Word of God, he must also,

James 1:22-25 Updated American Standard Version (UASV)

²² But be doers of the word, and not hearers only, deceiving yourselves. ²³ For if anyone is a hearer of the word and not a doer, he is like a man who looks intently at his natural face³² in a mirror.

²⁴ for he looks at himself and goes away, and immediately forgets what sort of man he was. ²⁵ But he that looks into the perfect law, the law of liberty, and abides by it, being no hearer who forgets but a doer of a work, he will be blessed in his doing.

Now that we have laid to rest the indwelling of the Holy Spirit and seen how context, even context that comes from other books by the same author, as well as books by other authors as well, can help us get at what the author meant by the words that he used. The one thing to keep in mind is this; it is not always this complex, or this much involved in an investigation to discover what was really meant. Nevertheless, if we want to get at the truth, from time to time, we will have to buy out the time in a deeper study.

Examine Parallel Passages

The third step in ascertaining the correct and precise meaning of a verse is the examination of parallel passages, i. e., passages that treat the same subject—passages, for example, that give another account of the same address or event, or passages that are evidently intended as a commentary on the passage in hand. Very often, after having carefully studied the words used and the context, we will still be in doubt as to which of two or three possible interpretations of a verse is the one intended by the writer or speaker. In such a case, there is always somewhere else in the Bible, a passage, which will settle this question.

Take, for example, John. 14:3, "And if I go and prepare a place for you, I will **come again** and receive you to myself, so that where I am, you may be also." A careful consideration of the words used in their relation to one another, will go far in determining the meaning of this passage, but still, we find among commentators whose opinion ought to have some weight, these four interpretations:

---

³² Lit *the face of his birth*

(1) The **coming** here referred to is Christ's coming at death to receive the believer unto himself, as in the case of Stephen.

(2) The **coming** again at the resurrection.

(3) The **coming** again through the Holy Spirit.

(4) The **coming** again of Christ when He returns personally and gloriously at the end of the age.

Which of these four interpretations is the correct one? What has already been said about verse 18 might seem to settle the question, but it does not; for it is not at all clear that the coming in verse 3 is the same as in verse 18, for what is said in connection with the two comings is altogether different. In the one case, it is a coming of Christ to "take you to myself, that where I am you may be also;" in the other case it is a coming of Christ to manifest himself unto us and make his abode with us. However, fortunately there is a verse, which settles the question, an inspired commentary on the Words of Jesus. This is found in 1 Thessalonians 4:16-17. This will be seen clearly if we arrange the two passages in parallel columns.

John 14:3	1 Thessalonians 4:16
Updated American Standard Version (UASV) ³ And if I go and prepare a place for you, I will come again and receive you to myself, so that where I am, you may be also.	Updated American Standard Version (UASV) ¹⁶ For the Lord himself will descend from heaven with a cry of command, with the voice of an archangel, and with the sound of the trumpet of God, and the dead in Christ will rise first. ¹⁷ Then we who are alive, who remain will be caught up together with them in the clouds to meet the Lord in the air, and so we shall always be with the Lord.

The two passages manifestly match exactly in the three facts stated, and beyond a doubt refer to the same event. However, if anyone will look at all closely at 1 Thess. 4:16-17, there can be no doubt as to what coming of our Lord is referred to there. Most Bibles (especially study Bibles) will be of great assistance in finding parallel passages. These are the three steps that lead us into the meaning of a verse. They require work, but it is work that anyone can do, and when the meaning of a verse is thus settled we arrive at conclusions that are correct and fixed. After taking these steps, it is well to consult commentaries, and see how our conclusions agree with those of others.[33]

Before we proceed to the next thing to be done with a verse after its meaning has been determined, let it be said, that God intended to convey some definite truth in each verse of scripture, and any one of from two to a dozen interpretations of a verse is not as good as another. With every verse of scripture we should ask, not what can this be made to teach? However, what was this intended to teach? In addition, we should not rest satisfied until we have settled that. Of course, it is admitted a verse may have what the author meant (one meaning for each verse) and what implications we can apply in our lives today, but the patterns must match.

IMPLICATION Excursion

The author had an intended meaning when he wrote his text, and that meaning is for all time, as long as that text is in existence. However, we need to understand that there are **implications** that belong to those words as well. What is an implication? Implications are principles that a reader can draw from the text, to apply it in his or her life. They fall within the pattern of the author's intended meaning. Let us look at a few examples from Jesus in his Sermon on the Mount. First, Paul's letter to the Galatians will set the stage.

Galatians 5:19-21 Updated American Standard Version (UASV)

[19] Now **the works of the flesh are** evident, which are: sexual immorality, impurity, sensuality, [20] idolatry, sorcery, enmity, strife, jealousy, fits of anger, rivalries, dissensions, divisions, [21] envy, drunkenness, orgies, and **things like these**. I warn you, as I warned you before, that those who do such things will not inherit the kingdom of God.

Look again at the very last expression in that list, "**things like these**." The Bible is not going to provide us with exhaustive lists of everything that we should understand as an example, a lesson, or **implication**, as this would mean a Bible with tens of thousands of additional pages. How long of a list would it be, if Paul had given the reader an exhaustive list of the works of the flesh? Do we believe that any Galatians who had this letter written to them, thought, 'Wow, that was close; he didn't list the one I do.' By closing the list with the words "things

---

[33] Holman New Testament Commentary of the individual book we are working on.

like these," Paul was making his readers aware that they should perceive or discern other things fit the pattern of "these things."

Matthew 5:21-22 Updated American Standard Version (UASV)

21 "You have heard that it was said to the ancients, 'You shall not murder; and whoever murders will be liable to judgment.' 22 But I say to you that everyone who is angry with his brother will be liable to judgment; whoever says to his brother, 'You fool,'34 will be brought before the Sanhedrin;35 and whoever says, 'You fool!' will be liable to the fire of Gehenna.36

We should take note in each of these that Jesus is giving an **implication** of what sin leads to, that is an act of heinous sinning. Furious anger is a sin, and in some cases does lead to murder. Let us put it another way; all murder is the result of furious anger.

Matthew 5:27-28 Updated American Standard Version (UASV)

27 "You have heard that it was said, 'You shall not commit adultery';37 28 but I say to you that everyone who looks at a woman with lust38 for her has already committed adultery with her in his heart.

We will notice the phrase "lustful intent," keying in on the word "intent." This is not a man walking along who catches sight of a beautiful woman and has an indecent thought, which he then dismisses. It is not even a man in the same situation that has an improper thought, who goes on to entertain and cultivate that thought. No, this is a man that is staring, gazing at a woman with the intent of lusting, and is looking at the woman, with the intention of peaking her interest and desire, to get her to lust.

---

34 Gr *Raca to*, an Aramaic term of contempt

35 The Jewish supreme court, which held life and death over the people in ancient Jerusalem before 70 C.E.

36 *geenna* 12x pr. *the valley of Hinnom*, south of Jerusalem, once celebrated for the horrid worship of Moloch, and afterwards polluted with every species of filth, as well as the carcasses of animals, and dead bodies of malefactors; to consume which, in order to avert the pestilence which such a mass of corruption would occasion, constant fires were kept burning—MCEDONTW

37 Ex. 20:14; Deut. 5:17

38 ἐπιθυμία [Epithumia] to strongly desire to have what belongs to someone else and/or to engage in an activity which is morally wrong—'to covet, to lust, evil desires, lust, desire.'— GELNTBSD

Therefore, the author determines the meaning of a text **by the words he chose** to use, as should have been understood by his intended audience. Within the *one intended meaning* are **implications** that must conform to the pattern of the author's intended meaning. All readers are to discover the intended meaning, as well as any **implications**. **Implications** are principles that a reader can draw from the text, to apply it in his or her life. They fall within the pattern of the author's intended meaning. The Apostle Paul's command at Ephesians 5:18 is a good example. There Paul writes, "do not get drunk with wine, for that is debauchery." Are we to believe that Paul would be fine if the Ephesian congregation members were to get drunk with beer instead? No. What about whiskey, since it was not invented until centuries later? No, the Christian would avoid this as an instrument for getting drunk as well. The principle of what Paul meant was that a Christian does not take in a substance that can affect his or her abilities to make good decisions, in excess. Therefore, this principle would apply to whiskey, wine, beer, bourbon, marijuana, and other things like these of which Paul would not be aware.

Please see the chart below the pattern of meaning, **implications** that fit, and the **implications** that do not.

Pattern of Meaning	Implications	No Pattern
Cold	Chilly	Warm
Sad	Unhappy	Joyful
Beer	Wine	Coffee
Nap	Sleep	Walk
Jog	Run	Fishing
Hop	Jump	Obstacle
Big	Large	Craving

Analyze the Verse after Meaning is Determined

This is most interesting and profitable work. It is also a rare education of the various faculties of the intellect. The way to do it is this: Look steadfastly at the verse and ask, What does this verse mean? Then, what implications are there within this verse that can be applicable to us today? This has these implications, 1st _____; 2nd _____; 3rd ____, etc. At the first glance very likely, you will see but one or two things the verse implies for us, but, as we look repeatedly, the implications will begin to multiply, we will wonder how one verse could imply so much, and we will have an ever-growing sense of the divine authorship of the Book.

Each verse has one absolute meaning, which is what the author meant to convey by the words he used. However, again, each verse may have multiple implications, which the author may have not even been aware of, but falls within the pattern of meaning.

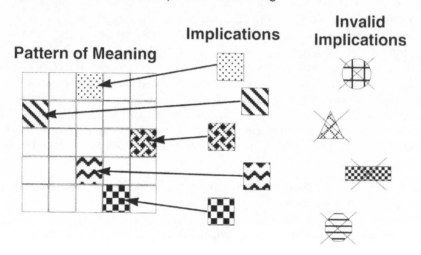

Our **first step** is *observation*, to get as close to the original text as possible. If we do not read Hebrew or Greek; then, two or three literal translations are preferred (ASV, NASB, and UASV). The **second step** is *interpretation*, What did the author mean by the words that he used, as should have been understood by his original audience. A part of this second step would be what the differences between the biblical audience and us are? As mentioned above, the Christian today is separated from the biblical audience by differences in culture, language, situation, time, and often covenant. The **third step** is the *implications* or *principles* in this text? This is perhaps the most challenging step. In it, we are looking for the implications or principles that are reflected in the meaning of the text we identified in the second step. Part of this third step is making sure that we stay within the pattern of the original meaning when we determine any implications for us. The **fourth step** is the *application*. How should individual Christians today live out the implications and principles?

Galatians 1:6-9 Updated American Standard Version (UASV)

⁶ I am amazed that you are so quickly deserting him who called you in the grace of Christ and are turning to a different gospel; ⁷ not that there

is another, but there are some who trouble you and want to distort the gospel of Christ. [8] But even if we or an angel from heaven should proclaim to you a gospel contrary to[39] the one we preached to you, let him be accursed![40] [9] As we said before, and now I say again, if anyone is proclaiming a gospel to you contrary to[41] what you have received, let him be accursed![42]

1:6. Paul was astonished the Galatians were so quickly deserting (like a military desertion) from the gospel of grace. This meant they were deserting God, turning their backs on him. It was almost beyond Paul's comprehension that they, having once been delivered from the bondage of law, would go back into this religious prison. Paul calls the Judaizer's blend of law and grace a different gospel, thus declaring that mixing law with the gospel is a distortion of truth. Even today, this Galatian error is repeated when people say, "This is what you have to do to be saved; join our church, obey our rules, submit to our baptism, practice our liturgy, worship the way we do, work hard, prove your worth, and earn God's love. In the end, if you are good enough, God will accept you." A works-based gospel is different from the message of grace.

1:7. In fact, a works-based, human-effort driven gospel is no gospel at all. How is a demand for impossible human achievement good news? Anyone who presents a way of salvation that depends in any way on works, rather than God, has contaminated the gospel message. They confuse honest, sincere believers. They have no gospel, no good news.

1:8. A hypothetical case shows the seriousness of legalism's perversion of grace. Through hyperbole (a deliberate exaggeration for emphasis), Paul declares that anyone who preaches a mixture of grace and law is worthy of eternal condemnation. A teacher who requires others to obey the law as a requirement for salvation is leading others to a Christless eternity. Paul uses strong language because he is dealing with a life-or-death situation. You must choose: the gospel of grace Paul

---

[39] Or *other than*

[40] Gr *anathema*

[41] Or *other than*

[42] Gr *anathema*

preached or the gospel of works the perverters preached.

1:9. Ditto! Paul repeated his curse for effect. Any person who preaches a gospel that requires more than God's grace for salvation deserves to suffer in hell for eternity.[43]

Excursion What James Said about Works Versus What Paul Said

James 2:21-26 Updated American Standard Version (UASV)

[21] Was not Abraham our father justified by works when he offered up Isaac his son on the altar? [22] You see that faith was working together with his works, and by the works the faith was perfected;[44] [23] and the Scripture was fulfilled that says, "Abraham believed God, and it was counted to him as righteousness,"[45] and he was called a friend of God. [24] You see that a man is justified by works and not by faith alone. [25] And in the same way was not also Rahab the prostitute justified by works when she received the messengers and sent them out by another way? [26] For as the body apart from the spirit[46] is dead, so also faith apart from works is dead.

Was not Abraham our father (2:21a)

James here now does something very significant to argue his point about faith and works by stating **was not Abraham, our father**. James makes his argument from the Old Testament scriptures using Abraham, who the Jews considered the father of their nation and perhaps the most respected man in all Old Testament history. The Jews took pride in their ancestry and could trace their lineage back to Abraham as the Father of the Jewish nation, which is why James says "Abraham, our father." The Jewish nation of Israel was God's chosen people, and that nation stemmed from the seed of Abraham, which God promised would happen.

The Jews highly esteemed their ethnicity and the father of their

---

[43] Max Anders, vol. 8, Galatians-Colossians, Holman New Testament Commentary; Holman Reference (Nashville, TN: Broadman & Holman Publishers, 1999), 6-7.

[44] Or *completed*

[45] Quoted from Gen. 15:6

[46] Or *breath*

nation because they were God's chosen that came through the lineage of Abraham. For this reason, the Jews looked at Abraham as the most prominent figure in their history, since he was the father of their nation. It is because of this that James would select Abraham to make his point that faith and works must exist together for it to be true saving faith. James purposely used one of the most significant men in Jewish history to make his point. This way, the Jewish audience he was writing to would be more apt to listen and take heed to what he was saying.

justified by works when he offered up Isaac his son on the altar? (2:21b)

Here James says that Abraham our father was **justified by works**. However, Paul wrote, "For by works of the law no human being will be justified." (Rom 3:20) How is it that these two were not contradicting one another? In Romans 4:2-3 Paul writes, "For if Abraham was justified by works, he has something to boast about, but not before God. For what does the Scripture say? 'Abraham believed God, and it was counted to him as righteousness.'" Paul is here quoting that same exact verse from Genesis 15:6 that James refers to in verse 23 of chapter 2. This verse that both are using was about Abraham's faith some 35 years before he ever attempted to offer up his son Isaac. This is the same event that James is referring to here in verse 21 of chapter 22. Thus, how are these two inspired New Testament authors in harmony?

If we look at the context of Genesis 15:1-6, we find that Abraham was declared righteous because of his trust in God's promise to make his offspring number like the stars of the heaven, even though Sarah was decades past being able to have a child. Therefore, how is it that James can say that Abraham was justified by works? Abraham's actions confirmed what God already knew was true of him. By Abraham's action, he proved, confirmed, demonstrated, beyond question that his faith in God for decades had been and was still real, i.e. genuine. Abraham evidenced that he had a living faith, not a dead one. It was not Abraham's works in and of themselves that made Abraham righteous, but rather his works were a result of his genuine faith, which God confirmed by declaring him righteous by way of this pronouncement or verdict.[47]

---

[47] Was God tempting or testing Abraham? Andrews writes, "God does **not** tempt us, but he does allow us to go through temptations. As we know from Abraham, God can test us, but never tempt us with sin ... The Greek word (*Peirazo*) can be rendered either as 'tempted' or 'tested,' and it is the context that determines which word should be chosen. In the case of Satan with Jesus in the wilderness, it should be rendered 'tempt.' However, in reference to God, in some very limited cases in history, he has put some to the test, i.e., Abraham, even his Son."—Hebrews 2:18.

You see that faith was working together with his works, and by the works the faith was perfected; (2:22)

James is calling his believers attention to Abraham's faith stating **you see that faith was working together with his works.** Abraham's faith was authenticated not because he believed intellectually but was authenticated in the fact that he was willing to follow through with the act of sacrificing his son. It for this reason that James says **by the works the faith was perfected.** God told Abraham to sacrifice his son, and yet it was the very son, which God promised would bring him his descendants. Therefore, if Abraham was to offer up his son then how could he bring about descendants if he was dead?

Abraham would not have been sure how this would happen either, but he truly trusted God enough to follow through with the act of killing his son. Abraham believed that God would somehow allow descendants to come despite whether or not he sacrificed his son, and he was willing to trust God at all costs. Abraham's act of attempting to offer up his son authenticated his faith in God, which was evidenced by his actions of obedience. The word for perfection means complete or finished. Abraham's faith was complete in the fact that works, which made his trust in God complete by his actions of obedience, accompanied his faith.[48]

and the scripture was fulfilled that says, "Abraham believed God, and it was counted to him as righteousness," and he was called a friend of God. You see that a man is justified by works and not by faith alone. (2:23-24)

James says, **and the scripture was fulfilled that says Abraham believed God and it was counted to him as righteousness.** Here James is referring to Genesis 15:6 about Abraham. In Genesis 15:4, God had told Abraham that he would provide an heir and many descendants from his seed. Then in Genesis 15:5, to confirm his promise, God asked Abraham to go out and count the stars. In the same way, the stars were too numerous to count so would Abraham's descendants be through the promised child. Despite being old and against all odds, it says in Genesis 15:6, "Then he believed in the Lord, and He reckoned it to him as

---

[48] An analogous situation might be a wealthy father testing his daughter's fiancé. The father offers the fiancé $50,000 to leave his daughter. This test will tell the father whether the poor fiancé is in love with his daughter, or after the father's money. Keep in mind, God never intended for Abraham to offer his son up, as he foreknew what Abraham would do in such a situation decades before even. Let us adapt apologist William Lane Craig's words to this situation. 'God had morally sufficient reasons for permitting the test, which he placed on Abraham.'

righteousness." Abraham had not seen his son and the child was not even conceived in the womb at this point. However, Abraham still believed God would carry out his promises. Since Abraham believed, what God said was firm and trustworthy, he was willing to kill his son, and as a result be declared righteous in God's sight. The word righteousness here, as stated before, carries with it the idea of being right, moral, and just.

Abraham not only believed in God but was also willing to put that into practice by killing his son; he was declared right in God's sight. God declared him right in the fact that Abraham acted upon his faith through his actions. As a result, he was also called **a friend of God**, which is the only time in the Bible where someone is called a friend of God. Abraham was first called a friend of God in Jehoshaphat's prayer in 2 Chronicles 20:7, "Did you not, O our God, drive out the inhabitants of this land before thy people Israel and give it to the descendants of Abraham thy friend forever?" Isaiah also makes mention of Abraham as a friend of God in Isaiah 41:8, "But you Israel, My servant, Jacob whom I have chosen, descendant of Abraham my friend."

Abraham's belief and actions were working together in a real, genuine faith and Abraham became a friend of God. James reaffirms the argument that he has been making by saying you see. James wants his readers to have a focused view of what he has been talking about in regards to faith and action. He has just offered Abraham as his example that faith is justified when accompanied by works. As a result, these Jews would have a hard time arguing against their forefather. Faith and works must go together, they are inseparably linked, and we cannot have one without the other. For this reason, as James says **a man is justified by works and not by faith alone**.

And in the same way was not also Rahab the prostitute justified by works when she received the messengers and sent them out by another way? (2:25)

In the same manner that Abraham's faith was evidenced by his actions, **was not also Rahab the prostitute justified by works**. The story of Rahab is found in the Old Testament book of Joshua chapter 2, shortly after Moses died, and Joshua took over in leading the nation of Israel. It would be Joshua, who would guide the nation of Israel into the promised land of Canaan. However, to get there many obstacles would be in their way and that through the power of God they would have to overcome. One of these major obstacles would be conquering the city of Jericho.

The problem is that Jericho had very thick and high walls that surrounded their city, and it was nearly impossible to penetrate. Joshua summoned two men who were to go and spy out the city and come to report to Joshua what they had seen and learned. When the spies got into the city, they went to the home of a prostitute whose name was Rahab. The king of the town somehow caught wind that the spies had come into town and were at Rahab's home, and he sent to have them killed. Rahab knew that the king wanted to kill the spies and so decided to hide them on the roof of her home under stalks of flax. The king's officials arrived at the house, but Rahab told them that the spies had already left. The king's officials went off trying to find the direction of the men to kill them.

When the king's officials had left, Rahab asked a favor of the spies found in Joshua 2:8-14, "Now therefore, please swear to me by the Lord, since I have dealt kindly with you, that you also will deal kindly with my father's household, and give me a pledge of truth, and spare my father and my mother and my brothers and my sisters, with all who belong to them, and deliver our lives from death." Therefore, the men said to her, "Our life for yours if you do not tell this business of ours; and it shall come about when the Lord gives us the land that we will deal kindly and faithfully with you."

The spies told Rahab that they would indeed spare her life if she tied a scarlet cord in her window. The scarlet cord was what Rahab used to let the spies down out of the city to spare their lives. Rahab could have just told the spies to get out of her house and never have let them in. Because she feared God and believed in the God of the spies, she took the risk of letting the men stay in her home. Rahab's belief in God was authenticated in that **she received the messengers and sent them out by another way**. It would be a direct result of the action of Rahab saving the spies that would help in giving Joshua the victory over the city of Jericho.

For the body apart from the spirit is dead, so also faith apart from works is dead. (2:26)

When a person (a soul) dies (beyond clinical death), there is no longer any animating force or "spirit" within any single cell out of the body's one hundred trillion cells. Many of us have seen the animation video in science classes at school, where the cell is shown to be like a microscopic factory with an enormous amount of work taking place. Therefore, no work is taking place within the lifeless body, as all of the cells that were animated by the spirit are dead. The body is not good for anything. This is the similarity that James is trying to draw as a faith that lacks works is just as lifeless, producing no results and of no use as a corpse. The literal eye cannot see faith; however, works is an evident demonstration that faith can be seen. When one has is not moved to good works, it is all too clear that this one has no real faith. Alternatively, any Christian that is motivated to good works possesses a genuine faith. [49]

End of Excursion

Galatians 2:19-20 Updated American Standard Version (UASV)

[19] For through the law I died to the law, so that I might live to God. [20] I have been crucified with Christ; and it is no longer I who live, but Christ lives in me; and the life which I now live in the flesh I live by faith in the Son of God, who loved me and gave himself up for me.

2:20. Now Paul expands upon verse 19. He died to the law (v. 19) by being crucified with Christ. He lives for God (v. 19) because Christ lives in him. Believers are in union with Christ. We are united with him in his death, burial, and resurrection. Thus, we died with him to the law.—see Romans 6.

Again, we are uncertain as to what Paul meant by I have been crucified with Christ. It certainly did not mean that he was physically crucified. Dead people do not write letters. In what sense was he crucified? He may have used the sentence as a figure of speech, referring to the effects of Christ's death which every believer experiences. It might be reworded, "I have been as good as crucified, since the results of Christ's crucifixion count for me." Or he may have referred to a sense in which every believer is required to endure a similar experience of spiritual crucifixion to the desires of self. We put to death our own plans to follow Jesus. It might be reworded, "I have crucified my right to self-control in life, in the same way that Christ was crucified physically. He gave up his right to physical life; I gave up my right to self-life."

Or he may have referred to some sense in which the believer, because he is "in Christ" is seen by God as having actually died. He may have been referring to the union between the believer and Jesus, when the believer in Jesus experiences, spiritually, everything Jesus experienced. More will be said of these options in the "Deeper Discoveries" section of this chapter.

Whatever Paul meant about having died in Christ, the point is that his death severed him from the requirements of the law. Therefore, for Peter and the Judaizers to go back to the law is to visit the graveyard.

---

[49] Brent Calloway, *THE BOOK OF JAMES: CPH Christian Living Commentary*, Volume 17 (Cambridge, OH: Christian Publishing House, 2019), 66-71

Paul goes on to say that he can live for God because Christ lives in him. Finally, Paul says that faith is the principle that unlocks the life of Christ in the believer. The more we exercise faith in Christ the more he is free to live through us. The more we are obedient to the Scripture and the leading of the Holy Spirit, the more our life approximates what Jesus would do if he were in our shoes. In that sense, the life he lives, he lives by faith in the Son of God.[50]

Galatians 5:7-10 Updated American Standard Version (UASV)

[7] You were running well; who hindered you from obeying the truth? [8] This persuasion is not from him who calls you. [9] A little leaven leavens the whole lump. [10] I have confidence in you in the Lord that you will adopt no other view; but the one who is disturbing you will bear his judgment, whoever he is.

5:7–10. The fourth negative consequence of returning to the law is that it hinders spiritual growth and development. Using the metaphor of a **race**, Paul states that the legalists had cut in on the Galatians' spiritual race and caused them to stumble spiritually. As a result, the Galatians were no longer **obeying the truth**. Turning to a yeast metaphor, Paul illustrates how quickly a little bit of legalism can contaminate a believer and, indeed, a whole church. Paul, however, expressed his confidence that the Galatians would not depart from the truth. He warned that those who are confusing them will experience God's judgment.[51]

The above is simply an illustration of what is meant
by analyzing a verse to find implications for us today.
The whole book should be gone through in this way.

There are three rules to be observed in this analytical work. **(1)** Do not put anything into your analysis that is not clearly in the verse. One of the greatest faults in Bible study is reading into passages what God never put into them. Some men have their pet doctrines, and see them everywhere, and even where God does not see them. No matter how true, precious or scriptural a doctrine is, do not put it into our analysis where it is not in the verse. Considerable experience with classes in this kind of study leads me to emphasize this rule. **(2)** Find all that is in the verse. This rule can only be carried out relatively. Much will escape us, the verses of the Bible are such a great deep, but do not rest until we have

---

[50] Ibid., 24-25.

[51] Ibid., 63.

52

dug, and dug, and dug, and there seems to be nothing more to find. **(3)** State what we do find just as accurately and exactly as possible. Do not be content with putting into our analysis something like what is in the verse, but state in our analysis precisely what is in the verse.

Classify the Results Obtained by Verse by Verse Analysis

By our verse-by-verse analysis, we have discovered and recorded a great number of facts. The work now is to get these facts into an orderly shape. To do this, go carefully through our analysis and note the subjects treated of in the Epistle. Write these subjects down as fast as noted. Having made a complete list of the subjects dealt with in the book, write these subjects on separate cards or sheets of paper, and then, going through the analysis again, copy each point in the analysis upon its appropriate piece of paper. This general classification should be followed by a more thorough and minute subdivision. Suppose that we are studying the First Epistle of Peter. Having completed our analysis of the Epistle, and gone over it carefully, we will find that the following subjects, at least, are treated in the Epistle: (1) God. (2) Jesus Christ. (3) The Holy Spirit. (4) The Believer. (5) Wives and Husbands. (6) Servants. (7) The New Birth. (8) The Word of God. (9) Old Testament Scripture. (10) The Prophets. (11) Prayer. (12) Angels. (13) The Devil. (14) Baptism. (15) The Gospel. (16) Salvation. (17) The World. (18) Gospel Preachers and Teachers. (19) Heaven. (20) Humility. (21) Love.

These will serve for general headings. However, after the material found in the analysis is arranged under these headings, it will be found to subdivide itself naturally into numerous subdivisions. For example, the material under the head God can be subdivided into these subdivisions: 1. His names. (The material under this head is quite rich). 2. His Attributes. (This should be subdivided again: (1) His Holiness. (2) His Power. (3) His Foreknowledge. (4) His Faithfulness. (5) His Long-suffering. (6) His Grace. There are twenty-five or more points on God's Grace in the Epistle. (7) His Mercy. (8) His Impartiality. (9) His Severity.) 3. God's Judgments. 4. God's Will. 5. What is Acceptable to God. 6. What is Due to God. 7. God's Dwelling Place. 8. God's Dominion. 9. God's Work. What God does. 10. The Things of God, e. g., "The mighty hand of God," "the house of God," "the gospel of God," "the flock of God," "the people of God," "the bondservants of God," "the Word of God," "the Oracles of God," etc., etc.

An illustration in full of the classified arrangement of the teaching of a book on one doctrine will probably show better how to do this work than any abstract statement, and it will also illustrate in part how fruitful is this method of study. We will take 1, Peter, again—it's teaching regarding the Believer.

What the Epistle Teaches About the Believer

I.—His Privileges.

1. His Election.

a, He is foreknown of the Father, 1:2.

b, He is elect or chosen of God, 1:1.

c, He is chosen of God, according to His foreknowledge, 1:2.

d, He is chosen unto obedience, 1:2.

e, He is chosen unto the sprinkling of the blood of Jesus, 1:2.

f, He is chosen in sanctification of the Spirit, 1:2.

2. *His Calling.*

a, By whom called:

God, 1:15.

The God of all grace, 5:10.

b, To what called:

The imitation of Christ in the patient taking of suffering for well doing, 2:20, 21.

To render blessings for reviling, 3:9.

Out of darkness into God's marvellous light, 2:9.

To God's eternal glory, 5:10.

c, In whom called:

In Christ, 5:10.

d, The purpose of his calling:

That he may show forth the praises of Him who called, 2:9.

That he may inherit a blessing, 3:9.

3.   *His Regeneration.*

He has been begotten again

a, of God, 1:3.

b, unto a living hope, 1:3.

c, unto an inheritance incorruptible, undefiled, that fadeth not away, reserved in heaven, 1:4.

d, By the resurrection of Jesus Christ, 1:3.

e, Of incorruptible seed by the word of God that liveth, etc., 1:23.

4. *His Redemption.*

He has been redeemed,

a, not with corruptible things, as silver and gold,: 1:18.

b, with precious blood, even the blood of Christ, 1:19.

c, from his vain manner of life, handed down from his fathers, 1:18.

d, His sins have been borne by Christ, in His own body, on the tree, 2:24.

5. *His Sanctification.*

He is sanctified by the Spirit, 1:2.

6. *His Cleansing.*

He is cleansed by the blood, 1:2.

7. *His Security.*

a, He is guarded by the power of God, 1:5.

b, He is guarded unto a salvation ready, or prepared, to be revealed in the last time, 1:5.

c, God careth for him, 5:7.

d, He can cast all his anxiety upon God, 5:7.

e, The God of all grace will perfect, stablish, strengthen him, after a brief trial of suffering, 5:10. R. V.

f, None can harm him if he is zealous of that which is good, 3:13.

g, He shall not be put to shame, 2:6.

8. His Joy.

a, The character of his joy.

(1) His present joy.

A great joy, 1:8. R. V.

An unspeakable joy, 1:8.

A joy full of glory, 1:8.

(Note—*This present joy cannot be hindered by being put to grief, because of manifold temptations,* 1:6.)

(2) His future joy: exceeding, 4:13.

b, In what he rejoices:

(1) In the salvation prepared to be revealed in the last time, 1:6.

(2) Because of his faith in the unseen Jesus Christ, 1:8.

(3) In fellowship in Christ's sufferings, 4:13.

c, In what he shall rejoice.

(1) In the revelation of Christ's glory, 4:13.

(Note—*Present joy in fellowship with the sufferings of Christ, is the condition of exceeding joy at the revelation of Christ's glory,* 4:13.

9. His Hope.

a, Its character.

(1) A living hope, 1:3.

(2) A reasonable hope, 3:15.

(3) An inward hope, "in you," 3:15.

b, In whom is his hope.

(1) In God, 1:21.

c, The foundation of his hope.

(1) The resurrection of Jesus Christ, 1:3–21.

10. His Salvation.

a, A past salvation.

(1) Has been redeemed, 1:18–19.

(2) Has been healed, 2:24.

(Note—*By baptism, after a true likeness, the Believer, as Noah by the flood, has passed out of the old life of nature into the new resurrection life of grace, 3:21.*

b, A present salvation.

(1) He is now receiving the salvation of his soul, 1:9.

c, A growing salvation, through feeding on His word, 2:2, R. V.

d, A future salvation: ready or prepared to be revealed in the last time, 1:5.

11. *The Believer's Possessions.*

a, God as his Father, 1:17.

b, Christ as his

(1) Sin bearer, 2:24.

(2) Example, 2:21.

(3) Fellow sufferer, 4:13.

c, A living hope, 1:3.

d, An incorruptible, undefiled, unfading inheritance reserved in heaven, 1:4.

e, Multiplied grace and peace, 1:2.

f, Spiritual milk without guile for his food, 2:2.

g, Gifts for service—each believer has, or may have, some gift, 4:10.

12. *What Believers Are.*

a, An elect race, 2:9.

b, A royal priesthood, 2:9.

c, A holy priesthood, 2:5.

d, A holy nation, 2:9.

e, A people for God's own possession, 2:9, R. V.

f, Living stones, 2:5.

g, The House of God, 4:17.

h, A spiritual House, 2:5.

i, The flock of God, 5:2.

j, Children of obedience, 1:14, R. V.

k, Partakers of, or partners in, Christ's sufferings, 4:13.

l, Partakers of, or partners in, the glory to be revealed, 5:1.

m, Sojourners or strangers, 1:1.

n, Foreigners on earth: he has no civil rights here: his Citizenship is in heaven, 2:11, com. Phil. 3:20, R. V.

o, A sojourner on his way to another country, 2:1.

p, A Christian: representative of Christ, 4:16.

13. *The Believer's Possibilities.*

a, He may die unto sin, 2:24.

b, He may live unto righteousness, 2:24.

(Note—*We must die unto sin if we are to live unto righteousness*, 2:24.

c, He may follow in Christ's steps, 2:21.

d, He may cease from sin, 4:1.

e, He may cease from living to the lusts of men, 4:2.

f, He may live unto the will of God, 4:2.

(Note—*It is through suffering in the flesh that he ceases from sin and living to the lusts of men, and lives to the will of God.*

14. *What was for the Believer.*

a, The ministry of the Prophets was in his behalf, 1:12.

b, The preciousness of Jesus is for him, 2:7, R. V.

15. *Unclassified.*

a, Has the gospel preached to him in the Holy Ghost, 1:12.

b, Grace is to be brought unto him at the revelation of Jesus Christ, 1:3, com. Eph. 3:7.

c, Has tasted that the Lord is gracious, 2:3.

II.—The Believer's Trial and Sufferings.

1. *The fact of the Believer's sufferings and trials, 1:6.*

2. *The nature of the Believer's sufferings and trials.*

a, He endures griefs, suffering wrongfully, 2:19.

b, He suffers for righteousness' sake, 3:14.

c, He suffers for well doing, 3:17; 2:20.

d, He suffers as a Christian, 4:16.

e, He is subjected to manifold temptations, 1:6.

f, He is put to grief in manifold temptations, 1:6.

g, He is spoken against as an evil doer, 2:12.

h, His good manner of life is reviled, 3:16.

i, He is spoken evil of because of his separated life, 4:4.

j, He is reproached for the name of Christ, 4, 14.

k, He is subjected to fiery trials, 4:12.

3. *Encouragements for believers undergoing fiery trials and suffering.*

a, It is better to suffer for well doing than for evil doing, 3:17.

b, judgment must begin at the House of God, and the present judgment of believers through trial, is not comparable to the future end of those who obey not the gospel, 4:17.

c, Blessed is the believer who does suffer for righteousness' sake, 3:14, comp. Matt. 5:10–12.

d, Blessed is the believer who is reproached for the name of Christ, 4:14.

e, The Spirit of Glory and the Spirit of God rests upon the believer who is reproached for the name of Christ, 4:14.

f, The believer's grief is for a little while, 1:6, R. V.

g, The believer's suffering is for a little while, 5:10, R. V.

h, Suffering for a little while will be followed by God's glory in Christ, which is eternal, 5:10.

i, The suffering endured for a little while is for the testing of faith, 1:7.

j, The fiery trial is for a test, 4:12.

k, The faith thus proved is more precious than gold, 1:7.

l, Faith proven by manifold temptations will be found unto praise, and honor, and glory, at the revelation of Jesus Christ, 1:7.

m, It is that his proved faith may be found unto praise and glory and honor at the revelation of Jesus Christ, that the believer is for a little while subjected to manifold temptations, 1:7.

n, It is pleasing to God when a believer, for conscience toward God, endures grief, suffering wrongfully, 2:19, R. V.

o, It is pleasing to God when a believer takes it patiently, when he does well and suffers for it, 2:20.

p, Through suffering in the flesh we cease from sin, 4:1.

q, Those who speak evil of us shall give account to God, 4:5.

r, Sufferings are being shared by fellow believers, 5:9.

s, Christ suffered for us, 2:21.

t, Christ suffered for sins once (or once for all), the righteous for the unrighteous, that He might bring us to God, being put to death in the flesh, but quickened in the spirit, 3:18.

u, Christ left the believer an example that he should follow in His steps, 2:21.

v, In our fiery trials we are made partakers of, or partakers in, Christ's sufferings, 4:13.

w, When His glory is revealed we shall be glad also with exceeding joy, 4:13.

4.   *How the believer should meet his trial and sufferings.*

a, The believer should not regard his fiery trial as a strange thing, 4:12.

b, The believer should expect fiery trial, 4:12.

c, When the believer suffers as a Christian let him not be ashamed, 4:16.

d, When the believer suffers as a Christian let him glorify God in this name, 4:16.

e, When the believer suffers fiery trials he should rejoice, insomuch as he is made partaker of Christ's suffering, 4:13, R. V.

f, When the believer suffers, let him not return reviling with reviling, or suffering with threatening; but commit himself to Him that judgeth righteously, 2:23.

g, When the believer suffers, he should in well-doing commit the keeping of his soul unto God, as unto a faithful Creator, 4:19.

III.—The Believer's Dangers.

1. *The believer may fall into fleshly lusts that war against the soul, 2:11.*

2. *The believer may sin, 2:20, R. V.*

3. *The believer may fall into sins of the gravest character, 4:15.* (Note in this verse the awful possibilities that lie dormant in the heart of at least a sincere professed believer.)

4. *The believer's prayers may be hindered, 3:7.*

5. *The believer is in danger that his high calling and destiny tempt him to despise human laws and authority, 2:13.*

6. *The believer is in danger that his high calling lead him to lose sight of his lowly obligations to human masters, 2:18.*

7. *Young believers are in danger of disregarding the will and authority of older believers, 5:5.*

IV.—The Believer's Responsibility.

1. *Each believer has an individual responsibility, 4:10, R. V.*

2. *Each believer's responsibility is for the gift he has received, 4:10.*

V.—The Believer's Duties.

1. What the believer should be.

a, Be holy in all manner of living.

(1) Because God is holy, 1:15.

(2) Because it is written "ye shall be holy," 1:16, R. V.

b, Be like Him who called him, 1:15–16.

c, Be sober, (or of a calm, collected, thoughtful spirit,) 1:13; 4:7; 5:8.

d. Be sober, or of a calm, etc., unto prayer, 4:7.

e. Be of a sound mind: because the end of all things is approaching, 4:7.

f. Be watchful, 5:8.

g. Be steadfast in the faith, 5:9.

h. Be subject to every ordinance of man.

(1) For the Lord's sake, 2:13.

(2) To the King, as supreme, 2:13.

(3) To governors, as sent by the King for the punishment of evil doers, and for praise to them that do well, 2:14.

(4) Because this is God's will, 2:15.

i. Be like minded, 3:8.

j. Be sympathetic, 3:8.

k. Be tenderhearted, 3:8.

l. Be humble minded, 3:8.

m. Be ready.

(1) Always.

(2) To give an answer to every man that asketh a reason of the hope that is in him.

(3) With meekness and fear.

(4) In order to put to shame those who revile their good manner of life in Christ, 3:16.

n, Should *not* be troubled, 3:14.

2. *What the Believer should not do.*

a, The believer should not fashion himself according to the lusts of the old life of ignorance, 1:14.

b, The believer should not render evil for evil, 3:9.

c, The believer should not render reviling for reviling, 3:9.

d, The believer should not fear the world's fear, 3:14.

e, The believer should not live his remaining time in the flesh to the lusts of men, 4:2.

3. *What the Believer should do*

a, He should live as a child of obedience, 1:14.

b, Pass the time of his sojourning here in fear, 1:17.

c, Abstain from fleshly lusts that war against the soul, 2:11.

d, Observe God's will as the absolute law of life, 2:15.

e, Let his conscience be governed by the thought of God and not by the conduct of men, 2:19.

f, Sanctify Christ in his heart as Lord, 3:15. R. V. Comp. Is. 8:13.

g, Live his remaining time in the flesh to the will of God, 4:2.

h, Put away

(1) All malice, 2:1.

(2) All guile, 2:1.

(3) Hypocrisies, 2:1,

(4) Envies, 2:1.

(5) All evil speaking, 2:1.

i. Come unto the Lord as unto a living stone, 2:4.

j, Show forth the excellencies of him who called him out of darkness into His marvellous light, 2:9.

k, Arm himself with the mind of Christ: *i. e.* to suffer in the flesh, 4:1.

l, Cast all his care upon God because he careth for him, 5:7.

m, Stand fast in the true grace of God, 5:12.

n, Withstand the devil, 5:9.

o, Humble himself under the mighty hand of God, 5:5.

(1) Because God resisteth the proud and giveth grace unto the humble, 5:5–6.

(2) That God may exalt him in due time, 5:6.

p, Glorify God when he suffers as a Christian, 4:16.

q, See to it that he does not suffer as a thief or as an evil doer or as a meddler in other men's matters, 4:15.

r, Rejoice in fiery trial, 4:13.

s, Toward various persons.

(1) Toward God—fear, 2:17.

(2) Toward the King—honor, 2:17.

(3) Toward Masters—be in subjection with all fear (not only to the good and gentle, but to the forward) 2:18.

(4) Toward the Brotherhood,

Love, 2:17; 1:22; 4:8.

Love from the heart, 1:22, R. V.

Love fervently—intensely, 1:22; 4:8.

Gird themselves with humility as with a slave's apron unto one another, *i. e.,*

1st. Be one another's slaves.

2nd. Wear humility as a token of their readiness to serve one another, 5:5, com. Jno. 13:4–5.

Minister the gift he has received from God among the brethren as a good steward of the manifold grace of God, 4:10.

Use hospitality one to another without murmuring, 4:9.

Salute one another with a holy kiss, 5:14.

5. Toward his revilers.

Render blessing for reviling, 3:9.

6. Toward the Gentiles.

Have his behavior seemly among the Gentiles, 2:12.

(Notes—*1st. The reason why he should have his behavior seemly among the Gentiles; that the Gentiles might glorify God in the day of* visitation, 2:12: 2nd. This seemly behavior should consist in good works which the Gentiles could behold, 2:12.

7. Toward foolish men.

By well doing put to silence their ignorance, 2:15.

8. Toward all men—honor, 2:17.

(Note—The especial duties of believing husbands and wives, toward one another, comes under a special classification.

t, Long for the sincere milk of the word, 2:2.

u, Gird up the loins of his mind, 1:13.

v, Grow, 2:2.

w, Set his hope perfectly on the grace to be brought unto him at the revelation of Jesus Christ, 1:13, R. V.

VI.—The Believer's Characteristics.

1. His faith and hope is in God, 1:21.

2. Believes in God through Jesus Christ, 1:21.

3. Calls on God as Father, 1:17.

4. Believes in Christ, though he has never seen Him, 1:8.

5. Loves Christ though he has never seen Him, 1:8.

6. Is returned unto the Shepherd and Bishop of his soul, 2:25.

7. Has purified his soul in obedience to the truth, 1:22.

8. Has unfeigned love for the Brethren, 1:22.

9. Has a good manner of life, 3:16.

10. Does not run with the Gentiles among whom he lives, to the same excess of riot, (lives a separated life), 4:4.

11. Refrains his tongue from evil. 3:10. Refrains his lips that they speak no guile, 3:10.

12. Turns away from evil, 3:11.

13. Does good, 3:11.

14. Seeks peace, 3:11.

15. Pursues peace, 3:11.

(Note—*From 11 to 14 would very properly come under duties.*

VII.—The Believer's Warfare.

The believer has a warfare before him, 4:1.

The mind of Christ is the proper armament for this warfare, 4:1.

The warfare is with the devil, 5:8–9.

Victory is possible for the believer, 5:9.

Victory is won through steadfastness in the faith, 5:9.

Meditate on the Results Obtained

At first thought, it might seem that when we had completed our classification of results, our work was finished, but this is not so. These results are for use: first, for personal enjoyment and appropriation, and afterward to give out to others. The provision of results is affected by meditation upon them. We are no more through with a book when we have carefully and comprehensively classified its contents than we are through with a meal when we have it arranged in an orderly way upon the table. It is there to eat, digest and assimilate. One of the significant failures in much of the Bible study of the day is just at this point. There is observation, analysis, classification, but no meditation. There is perhaps nothing as important in Bible study as meditation. (See Josh. 1:8; Ps. 1:2, 3.) Take our classified teachings and go slowly over them, and ponder them, point by point, until these beautiful truths live before you and sink into your soul, and live in you, and become part of your life. Do this repeatedly. Nothing will go further than meditation to make one great and fresh and original as a thinker and speaker. Very few people in this world think.

The method of study outlined in this chapter can be shortened to suit the time and industry of the student. For example, one can omit the Fifth work (V.), and proceed at once to go through the Book as a whole and note down its teachings on different doctrines. This will significantly shorten and lighten the work. It will also greatly detract from the richness of the results, it will not be as thorough, as accurate or as scholarly, and will not be nearly so good a mental discipline. But many people are lazy, and everybody is in a hurry. So if you will not follow out the fuller plan the shorter is suggested. However, any man can be, if he will, a scholar at least in the most important line—that of Biblical study.

A still briefer plan of Book Study and yet very profitable, if one has no time for anything better, is to do the Second work (II.) and then go through the Epistle verse by verse looking up all the references given in "The Treasury of Scripture Knowledge." However, we urge every reader to try the full method described in this chapter with at least one short book in the Bible. Moreover, after we have pondered the above outline, we must consider the books mention earlier. We must compare it against our Holman Bible Handbook and Holman New Testament Commentary Volume. Moreover, we must see what our IVP Bible Background Volume has to say. Lastly, we must see if there are any Bible Difficulties in 1 Peter. We will find that Geisler and Howe have five Bible difficulties listed, while Archer has but one.

CHAPTER 3 Topical Study

The second method of Bible study is the Topical Method. This consists of searching through the Bible to find out what its teaching is on various topics. It is perhaps the most fascinating method of Bible study. It yields the largest immediate results, though not the largest ultimate results. It has advantages. The only way to master any topic is to go through the Bible and find what it has to teach on that topic. Almost any great subject will take a remarkable hold upon the heart of a Christian man, if he will take time to go through the Bible, from Genesis to Revelation, and note what it has to say on that topic. He will have a more full and more correct understanding of that topic than he ever had before. It is said of Mr. Moody, that many years ago he took up the study of "Grace" in this way. Day after day he went through the Bible, studying what it had to say about "grace." As the Bible doctrine unfolded before his mind his heart began to burn, until at last, full of the subject and on fire with the subject, he ran out onto the street, and, taking hold of the first man he met, he said: "Do you know grace?" "Grace who?" was the reply. "The grace of God that bringeth salvation." Then he just poured out his soul on that subject. If any child of God will study "Grace," or "Love," or "Faith," or "Prayer," or any other great Bible doctrine, in that way, his soul too will become full of it. Jesus evidently studied the Old Testament Scriptures in this way, for we read that "beginning at Moses and all the prophets, He expounded unto them in all the scriptures the things concerning Himself." (Luke, 24:27.) This method of study made the hearts of the two who walked with Him to burn within them. (Luke 24:32.) Paul seems to have followed his Master in this method of study and teaching. (Acts 17:2, 3.)

But the method has its dangers. It's very fascination is a danger. Many are drawn by the fascination of this method of study to give up all other methods of study, and this is a great misfortune. A well-rounded, thorough-going knowledge of the Bible is not possible by this method of study. No one method of study will answer if one desires to be a well-rounded and well-balanced Bible student. But the greatest danger lies in this, that every man is almost certain to have some line of topics in which he is especially interested, and if he studies his Bible topically, unless he is warned, he is more than likely to go over certain topics again and again, and be very strong in this line of truth, but other topics of equal importance he neglects, and thus becomes a one-sided man. We never know one truth correctly until we know it in its proper relations to other truths. I know of people, for example, who are interested in the great

68

doctrine of the Lord's Second Coming, and nearly all their Bible studies are on that line. Now this is a precious doctrine, but there are other doctrines in the Bible which a man needs to know, and it is folly to study this doctrine alone. I know others whose entire interest and study seems to center in the subject of "Divine Healing." It is related to one man that he confided to a friend that he had devoted his time for years to the study of the number "seven" in the Bible. This last is doubtless an extreme case, but it illustrates the danger in Topical Study. It is sure that we will never master the whole range of Bible truth if we pursue the Topical Method alone. A few rules concerning topical study will probably be helpful to most of the readers of this book.

I.—*Be systematic.* Do not follow your fancy in the choice of topics. Do not take up any topic that happens to suggest itself. Make a list of all the subjects that you can think of that are touched upon in the Bible. Make it as comprehensive and complete as possible. Then take these topics up one by one in a logical order. The following list of subjects is given as a suggestion. Each one can add to the list for himself and subdivide the general subjects into proper sub-divisions.

List of Topics

God.

God as a Spirit.

The Unity of God.

The Eternity of God.

The Omnipresence of God.

The Personality of God.

The Omnipotence of God.

The Omniscience of God.

The Holiness of God.

The Love of God.

The Righteousness of God.

The Mercy or Loving Kindness of God.

The Faithfulness of God.

The Grace of God.

Jesus Christ.

The Divinity of Christ.

The Subordination of Jesus Christ to the Father.

The Human Nature of Jesus Christ.

The Character of Jesus Christ.

His Holiness.

His Love to God.

His Love to Man.

His Love for Souls.

His Compassion.

His Prayerfulness.

His Meekness and Humility.

The Death of Jesus Christ.

The Purpose of Christ's Death;

Why did Christ die?

For Whom did Christ Die?

The Results of Christ's Death.

The Resurrection of Jesus Christ.

The Fact of the Resurrection.

The Results of the Resurrection.

The Importance of the Resurrection.

The Manner of the Resurrection.

The Ascension and Exaltation of Jesus Christ.

The Return or Coming Again of Jesus Christ.

The Fact of His Coming Again.

The Manner of His Coming Again.

The Purpose of His Coming Again.

The Results of His Coming Again.

The Time of His Coming Again.

The Reign of Jesus Christ.

The Holy Spirit.

Personality of the Holy Spirit.

Deity of the Holy Spirit.

Distinction of the Holy Spirit from God the Father, and the Son, Jesus Christ.

The Subordination of the Holy Spirit to the Father and to the Son.

Names of the Holy Spirit.

The work of the Holy Spirit:

In the Universe.

In Man in General.

In the Believer.

In the Prophet and Apostle.

In Jesus Christ.

Man.

His Original Condition.

His Fall.

The Present Standing before God and Present Condition of Man outside of the Redemption that is in Jesus Christ.

The Future Destiny of those who Reject the Redemption that is in Jesus Christ.

Justification.

The New Birth.

Adoption.

The Believer's Assurance of Salvation.

The Flesh.

Sanctification.

Cleansing.

Their Work.

Their Destiny.

For a student who has the perseverance to carry it through, it might be recommended, to begin with, the first topic on a list like this, and go right through it to the end, searching for everything the Bible has to say on these topics. This the author of this book has done, and, thereby, gained a fuller knowledge of truth along these lines, and an immeasurably more vital grasp of the truth, than he ever obtained by somewhat extended studies in Systematic Theology. Many, however, will stagger at the *seeming* immensity of the undertaking. To such it is recommended to begin by selecting those topics that seem more important. But sooner or later settle down to a thorough study of what the Bible has to teach about God and Man. The "Abstract of Subjects, Doctrinal and Practical," in the back of "The Bible Text Cyclopedia" is very suggestive.

II.—*Be thorough.* Whenever you are studying any topic, do not be content with examining some of the passages in the Bible that bear upon the subject, but find, as far as possible, *every passage in the Bible that bears on this subject.* As long as there is a single passage in the Bible on any subject that you have not considered, you have not yet gotten a thoroughly true knowledge of that subject. How can we find all the passages in the Bible that bear on any subject? 1st. By the use of the Concordance. Look up every passage that has the word in it. Then look up every passage that has synonymous words in it. If, for example, you are studying the subject of prayer, look up every passage that has the word "pray" and its derivatives in it, and also every passage that has such words as "cry," "call," "ask," "supplication," "intercession," etc., in it. 2nd. By the use of a Bible textbook. A textbook arranges the passages of Scripture, not by the words used, but by the subjects treated, and there is many a verse, for example on prayer, that does not have the word "prayer" or any synonymous word in it. Incomparably the best Bible textbook is Inglis' "The Bible Text Cyclopedia." 3rd. Passages not discovered by the use of either concordance or textbook will come to light as we study by books, or as we read the Bible through in course, and so our treatment of topics will be ever broadening.

III.—*Be exact.* Get the precise meaning of each passage considered. Study each passage in its connection, and find its meaning in the way suggested in the chapter on "Study of Individual Books." Topical study is frequently carried on in a very slip-shod fashion. Passages, torn from their connection, are strung or huddled together because of some superficial connection with one another, and without much regard to their real sense and teaching, and this is called "topical study." This has brought the whole method of topical study into disrepute. But is possible to be as exact and scholarly in topical study as in any other method, and when we are the results will be instructive and gratifying, and not misleading. But the results are sure to be misleading and unsatisfactory if the work is done in a careless, inexact way.

IV.—*Classify and write down your results.* In the study of any large subject one will get together a great mass of matter. Having gotten it, it must now be gotten into shape. As you look it over carefully, you will soon see the facts that belong together. Arrange them together in a logical order. An illustrative topical study is given below. What the Bible teaches concerning the Deity of Jesus Christ.

JESUS CHRIST: HIS DEITY

1. Divine names.

a. Luke, 22:70.

"The Son of God." This name is given to Christ forty times. Besides this the synonymous expression "His son," "My son," are of frequent occurrence. That this name as used of Christ is a distinctly Divine name appears from Jno. 5:18.

b. Jno. 1:18.

"The only begotten Son." This occurs five times. It is evident that the statement, that "Jesus Christ is the Son of God only in the same sense that all men are sons of God" is not true. Compare Mark 12:6. Here Jesus Himself, having spoken of all the prophets as servants of God, speaks of Himself as "one," "a beloved Son."

c. Rev. 1:17.

"The first and the last." Comp. Is. 41:4; 44:6. In these latter passages it is "Jehovah," "Jehovah of hosts," who is "the first and the last."

d. Rev. 22:12, 13, 16.

First, "the Alpha and Omega."

Second, "the beginning and the ending."

In Rev. 1:8, R. V. It is the Lord God who is the Alpha and Omega.

e. Acts 3:14.

"The Holy One." In Hosea 11:9, and many other passages, it is God who is "the Holy One."

f. Mal. 3:1; Luke 2:11; Acts 9:17; Jno. 20:28; Heb. 1:11.

"The Lord." This name or title is used of Jesus several hundred times. The word translated "Lord" is used in the New Testament in speaking of men nine times, e. g., Acts 16:30, Eph. 4:1, Jno. 12:21, but not at all in the way in which it used of Christ. He is spoken of as "*the* Lord" just as God is, cf. Acts 4:26 with 4:33. Note also Matt. 22:43–45, Phil. 2:21, Eph. 4:5. If anyone doubts the attitude of the Apostles of Jesus toward Him as Divine, they will do well to read one after another the passages which speak of Him as Lord.

g. Acts 10:36.

"Lord of all."

h. 1 Cor. 2:8.

"The Lord of Glory." In Ps. 24:8–10, it is "the Lord of Hosts" who is the King of Glory.

i. Is. 9:6.

(1) "Wonderful" (cf. Judges 13:18, R. V.)

(2) "Mighty God."

(3) "Father of Eternity." See R. V. margin.

j. Heb. 1:8.

"God." In Jno. 20:28, Thomas calls Jesus "my God," and is gently rebuked for not believing it before.

k. Matt. 1:23.

"God with us."

l. Tit. 2:13, R. V.

"Our great God."

m. Rom. 9:5.

"God blessed forever."

Proposition: Sixteen names clearly implying Deity are used of Christ in the Bible, some of them over and over again, the total number of passages reaching far into the hundreds.

2. *Divine Attributes.*

a. Omnipotence.

(1) Luke 4:39. Jesus has power over disease; it is subject to His word.

(2) Luke 7:14–15; 8:54–55; Jno. 5:25. The Son of God has power over death; it is subject to His word.

(3) Matt: 8:26–27.

Jesus has power over the winds and sea; they are subject to His word.

(4) Matt. 8:16; Luke 4:35, 36, 41.

Jesus, the Christ, the Son of God, has power over demons, they are subject to His word.

(5) Eph. 1:20–23.

Christ is far above *all* principality and power and might, and dominion and every name that is named, not only in this world but also in that which is to come. All things are in subjection (R. V.), under His feet. All the hierarchies of the angelic world are under Him.

(6) Heb. 1:3.

The Son of God upholds *all* things by the word of His power.

Proposition. Jesus Christ, the Son of God, is omnipotent.

b. Omniscience.

(1) Jno. 4:16–19.

Jesus knows men's lives, even their secret history.

(2) Mark 2:8; Luke 5:22; Jno. 2:24–25; (Acts 1:24.)

Jesus knows the secret thoughts of men. He knew all men. He knew what was in man. (cf. 2 Chron. 6:30; Jer. 17:9, 10. Here we see that God "only knoweth the hearts of the children of men.")

(3) Jno. 6:64.

Jesus knew from the beginning that Judas would betray Him. Not only men's present thoughts but their future choices were known to Him.

(4) Jno. 1:48.

Jesus knew what men were doing at a distance.

(5) Luke 22:10, 12; Jno. 13:1; Luke 5:4–6.

Jesus knew the future regarding not only God's acts, but regarding the minute specific acts of men, and even the fishes of the sea.

Note—*Many, if not all, of these items of knowledge up to this point could possibly, if they stood alone, be accounted for by saying that the Omniscient God revealed these specific things to Jesus.*

(6) Jno. 21:17; 16:30; Col. 2:3. Jesus knew all things, in Him are hid all the treasures of wisdom and knowledge.

Proposition. Jesus Christ is omniscient.

(Note—*There was, as we shall see when we study the Humanity of Christ, a voluntary veiling and abnegation of the exercise of His inherent Divine omniscience. (Mark 11:12–14; Phil. 2:7.)*

c. Omnipresence.

(1) Matt. 18:20.

Jesus Christ is present in every place where two or three are gathered together in His name.

(2) Matt. 28:20.

Jesus Christ is present with everyone who goes forth into any part of the world to make disciples, etc.

(3) Jno. 3:13.

The Son of man was in heaven while He was here on earth.

(Note—*This text is doubtful. (See R. V and the Variorum Bible.)*

(4) Jno. 14:20; 2 Cor. 13:5.

Jesus Christ is in each believer.

(5) Eph. 1:23.

Jesus Christ filleth all in all.

Proposition. Jesus Christ is omnipresent.

d. Eternity.

Jno. 1:1; Mic. 5:2; Col. 1:17; Is. 9:6; Jno. 17:5 (Jno. 6:62; Jno. 8:58; 1 Jno. 1:1, 2); Heb. 13:8.

Proposition. The Son of God was from all eternity.

e. Immutability.

Heb. 13:8; 1:12. Jesus Christ is unchangeable. He not only always is, but always is *the same.*

f. Phil. 2:6.

Jesus Christ before His incarnation was in the *form* of God.

(Note—"Morphe" *translated* "form" *means* "the form by which a person or thing strikes the vision; the external appearance."* (Thayer, Grk-Eng. Lexicon of the N. T.)

g. Col. 2:9.

In Christ dwelleth all the fulness of the Godhead in a bodily way.

Proposition. Five or more distinctively divine attributes are ascribed to Jesus Christ, and all the fulness of the Godhead is said to dwell in Him.

3. *Divine Offices.*

a. Creation.

Heb. 1:10; Jno. 1:3; Col. 1:16.

The Son of God, the eternal Word, the Lord, is the creator of all created things.

b. Preservation.

Heb. 1:3. The Son of God is the preserver of all things.

c. The forgiveness of sin.

Mark 2:5–10; Luke 7:48–50.

Jesus Christ had power on earth to forgive sins.

Note—*He taught that sins were sins* against Himself. *Luke 7:40–47, both Simon and the woman as sinners were debtors to Him, but in Ps. 51:4 sin is seen to be against God and God only.)*

d. Raising of the dead.

Jno. 6:39–44; 5:28–29.

It is Jesus Christ who raises the dead.

Ques. Did not Elijah and Elisha raise the dead? No; God raised the dead in answer to their prayer, but Jesus Christ will raise the dead by His own word. During the days of His humiliation, it was by prayer that Christ raised the dead. Jno. 11:41.

e. Transformation of bodies. Phil. 3:21, R. V.

Jesus Christ shall fashion the body of our humiliation anew into the likeness of His own glorious body.

f. Judgment. 2 Tim. 4:1, R. V.

Christ Jesus shall judge the quick and the dead.

Note—*Jesus Himself emphasized the Divine character of this office.* (Jno. 5:22–23.)

g. The bestowal of eternal life.

Jno. 10:28; 17, 2.

Jesus Christ is the bestower of eternal life.

Proposition. Seven distinctively Divine offices are predicated of Jesus Christ.

4. Statements which in the O. T. are made distinctly of Jehovah God taken in the N. T. to refer to Jesus Christ.

a. Ps. 102:24–27, comp. Heb. 1:10–12.

b. Is. 40:3–4, comp. Matt. 3:3, Luke 1:68, 69, 76.

c. Jer. 11:20; 17, 10, comp. Rev. 21:23.

d. Is. 60:19 (Zech. 2:5) comp. Luke 2:32.

e. Is. 6:1; 3:10, comp. Jno. 12:37–41.

f. Is. 8:13–14, comp. 1 Pet. 2:7–8.

g. Is. 8:12–13, comp. 1 Pet. 3:14–15, R. V.

h. Num. 21:6–7, comp. 1 Cor. 10:9. (See R. V.)

i. Ps. 23:1; Is. 40:10–11, comp. Jno. 10:11.

j. Ez. 34:11; 12:16, comp. Luke 19:10.

k. Lord in the O. T. always refers to God except when the context clearly indicates otherwise: Lord in the N. T. always refers to Jesus Christ except where the context clearly indicates otherwise.

Proposition. Many statements which in the O. T. are made distinctly of Jehovah God are taken in the N. T. to refer to Jesus Christ, *i. e.,* in N. T. thought and doctrine Jesus Christ, occupies the place that Jehovah occupies in O. T. thought and doctrine.[52]

---

[52] Jehovah is the name of the Father in the OT and Jesus is the name of the Son in the NT. They are two separate persons. Those texts in the NT applying to Jesus that had applied to the Father in the OT are merely conveying that Jesus, the Son is carrying out the will of Jehovah, the Father. Jesus said, "The Father judges no one, but has given all judgment to the

5. The way in which the name of God the Father and Jesus Christ the Son are coupled together.

2 Cor. 13:14.

Matt. 28:19.

1 Thess. 3:11.

1 Cor. 12:4–6.

Tit. 3:4, 5, comp. Tit. 2:13.

Rom. 1:7. Many instances of this sort (see all the Pauline Epistles).

Jas. 1:1.

Jno. 14:23, "we," i. e., God the Father and I.

2 Pet. 1:1. (Comp. R. V.)

Col. 2:2. (See R. V.)

Jno. 17:3.

Jno. 14:1, comp. Jer. 17:5–7.

Rev. 7:10.

Rev. 5:13; comp. Jno. 5:23.

Prop. The name of Jesus Christ is coupled with that of God the Father in numerous passages in a way in which it would be impossible to couple the name of any finite being with that of the Deity.

6. Divine Worship to be given to Jesus Christ.

a. Matt. 28:9; Luke 24:52; Matt. 14:33, comp. Acts 10:25–26; Rev. 22:8–9; Matt. 4:9–10.

Jesus Christ accepted without hesitation a worship which good men and angels declined with fear (horror).

Ques. Is not the verb translated worship in these passages used of reverence paid to men in high position? Yes; but not in this way by worshippers of Jehovah, as is seen by the way in which Peter and the angel drew back with horror when such worship was offered to them.

b. 1 Cor. 1:2; 2 Cor. 12:8, 9; Acts 7:59. (R. V.)

Son" (John 5:22) Just before Jesus said to them, "Truly, truly, I say to you, the Son can do nothing of his own accord, but only what he sees the Father doing. For whatever the Father does, that the Son does likewise. (John 5:19)

Prayer is to be made to Christ.

c. Ps. 45:11; Jno. 5:23; comp. Rev. 5:8, 9, 12, 13.

It is God the Father's will that all men pay the same divine honor to the Son as to Himself.

d. Heb. 1:6; Phil, 2:10, 11. (Comp. Is. 45:21, 23.)

The Son of God, Jesus, is to be worshiped as God by angels and men.

Proposition. Jesus Christ is a person to be worshiped by angels and men even as God the Father is worshiped.

General Proposition. By the use of numerous Divine names, by the ascription of all the distinctively divine attributes, by the predication of several divine offices, by referring statements which in the O. T. distinctly name Jehovah God as their subject to Jesus Christ in the N. T., by coupling the name of Jesus Christ with that of God the Father in a way in which it would be impossible to couple that of any finite being with that of the Deity, and by the clear teaching that Jesus Christ should be worshiped even as God the Father is worshiped—in all these unmistakable ways, God in His word distinctly proclaims that Jesus Christ is a Divine Being, is God.

One suggestion remains to be made in regard to topical study. Get further topics for topical study from our book studies.

Topical Studies by Edward D. Andrews

One of the best additional studies that any Christian can do is topical studies. Exactly what are topical studies? What is involved in such a study? Moreover, what is the best way to accomplish them in a timely and proficient manner? How are we to go about collecting our information for such a study?

A topical study is merely what we might think from the title itself. It is covering a person, place, event, or doctrine in a comprehensive manner. We will soon find that many people offer their opinions about what God's Word has to say on a particular subject and that it is usually just that, an opinion. After we have completed our first topical study, we will likely find that we only had a scrap of knowledge about the topic, and most of it was in error.

These studies require quite a bit of time and energy, so I would personally recommend that we not do any more than one topic at a time. In addition, we will not want to be consumed by the topic. Just choose our first topic, and the amount of time that we can give to it, which will not deprive our family, or rob our time for preparing for regular religious services, our personal Bible studied outlined in this book (Bible Reading and Book Study), and our ministry.

To find all of the references to our topic, we will need an exhaustive concordance, or a topical Bible. If we use the concordance at the back of our study Bible, remember that it will not cover every reference. We will investigate the tem "earth." Keep in mind that we will find, for example every mention of the English word "earth" as well as every mention of the original language words, but they may not be rendered as "earth" in other translations; it might be rendered in other Bible versions as "world."

Initially we will want to pick our topic. For the sake of an example, we will pick the word "earth." At the top of our document, type or write **EARTH**, and make it large and bold, as our paper title. Initially we will want to ask ourselves questions, to generate a thought process that we would like to see answers to, but not in such a way as to form any kind of preconceived ideas. Questions such as:

(1) Why did God create the earth?

(2) What were his intentions for man on the earth?

(3) Did those intentions changed after the sin of Adam and Eve?

(4) What is the future for the earth and its inhabitants?

These questions are certainly not exhaustive, but are enough to see what we would like to know about the earth, but not so leading that we influence the outcome. The next step in our process is to find our subject in all the related passages, making sure that they fall within the same context. As we go, we will generate headings and subheadings from our findings that may be adjusted as we grow in knowledge of our topic. In addition, we may want to consider whether we want to include other related word, like "world." Moreover, in some way (underline, italicize, bold, highlight), we may want to mark each text that we list, to remind ourselves of how it is adding to our knowledge of the topic, and later we can see if it is a literal addition, or symbolic or figurative one.

(1) **The Original Language Terms**: Here we will look up all of the original language terms that are related to our topic. In this, we will need to look at a Mounce's *Complete Expository Dictionary of Old & New Testament Words*. We may choose to read some

of his commentary on each of these terms, and then list the words and their range of meaning on our paper.

a) (Heb) erets: land earth, ground

b) (Heb) adhamah': ground, soil, earth, land, regions below the ground

c) (Grk) ge: Earth, land, region, humanity

d) (Grk) Oikoumene: the inhabited earth

(2) **The Creation of the Earth**: Here we will want to look at every verse that discusses the earth's initial creation. Of course, we do not have the space, to consider every verse as we generate our example topic headings here.

Genesis 1:1 Updated American Standard Version (UASV)

1 In the **beginning**, God **created** the heavens and the earth.

As we generate verses under sections, we start to see questions that we would like to have answers to, such as, 'what exactly is meant by "in the beginning"?' We may want to know what is meant by the word "create" *bara*, as opposed to the word "make" *asah* that is used later in the creation account.

(3) **The Purpose for the Creation of the Earth**: This thought logically follows the creation of the earth. If an all-powerful person creates something, such as the earth, the question that follows is, why? Is the earth permanent; or is it a temporary home? Was it created specifically for humans? Many other questions could be asked.

Genesis 1:28 Updated American Standard Version (UASV)

28 And God blessed them. And God said to them, "**Be fruitful and multiply** and **fill** the earth and **subdue** it, and have dominion over the fish of the sea and over the birds of the heavens and over every living thing that moves on the earth."

And God blessed them. And God said to them, "Be fruitful and multiply and fill the earth and subdue it and have dominion over the fish of the sea and over the birds of the heavens and over every living thing that moves on the earth."

Psalm 78:69 Updated American Standard Version (UASV)

⁶⁹ And he built his sanctuary like the heights,
like the earth, which he has founded **forever**.

Psalm 104:5 Updated American Standard Version (UASV)

⁵ He established the earth on its **foundations**,
So that it will not totter **forever and ever**.

Psalm 119:90 Updated American Standard Version (UASV)

⁹⁰ Your faithfulness endures to all generations;
you have **established the earth**, and it **stands**.

Ecclesiastes 1:4 Updated American Standard Version (UASV)

⁴ A generation goes, and a generation comes,
but **the earth stands forever**.

Isaiah 45:18 Updated American Standard Version (UASV)

¹⁸ For thus says Jehovah,
who created the heavens
(he is God!),
who **formed the earth** and **made it**
(he **established it**;
he **did not create it empty**,
he **formed it to be inhabited**!):
"I am Jehovah, and there is no other.

(4) **The Bible and Science**: Is the Bible an enemy of science? Does the Bible contradict science? Is the Bible attempting to be a science textbook? When it touches on science is it accurate?

Many truths about God are beyond the scope of science. Science and the Bible are not at odds. In fact, we can thank modern day science, as it has helped us to better under the creation of God, from our solar system, to the universes, to the human body and mind. What we find is a level of order, precision, design and sophistication, which points to a Designer, the eyes of many Christians, to an Almighty God, with infinite intelligence and power. The apostle Paul makes this all too clear, when he writes, "For his invisible attributes, namely, his eternal power and divine nature, have been clearly perceived, ever since the creation of the world, in the things that have been made. So they are without excuse."—Romans 1:20.

Back in the seventeenth century, the world-renowned scientist Galileo proved beyond any doubt that the earth was not the center of the universe, nor did the sun orbit the earth. In fact, he proved it to be the other way around (no pun intended), with the earth revolving around the sun. However, he was brought up on charges of heresy by the Catholic Church and ordered to recant his position. Why? From the viewpoint of the Catholic Church, Galileo was contradicting God's Word, the Bible. As it turned out, Galileo and science were correct and the Church was wrong, for which it issued a formal apology in 1992. However, the point we wish to make here is that in all the controversy, the Bible was never in the wrong. It was a misinterpretation on the part of the Catholic Church, and not a fault with the Bible. One will find no place in the Bible that claims the sun orbits the earth. So where would the Church get such an idea? The Church got such an idea from Ptolemy (b. about 85 C.E.), an ancient astronomer, who argued for such an idea.

As it usually turns out, the so-called contradiction between science and God's Word lies at the feet of those who are interpreting Scripture incorrectly. To repeat the sentiments of Galileo when writing to a pupil— Galileo expressed the same sentiments: "Even though Scripture cannot err, its interpreters and expositors can, in various ways. One of these, very serious and very frequent, would be when they always want to stop at the purely literal sense."[53] I believe that today's scholars, in hindsight, would have no problem agreeing.

While the Bible is not a science textbook, it is scientifically accurate when it touches on matters of science.

The Circle of the Earth Hangs on Nothing

Isaiah 40:22 Updated American Standard Version (UASV)

[22] It is he who sits above the **circle of the earth,**
    and its inhabitants are like grasshoppers;
who stretches out the heavens like a curtain,
    and spreads them like a tent to dwell in.

More than 2,500 years ago, the prophet Isaiah wrote that the earth is a circle or sphere. First, how would it be possible for Isaiah to know the earth is a circle or sphere, if not from inspiration? Scientific America writes, "As countless photos from space can attest, Earth is round—the "Blue Marble," as astronauts have affectionately dubbed it. Appearances, however, can be deceiving. Planet Earth is not, in fact, perfectly round."[54]

---

[53] Letter from Galileo to Benedetto Castelli, December 21, 1613.

[54] Charles Q. Choi (April 12, 2007). Scientific America. Strange but True: Earth Is Not Round. Retrieved Monday, August 03, 2015.

Scientifically speaking, the sun is not perfectly, absolutely 100 percent round but in everyday speech, this verse is both acceptable and accurate, when we keep in mind it is written from a human perspective, not from a scientific perspective. Moreover, Isaiah was not discussing astronomy; he was simply making an inspired observation that man came to realize once he was in space, looking back at the earth, it is round. See the section about title, "Intended Meaning of Writer."

Job 26:7 Updated American Standard Version (UASV)

7 "He stretches out the north over empty space
and hangs the earth on nothing.

Here the author describes the earth as hanging upon nothing. Many have never heard of the Greek mathematician and astronomer Eratosthenes. He was born in about 276 B.C.E. and received some of his education in Athens, Greece. In 240 B.C., the "Greek astronomer, geographer, mathematician and librarian Eratosthenes calculates the Earth's circumference. His data was rough, but he wasn't far off."[55] While man very early on used their God given intelligence to arrive at some outstanding conclusion that were actually very accurate, we learn two points here. Eratosthenes was a very astute scientist, while Isaiah, who wrote some 500 years earlier, was no scientist at all. Moreover, Moses, who wrote the book of Job over 1,230 years before Eratosthenes, knew that the earth hung upon nothing.

How Is the Sun Standing Still Possible?

Joshua 10:13 Updated American Standard Version (UASV)

13 And the sun stood still, and the moon stopped,
until the nation avenged themselves of their enemies.

Is this not written in the Book of Jashar? The sun stopped in the midst of heaven and did not hurry to set for about a whole day.

The Canaanites had besieged the Gibeonites, a group of people that gained Jehovah God's backing because they had faith in Him. In this battle, Jehovah helped the Israelites continue their attack by causing "the sun [to stand] still, and the moon stopped, until the nation took vengeance on their enemies." (Jos 10:1-14) Those who accept God as the creator of the universe and life can accept that he would know a way of

---

http://www.scientificamerican.com/article/earth-is-not-round/

55 Alfred, Randy (June 19, 2008). "June 19, 240 B.C.E: The Earth Is Round, and It's This Big". Wired. Retrieved Monday, August 03, 2015.

stopping the earth from rotating. However, there are other ways of understanding this account. We must keep in mind that the Bible speaks from an earthly observer point of view, so it need not be that he stopped the rotation. It could have been a refraction of solar and lunar light rays, which would have produced the same effect.

Psalm 136:6 Updated American Standard Version (UASV)

⁶ to him who spread out the earth above the waters,
for his lovingkindness is everlasting;

Hebrews 3:4 Updated American Standard Version (UASV)

⁴ For every house is built by someone, but the builder of all things is God.

2 Kings 20:8-11 Updated American Standard Version (UASV)

⁸ And Hezekiah said to Isaiah, "What shall be the sign that Jehovah will heal me, and that I shall go up to the house of Jehovah on the third day?" ⁹ And Isaiah said, "This shall be the sign to you from Jehovah, that Jehovah will do the thing that he has spoken: shall the shadow go forward ten steps or go back ten steps?" ¹⁰ And Hezekiah answered, "It is an easy thing for the shadow to decline ten steps; no, but let the shadow turn backward ten steps." ¹¹ And Isaiah the prophet cried to Jehovah, and he brought the shadow on the steps back ten steps, by which it had gone down on the steps of Ahaz.

How is it that the stars fought on behalf of Barak?

Judges 5:20 Updated American Standard Version (UASV)

²⁰ The stars fought from heaven,
from their courses they fought against Sisera.

Judges 4:15 Updated American Standard Version (UASV)

¹⁵ And Jehovah routed Sisera and all his chariots and all his army with the edge of the sword before Barak; and Sisera alighted from his chariot and fled away on foot.

In the Bible, you have Biblical prose, and Biblical poetry.

Prose: language that is not poetry: (1) writing or speech in its normal continuous form, without the rhythmic or visual line structure of poetry **(2)** ordinary style of expression: writing or speech that is ordinary or matter-of-fact, without embellishment.

Poetry: literature in verse: (1) literary works written in verse, in particular verse writing of high quality, great beauty, emotional sincerity or intensity, or profound insight **(2) beauty or grace:** something that resembles poetry in its beauty, rhythmic grace, or imaginative, elevated, or decorative style.

We have a beautiful example of both of these forms of writing-communication in chapters four and five of the book of Judges. Judges Chapter 4 is a prose account of Deborah and Barak, while Judges Chapter 5 is a poetic account. As we have learned from the above, poetry is less concerned with accuracy than evoking emotions. Poetry has a license to say things like what we find in of 5:20, which is in the poetry chapter: "from heaven the stars fought." This can be said and the reader is expected to not take the language literally. What we can surmise from it though, is that God was acting against Sisera in some way, there was divine intervention.

(5) **The Earth Metaphorically**: the use to describe the earth that is not meant literally but by means of a vivid comparison expresses something about it, e.g. saying that the earth is a . . . . . This can be done **symbolically**, where one thing is used or considered to represent another. Revelation 12:16 is a good example of this: "But the earth came to the help of the woman, and the earth opened its mouth and swallowed the river that the dragon had poured from his mouth." This can also be done **figuratively**, where the language does not literally represent real things. Job 38:14 is a good example of this: It [the earth] is changed like clay under the seal, and its features stand out like a garment." Keep in mind, right now; we are just generating our list of texts.

Job 38:4-6 Updated American Standard Version (UASV)

4 "Where were you when I laid the foundation of the earth?
   Tell me, if you have understanding.
5 Who set its measurements? Since you know.
   Or who stretched the measuring line upon it?
6 On what were its bases sunk?
   Or who laid its cornerstone,

2 Peter 3:7 Updated American Standard Version (UASV)

7 But by the same word the heavens and earth that now exist **are stored up for fire**, being kept until the day of judgment and **destruction of ungodly men**.

Is the earth to be destroyed by fire, some nuclear holocaust? Is this a contradiction of the other texts, which suggest the earth is to be here forever? Will context answer these questions? Notice that the latter part of verse 7 shows us how we are to understand that the earth is being used figuratively here, as wicked mankind and fire figuratively for the destruction of wicked mankind.

The Second Step in Our Topical Study

By now, we should have some subheadings, and should have organized the texts concerning where they should be in relation to those headings, noting that this is just our initial sense. Now it is time to investigate the texts ourselves, each one, knowing that we may have to move one text or another under another heading or it may remain right where we initially placed it. In addition, we may need to generate more headings during this stage as well. When we investigate the passage, find its meaning by context, using a good exegetical commentary, or a background commentary, and list how our topic is used in the passage. What did the author mean to convey by the use of our topical word in this passage? Once we are through the whole of our texts, make a note how our understanding progressed.

The Third Step in Our Topical Study

It is time to organize all those notes. It is advisable to create an outline. Place our title at the top, and our headings and subheading in a logical way, with the texts that apply to each heading and subheading throughout our paper. Once we have this skeleton, it is time to add the meat, the information that we have discovered about each text. Do not get excessive here, just the facts in concise sentences. We can do it one of two ways. We can write out what we know, cite our Scripture, and then add to that, and cite another Scripture. On the other hand, we may follow, the pattern that was used above, the heading, and the texts fully quoted, placing the basic information in brackets after it. Below is an example of the former:

Throughout the Bible, the earth is spoken of in a figurative sense. In Job 38:4-6, it is compared to a building, as Jehovah God questions Job about the creation of the earth, as well as his management of it, leaving Job speechless. The earth is also symbolically used to mean the steadier, more unwavering basics of humankind. The uneasy, disturbed elements of humankind are demonstrated by the representative restlessness of the sea.—Isaiah 57:20; James 1:6; Jude 13; compare Rev 12:16; 20:11; 21:1.

CHAPTER 4 Biographical Study

The third method of study is the Biographical. This needs no definition. It consists of taking up the various persons mentioned in Scripture and studying their life, work and character. It is really a special form of Topical Study. It can be made fascinating and instructive. It is especially useful to the minister with a view to sermon building but is profitable for all Christians. The following suggestions will help those who are not already experienced in this line of work.

1. Collect all the passages in the Bible in which the person to be studied is mentioned. This is readily done by turning in Strong's Concordance to the person's name, and we will find every passage in which he is mentioned given.

2. Analyze the character of the person. This will require a repeated reading of the passages in which he is mentioned. This should be done with pencil in hand, that any characteristic may be noted down at once.

3. Note the elements of power and success.

4. Note the elements of weakness and failure.

5. Note the difficulties overcome.

6. Note the helps to success.

7. Note the privileges abused.

8. Note the opportunities neglected.

9. Note the opportunities improved.

10. Note the mistakes made.

11. Note the perils avoided.

12. Make a sketch of the life in hand. Make it as vivid, living and realistic as possible. Try to reproduce the subject as a real, living man. Note the place and surroundings of the different events, e. g., Paul in Athens, Corinth, Philippi. Note the time relations of the various events. Very few people in reading the Acts of the Apostles, for example, take notice of the rapid passage of time, and so regard events separated by years as following one another in close sequence. In this connection note the age or approximate age of the subject at the time of the events recorded of him.

13. Summarize the lessons we should learn from the story of this person's life.

14. Note the person in hand in his relations to Jesus, e. g., as a type of Christ (Joseph, David, Solomon and others), forerunner of Christ, believer in Christ, enemy of Christ, servant of Christ, brother of Christ (James and Jude), friend, etc., etc.

It will be well, to begin with some person who does not occupy too much space in the Bible, as, e. g., Enoch or Stephen. Of course, many of the points mentioned above cannot be taken up with some characters.[56]

---

[56] Suggestive books in character studies are *People of the Old Testament World* and *Peoples of the New Testament World: An Illustrated Guide*.

CHAPTER 5 Study of Types

The fourth method of study is the Study of Types. We have illustrations of this in the Bible itself, as in the Epistle to the Hebrews. It is both an interesting and instructive method of study. It shows us the most precious truths buried away in what once seemed to us a very dry and meaningless portion of the Bible. It need scarcely be said that this method of study is greatly abused and overdone in some quarters. But that is no reason why we should neglect it altogether, especially when we remember that not only Paul but Jesus were fond of this method of study. The following may serve as principles to govern us in this method of study:

1. *Be sure we have Bible warrant for our supposed type.* If one gives free rein to his fancy in this matter, he can imagine types everywhere, even in places that neither the human or divine author of the book had any intention of a typical sense. Never say this is a type unless we can point to some clear passage of Scripture where the truth said to be typified is definitely taught.

2. *Begin with the more simple and evident types,* e g., the Passover (comp. Ex. 12 with 1 Cor. 5:7, etc.), the High Priest, the Tabernacle.

3. *Be on our guard against the fanciful and overstrained.* Fancily is almost sure to run away with any man who is blessed with any imagination and quickness of typical discernment unless he holds it in check. Our typical sensitiveness and sensibleness will become both quickened and chastened by careful and circumspect exercise.

4. *In studying any passage of possible typical suggestion, look up all the Scripture references.* The best collection of references is that given in "The Treasury of Scripture Knowledge."

5. *Study carefully the meaning of the names of persons and places mentioned.* Bible names often have a very deep and far reaching suggestiveness. Thus, for example, Hebron, which means "joining together," "union" or "fellowship," is deeply significant when taken in connection with its history, as are all the names of the Cities of Refuge, and indeed very many Scripture names. Was it accidental that Bethlehem, the name of the place where the Bread of Life was born, means "House of bread"?[57]

---

[57] We recommend *A Dictionary of Bible Types* by Walter L. Wilson and *Connections: A Guide to Types and Symbols in the Bible* by Glen Carpenter

Typological Interpretation is the study of religious texts for identifying entities (people, objects, institutions and events) in them that appear to prefigure subsequent corresponding entities. For example, King David is viewed as a type of Christ.

A biblical "type" is an illustration, an example, or a pattern of God's activity in the history of his people Israel and the church through persons, events, or institutions. Typology is not the same thing as an exegesis of a passage, for a biblical text has only one meaning, its natural or normal meaning as determined by means of grammatico-historical study. If the typical sense is not indicated by the original author or his text, then it probably is not consistent with the normal or natural (some read: literal) meaning of the text.[58]

Like allegory, typological interpretation is subjective, meaning one's opinion. Therefore, it is fine that a New Testament writer used typological interpretation, because they were inspired, and the result was/is the Word of God.[59] However, we are not inspired, so like allegory, we do not use typological interpretation, unless we are using what the New Testament writer already established as typological. Again, the New Testament writer did not need to use historical-grammatical hermeneutics, because Holy Spirit led him.

---

[58] Kaiser Jr., Walter C.; Silva, Moises (2009-08-12). Introduction to Biblical Hermeneutics: The Search for Meaning (Kindle Locations 2100-2104). Zondervan. Kindle Edition.

[59] The NT typologists did not get their typological correspondence from their exegetical analysis of the context of the OT. Hermeneutics is incapable of extracting a typological meaning from the OT context because hermeneutics operates objectively while the typological identification can only be made subjectively.—Page(s): 6, Inspired Subjectivity and Hermeneutical Objectivity by John H. Walton Master's Seminary Journal March 01, 2002.pdf

CHAPTER 6 The Study of the Books of the Bible in the Order Given in the Bible and in Their Chronological Order

The fifth method of Bible study is the old fashioned method of the study of the Bible in course, beginning with Genesis and going right on until Revelation is finished. This method of study is ridiculed a good deal in these days, but it has some advantages, which no other method of study possesses. It is sometimes said, we might as well begin at the top shelf of our library and read right through, as to begin at the beginning of this library of sixty-six books and read right through. To this, it is a sufficient answer if we had a library that it was important to master as a whole, that we might understand the separate books in it, and that was as well arranged as the Bible is, then this method of going through our library would be excellent.

We can go about this in three different methods. We can buy a one-volume commentary that deals with the entire Bible, or we can buy a Bible handbook that covers every book the Bible and far more or we can buy an entire set of individual volumes that include the Old Testament and the New Testament. We would highly recommend number three, studying the Bible with commentary volumes.

Holman Concise Bible Commentary From Holman Reference

Product Description

With solid scholarship and exceptional clarity, the Holman Concise Bible Commentary gives readers a feel for the key themes and intentions of all 66 books in the Bible. But don't mistake concise for incomplete; this volume also contains detailed introductions to the ten major units of Scripture (the Gospels, Paul's letters, etc.), maps related to biblical history, informational charts, and in-depth sidebars. It's a perfect resource for adding an extra level of insight to Sunday school lessons, sermons, and personal devotional times.

Holman Bible Handbook From Holman Reference Price: $16.48

Product Description

This practical tool brings an understanding of the ancient world together with the timeless message of God's Word to expand Biblical insights for the modern readers. Features include articles, outlines, and commentary from leading evangelical scholars, full-color photos, illustrations, charts and maps, a special section on historical background and recent findings in Biblical archaeology, highlighted, theological teaching and ethical message of each Bible book, and study questions for further reflection.

Holman Old Testament Commentary Series (20 volume set)

Product Description

No other reference series gets to the heart of the Old Testament as efficiently as the Holman Old Testament Commentary (HOTC). When a reader's time allows, the series offers a detailed interpretation based on the popular New International Version text. When time is short, it delivers an essential understanding of the Old Testament with unsurpassed clarity and convenience.

Now all twenty volumes in the HOTC series are available in one generously discounted set. The twelve volume Holman New Testament Commentary series is also offered at a reduced rate.

Holman New Testament Commentary (12 volume set)

Product Description

One in a series of twelve New Testament verse-by-verse commentary books edited by Max Anders. Includes discussion starters, teaching plan, and more. Great for lay teachers and pastors alike.

In the works, (We just finished Philippians and Esther is almost complete)

CPH Old and New Testament Commentary Volumes

This commentary volume is part of a series by Christian Publishing House (CPH) that covers all of the sixty-six books of the Bible. These volumes are a study tool for the pastor, small group biblical studies leader, or the churchgoer. The primary purpose of studying the Bible is to learn about God and his personal revelation, allowing it to change our lives by drawing closer to God. The Book of Philippians volume is written in a style that is easy to understand. The Bible can be difficult and complicated at times. Our effort herein is to make it easier to read and understand, while also accurately communicating truth. CPH New Testament Commentary will convey the meaning of the verses in the book of Philippians. In addition, we will also cover the Bible background, the custom, and culture of the times, as well as Bible difficulties.

Another important feature of CPH New Testament Commentary is its range of information. We have made every effort to supply our readers with relevant textual information in an easy way. In addition, the reader will be introduced to one of the original languages of the Bible by way of transliteration (English letters), Greek. This thorough information should benefit our readers in becoming more in-depth students of the fully inerrant, inspired Word of God, as well as being better qualified to defend to anyone who asks them for a reason for their hope.—1 Peter 3:15.

CHAPTER 7 Interpreting Biblical Word Pictures

Most have heard the saying 'a picture is worth a thousand words.' However, the Bible has a real knack of painting a picture with just a few words. The word pictures found in God's Word creates an image in the mind of the reader that will likely never be forgotten. The phrase that I am using, 'word picture,' is to be understood as all of the different figures of speech found in God's Word: metaphors, similes, as well as other forms of literary devices that involve figures of speech. If we were to read Jesus' Sermon on the Mount meticulously, we would discover that he used over fifty different word pictures.

It is significant that we learn how to discover the meaning behind these word pictures. Without discovering their true meaning, we will misinterpret the Bible, and misapply it in our lives. As we have already seen in the above, misapplication cannot only cause one not to have the success that the Bible holds out, but can be dangerous at times, like the rod of the shepherd and the many proverbs, which talk about the disciplining of a rebellious boy. Of course, these word pictures throughout God's Word are not to be taken literally, but the message they convey by the picture is to be taken literally.

Correct Mental Grasp of Word Pictures

A word picture is one thing used or considered to represent or express something in another manner. The **topic** is compared with the **image**. Something about the topic and the image is similar. In order for us to discover the true meaning, we must find the similarities. The danger is in finding more than was intended by the author.

Proverbs 30:18-19

¹⁸Three things are too wonderful for me; four I do not understand: ¹⁹the way of an eagle in the sky, the way of a serpent on a rock, the way of a ship on the high seas, and the way of a man with a virgin.

There is a similarity to the above list. An eagle soars through the sky; the way of a serpent on a rock is that it crosses the rock, the way of a ship on the high seas as it cuts through the waves. The similarity is that none of these three leave a trail, which does not allow anyone to follow their path. This now helps us establish the similarity of number four, where the proverb was leading us, "the way of a man with a virgin."

A man may engage cunning ways of using insincere flattery and pleasantness, especially in order to persuade somebody to do something, to capitalize upon the friendliness of an innocent virgin. She is innocent and untested; she would not be able to discover his charms. It is near impossible for her to see the trail or path of a seductive man, yet he has a goal just as "the way of an eagle in the sky, the way of a serpent on a rock, the way of a ship on the high seas." The seductive man has the objective of exploiting her for sex.

Revelation 3:3

³ Remember, then, what you received and heard. Keep it, and repent. If you will not wake up, I will come <u>like a thief</u>, and <u>you will not know at what hour I will come against you</u>.

Jesus said, "I will come (topic) like a thief (image)." There must be a similarity. The context of verse 3 answers the question for us, as it reads: "you will not know at what hour I will come against you." Therefore, we can rule out that the verse is telling us *why* he is coming, but instead tells us of *how* he will come. It will be like a thief, unforeseen and without warning.

The context helps us. Jesus went on to say, "You will not know at all at what hour I shall come upon you." (Revelation 3:3) Therefore, the comparison does not point to the purpose of his coming. He was not implying that he would come to steal anything. Rather, the point of comparison involves the unforeseen, without the warning aspect of his arrival.

1 Thessalonians 5:2

²For you yourselves are fully aware that the day of the Lord will come <u>like a thief in the night</u>.

While the context here does not offer us a spelled out explanation of the similarity, like the words of Jesus, it is best to use one part of the Bible to interpret the other. So, then, let us wake up!

Word Pictures and God

Psalm 145:3 (Updated American Standard Version)

³Great is Jehovah, and greatly to be praised, and <u>his greatness is unsearchable</u>.

God's greatness is unlimited. Even in perfection, we could spend hundreds of trillions of years, and we would never even come close to understanding, comprehending, or measuring his greatness. There are many examples within Scripture, which point to his greatness. When we look up at the starry heavens and realize that it would take 100,000 years at the speed of light, to cross just our galaxy.[60] Then, we reflect on the fact that there are over 100 billion galaxies in our universe. Moreover, it boggles our mind when we contemplate that there are countless universes, at least 10 to the 500 universes, which is a 1 followed by 500 zeroes! Then, we are certainly confounded at the idea that space itself is expanding at an accelerating pace!—Isaiah 40:26

Job 26:14

[14]Behold, these are but the outskirts of his ways, and how small a whisper do we hear of him! But <u>the thunder of his power who can understand</u>?"

As we can see from the above, the study of our physical creation only touches 'the outskirts of God's ways,' and is but 'a small whisper,' in comparison to "the thunder of his power." However, this is even truer of God's creation of spiritual and physical life, as well as the salvation that he has offered his fallen people. Yes, the thoughts of God are so deep that the ungodly are unable to understand the significance (not the meaning) of his Word.

It is impossible for us to understand the greatness and the power of God fully. However, the Bible paints the best picture, for our limited minds. Walk with me as I list just a few of these word pictures: a King, a Lawmaker, a Judge, and a Warrior, obviously, someone we should esteem and revere. He is also described as a Counselor, a Shepherd, an Instructor, a Teacher, a Father, a Healer, Lawgiver, and a Savior, One we can hardly resist loving.

Psalm 16:7 (Updated American Standard Version)

[7]I bless Jehovah who gives me <u>counsel</u>; in the night also my heart [or mind][61] instructs me.

See footnote. The kidneys are deep inside the body, so this text means that the counsel of God has reached the deepest part of the inner man, correcting his deepest thoughts and emotions.

---

[60] The Milky Way galaxy is some 600 quadrillion miles **[about a quintillion km]** in diameter, yes, 600,000,000,000,000,000 miles, and this one galaxy contains over 400 billion stars! The average distance between stars within the galaxy is about 36 trillion miles.

[61] Literally *kidneys*, figurative for inner man

Psalm 23:1 American Standard Version (ASV)

¹Jehovah is my <u>shepherd</u>; I shall not want.

The Middle Eastern shepherd of Bible times would care for each of his sheep as a group and individually, even naming every one of them. Each day he will call every one of his sheep to him, and as he strokes it, lovingly calling out its name, talking to it, he will look to see if it has suffered any injuries. If he happens upon an injury, he will apply oil or an ointment to accelerate the process of headlining. There may even be times, when a sheep is sick that the shepherd will have to force medicine down its throat, holding it throughout the day and night, making sure it does not lie down and die. This word picture perfectly demonstrates the love and tenderness that God has for each of us.

Psalm 32:8

⁸I will <u>instruct</u> you and <u>teach</u> you in the way you should go; I will <u>counsel</u> you with <u>my eye upon you</u>.

Our heavenly Father has a school of success, where all are welcome to join and have him as their Grand Instructor. Yes, we have access to the greatest instructor, as well as his head instructor, the Son, who will teach and counsel us, with their eyes always upon us. In addition, we are privileged to have the opportunity to be a sort of admissions counselor, so that others may gain access to this Grand Instructor.

Are there any requirements to be in this school of success? Yes, if there are requirements to enter a seminary, certainly, there are requirements to enter a school where God Himself is our instructor. There are two major requirements to enter this school. "'And you shall love the Lord your God with all your heart and with all your soul and with all your mind and with all your strength.' The second is this: 'You shall love your neighbor as yourself.' There is no other commandment greater than these.'" (Mark 12.30-31) Moreover, the head instructor of the school, Jesus Christ also said, "Not everyone who says to me, 'Lord, Lord,' will enter the kingdom of heaven, but **the one** <u>who does the will of my Father</u> who is in heaven." (Matt 7:21) Therefore, if we are to enter into the school of success, we must do it willingly, and we must be willing to apply the rules and principles within the textbook, i.e., the Holy Bible. The students must choose to willing serve God out of love, and agree to do his will, and be willing to be molded into a new person. (Col. 3:9-10; Eph. 4:22-24) The greatest thing about this school is, there is not graduation date, as it runs for an eternity.

'In all that the student does, he prospers.' (Psa. 1:1-3) This is nothing like the former way of things, nor any human institution. Some are very proud to have studied under some of the greatest Christian instructors of the 20th century, such as Norman L. Geisler, Gleason L. Archer, or John Gresham Machen. However, every human has the opportunity to study under the Father and the Son, and to be taught by Holy Spirit, and no greater privilege exists. There is no grander experience, with everlasting benefits. Moreover, what human instructor has ever cared intimately for the needs of each student individually, being there for them 24/7/365? He says of himself, "I am the Lord your God, who teaches you to profit, who leads you in the way you should go. Oh that you had paid attention to my commandments! Then your peace would have been like a river, and your righteousness like the waves of the sea;" (Isa 48:17-18) We are told of his textbook, that it is 'inspired by God and profitable for teaching, for reproof, for correction, for training in righteousness; so that the man of God may be adequate, equipped for every good work.' – 2 Timothy 3:16-17

Inanimate

2 Samuel 23:3 (ESV)	Psalm 18:2 (ASV)	Deuteronomy 32:4 (ESV)
3The God of Israel has spoken; the <u>Rock of Israel</u> has said to me: When one rules justly over men, ruling in the fear of God,	2 Jehovah is my <u>rock</u> and my fortress and my deliverer, my God, my <u>rock</u>, in whom I take refuge, my <u>shield</u>, and the <u>horn of my salvation</u>, my <u>stronghold</u>.	4"The <u>Rock</u>, his work is perfect, for all his ways are justice. A God of faithfulness and without iniquity, just and upright is he.

God is here described as "the Rock of Israel," as "my rock," and as "my stronghold," thus carrying the sense that God is a rock-solid source of security.

Personality

Psalm 84:11

11For the LORD God is <u>a sun and shield</u>; the LORD bestows favor and honor. No good thing does he withhold from those who walk uprightly.

God is the Source of light, life, energy, who protects his people.

Psalm 121:5 (UASV)

⁵ Jehovah is your keeper; Jehovah is your <u>shade on your right hand.</u>

Isaiah 51:16 (ESV)

¹⁶And I have put my words in your mouth and covered you in <u>the shadow of my hand</u>, establishing the heavens and laying the foundations of the earth, and saying to Zion, 'You are my people.'"

If any have ever been to Death Valley, "which is a desert valley located in Eastern California. Situated within the Mojave Desert, it is the lowest and driest area in North America, and currently the hottest in the world. Death Valley's Furnace Creek holds the record for the highest reliably reported air temperature in the world, 134 °F (56.7 °C) on July 10, 1913."[62] If stranded, when the sweltering sun is beating down at midday, a place of shade could mean the difference between life and death. In the same way, God can protect us from the heat of the disasters of this human imperfection, and the evil world that surrounds us.

Psalm 17:8

⁸Keep me as the <u>apple of your eye</u>; hide me in <u>the shadow of your wings,</u>

The Hebrew word *'ishohn'* (Deut. 32:10; Pro 7:2), when used with *'a'yin* (eye), it literally means "little man of the eye"; likewise, *bath* (daughter) is used at Lamentations 2:18 with the idea "daughter of the eye," both denoting the pupil. The two are joined for emphasis at Psalm 17:8 (*'ishohn' bath-'a'yin*), literally, "little man, daughter of the eye" ("pupil of the eyeball"). "The black center of the eyeball, formally, "the little man (of the eye)," often translated as "the apple of the eye," an idiom of care and love."[63] The allusion is obviously to the small image of oneself, which can be seen reflected in that part of another's eye.

The eyes are one of the most tender and sensitive parts of the human body, and even a microscopic piece of dust can cause serious irritation if it gets between lid and eyeball. Even the slightest damage to the cornea covering the pupil, it will become cloudy through disease, resulting in distorted vision or possible blindness. Proverbs 7:2 reads "Keep my

---

⁶² http://en.wikipedia.org/wiki/Death_Valley

⁶³ William D. Mounce, *Mounce's Complete Expository Dictionary of Old & New Testament Words* (Grand Rapids, MI: Zondervan, 2006), 893.

commandments and live, And my teaching as the apple [lit., pupil] of your eye." This means that God's laws and teachings are to be guarded with paramount care. In the above Psalm, 17:8, David is asking God to be quick to come to his rescue when the enemies attacked, just as we would quickly react if some foreign object is getting in our eye.

Ephesians 1:18

18 having the eyes of your hearts enlightened, that you may know what is the hope to which he has called you, what are the riches of his glorious inheritance in the saints,

"Eyes of your heart" is a Hebrew Scripture expression, meaning spiritual insight, to grasp the truth of God's Word. So we could pray for the guidance of God's Spirit, and at the same time, we can explain why there are so many different understandings (many wrong answers), some of which contradict each other, as being human imperfection that is diluting some of those interpreters, causing them to lose the Spirit's guidance. When we say spiritual guidance, we are not saying the Holy Spirit is guiding the Christian along, but that the Word of God is inspirited, and it is a guide. Therefore, if we objectively apply biblical interpretation rules and principles in a balanced manner, Holy Spirit guides us.

A person sits down to study and prays earnestly for the guidance of Holy Spirit, that his mental disposition be in harmony with God's Word [or simply that his heart be in harmony with . . .], and sets out to study a chapter, an article, something biblical. In the process of that study, he allows himself to be moved, not by a mental disposition in harmony with the Spirit, but by human imperfection, by way of his wrong worldview, his biases, his preunderstanding.[64]

Psalm 36:7

7How precious is your steadfast love, O God! The children of mankind take refuge in the shadow of your wings.

God's "steadfast love" is nothing like any human ruler could ever hope to possess. Rather, there is a strong and secure sense, as well as loyalty essential in it. This quality is displayed naturally toward all, but especially to those, who remain loyal to him. An eagle is a large bird of prey, and any eaglet that might sour beneath its wings would have no need of fearing anything. King David received such protection from God

---

[64] Preunderstanding is all of the knowledge and understanding that we possess before we begin the study of the text.

on many occasions, so well could David write the words found in Psalm 36:7.

Psalm 103:12

[12]as far as the east is from the west, so far does he remove our transgressions from us.

We will notice in Psalm 103:12, that God removes the sins of the repentant one as far as the east is from the west. The picture being painted is, to the human mind that is the farthest we can remove something, as there is no greater distance.

Isaiah 38:17

[17] Behold, it was for my welfare that I had great bitterness; but in love you have delivered my life from the pit of destruction, for you have cast all my sins behind your back.

In Isaiah 38, we are given another visual, God throwing our sins behind his back, meaning he can no longer see them, as they are out of sight, thus out of mind.

Micah 7:19

[19]He will again have compassion on us; he will tread our iniquities underfoot. You will cast all our sins into the depths of the sea.

In Micah, our last example, we see that God hurls all of the sins of a repentant person into the depths of the sea. In the setting of the ancient person, this meant that retrieving them was literally impossible. In other words, God has removed them, never to be retrieved or brought to mind ever again. This was the viewpoint that he had before Jesus ever even offered himself as a ransom sacrifice.

Word Pictures and Jesus

John 1:34

[34]And I have seen and have borne witness that this is the Son of God.

Of course, God, the Father, does not literally have a wife, producing a Son, as he is Spirit. So this expression, Son of God, is a word picture, to better help us understand the relationship between two different persons.

John 15:1, 4

[1] "I am the <u>true vine</u>, and my <u>Father is the vinedresser</u>. [4] Abide in me, and I in you. As the branch cannot bear fruit by itself, unless it abides in the vine, neither can you, unless you abide in me."

These are word pictures, used to help us better understand the role that the Son is playing in the outworking of the Father's will and purposes. What point is this word picture making for us? If a literal branch is to remain alive, it must remain connected to the trunk. In this same way, a disciple of Christ must abide in Jesus (remain in him). Yes, 'apart from Jesus we can do nothing.' (John 15:5) In addition, the cultivator of a vine expects that it will produce fruit, the 'Father is glorified, that we bear much fruit and so prove to be Jesus' disciples.'--John 15:8

What important points does this word picture teach? To remain alive and fruitful, the branches of a literal vine must remain attached to the trunk. Similarly, Christ's disciples must remain in union with him. "Apart from me you can do nothing at all," Jesus said. (John 15:5) And just as a cultivator expects a vine to produce fruit, Jehovah expects those in union with Christ to produce spiritual fruitage.—John 15:8.

Word Pictures and the Similarity

One can never find the meaning of the word picture, without finding the similarity. In fact, as our example below illustrates, to miss the mark is dangerous, if taken the wrong way.

Romans 12:20

[20] To the contrary, "if your enemy is hungry, feed him; if he is thirsty, give him something to drink; for by so doing you will <u>heap burning coals on his head</u>."

Are we to infer that Paul was suggesting a retaliate attitude? No. Here we have to go back to the historical setting of the first-century. The melting of ore in order to get metal from it was accomplished by heaping the hot coals on top of the ore. This process was to soften the metal to cause impurities to separate. The similarity is that we are to soften the enemy with loving kindness, rapport and bring out the good in him.

Luke 11:4

[4] and forgive us our sins, for we ourselves forgive everyone who is <u>indebted</u> to us. And lead us not into temptation."

Do our sins feel like a debt to us? Therefore, we are moved emotionally, when God 'forgives our transgressions and covers our sins.'-- Psalm 32:1

Word Pictures

The word picture is capable of taking a difficult concept and using an easier one, to help us wrap our mind around the difficulty. There can be multiple word pictures, to highlight the different aspects of the subject. The word picture may be used to emphasize the concept the author is trying to bring out, more memorable, more appealing.

Recognizing the Different Features

WORD PICTURE: "He is like a tree planted by streams of water." (Psalm 1:3)

TOPIC: Us (those of us who love God's Word, vs. 1-2)

IMAGE: tree planted by streams of water

SIMILARITY IN CONTEXT: life is drawn through the root from the water; we draw spiritual vitality through God's Word

LESSON: Just as a tree that is most healthy by being next to its life-sustaining element of water, we are most healthy when we are in the Word of personal study, meeting, ministry, and evangelism.

Part II FUNDAMENTAL CONDITIONS OF PROFITABLE BIBLE STUDY

CHAPTER 8 The Fundamental Conditions of the Most Profitable Bible Study

We have considered seven profitable methods of Bible study. There is something, however, in Bible study more important than the best methods, that is, The Fundamental Conditions of Profitable Study. The one who meets these conditions will get more out of the Bible, while pursuing the poorest method, than the one who does not meet them will, while pursuing the best method. Many a one who is eagerly asking, "What method shall I pursue in my Bible study?" needs something that goes far deeper than a new and better method.

Buy Out the Time

Many want to understand, to be fearless, and capable of sharing Bible truth with others. However, if this is to be the case, we must be willing to buy out a small amount of time from the worldly wicked age that surrounds us, and invest it into a small study program. Many people want to do many things, but they allow the time to slip by. The thought of, 'oh! If only I had started six months ago, I would be so far along now!' Do not let another six months slip by.

Colossians 4:5-6 Updated American Standard Version (UASV)

⁵ Walk in wisdom toward outsiders, buying out for yourselves the time. ⁶ Let your speech always be gracious, seasoned with salt, so that you may know how you ought to answer each person.

The recommendation once more is to set aside one hour each day for God. If we are able to spend more time, this is entirely up to us. What must be realized is just how much time we give to the world around us, a world that lies in the hands of Satan. Is it too much to ask that we give one hour a day to the Creator of life? We simply get up one hour earlier than we normally do, and we will have our study in before the day even begins. The beautiful thing about that plan is; it will start our day on a spiritual track, meaning a better day from the beginning.

For a Love for the Bible

A man, who eats with an appetite, will get far more good out of his meal than a man who eats from a sense of duty. It is well when a student of the Bible can say with Job, "I have treasured up the words of his mouth more than my necessary food," (Job, 23:12 R. V.) or with

Jeremiah, "Thy words were found and I did eat them; and thy words were unto me a joy and the rejoicing of mine heart; for I am called by thy name, O, Lord God of hosts." (Jer., 15:16, R. V.) Many come to the table God has spread in His word with no appetite for spiritual food, and go mincing here and there and grumbling about everything. Spiritual indigestion lies at the bottom of much modern criticism of the Bible. But how can one get a love for the Bible? First of all by being born again. Where there is life there is likely to be appetite. A dead man never hungers. This brings us back to the first condition. But going beyond this, the more there is of vitality the more there is of hunger. Abounding life means abounding hunger for the Word. Study of the Word stimulates love for the Word. The author can well remember the time when he had more appetite for books about the Bible than he had for the Bible itself, but with increasing study there has come increasing love for the Book. Bearing in mind who the author of the Book is, what its purpose is, what its power is, what the riches of its contents are, will go far toward stimulating a love and appetite for the Book.

Be Willing to Work Hard

Solomon has given a graphic picture of the Bible student who gets the most profit out of his study,

The Value of Wisdom

Proverbs 2:1-6 Updated American Standard Version (UASV)

2 My son, if you receive my words
  and treasure up my commandments with you,
2 making your ear attentive to wisdom
  and inclining your heart to discernment;[65]
3 For if you cry for discernment[66]
  and raise your voice for understanding,
4 if you seek it like silver
  and search for it as for hidden treasures,
5 then you will understand the fear of Jehovah
  and find the knowledge of God.

---

[65] The Hebrew word rendered here as "discernment" (*tevunah*) is related to the word *binah*, translated "understanding." Both appear at Proverbs 2:3.

[66] See 2.2 ftn.

⁶ For Jehovah gives wisdom;
    from his mouth come knowledge and understanding;

Now, seeking for silver and searching for hid treasures, means hard work, and the one who wishes to get not only the silver but the gold as well out of the Bible, and find its "hid treasures," must make up his mind to dig. It is not glancing at the word, or reading the word, but studying the Word, meditating on the word, pondering the word that brings the richest yields. The reason why many get so little out of their Bible reading is simply because they are not willing to think. Intellectual laziness lies at the bottom of a large percent of fruitless Bible reading.

People are constantly crying for new methods of Bible study, but what many of them wish is simply some method of Bible study by which they can get all the good out of the Bible without work. If someone could tell lazy Christians some method of Bible study whereby they could put the sleepiest ten minutes of the day, just before they go to bed, into Bible study, and get the profit out of it that God intends His children shall get out of the study of His Word, that would be just what they desire. But it can't be done. Men must be willing to work and work hard, if they wish to dig out the treasures of infinite wisdom and knowledge and blessing which He has stored up in His Word. A business friend once asked me in a hurried call to tell him "in a word" how to study his Bible. I replied, "Think." The Psalmist pronounces that man "blessed" who "*meditates* in the law of the Lord, *day and night*." (Ps. 1:2.) The Lord commanded Joshua to "*meditate therein day and night*," and assured him that as a result of this meditation "*then* thou shalt make thy way prosperous, and *then* thou shalt have good success." (Josh. 1:8.)

Of Mary, the mother of Jesus, we read, "Mary kept all these sayings, pondering them in her heart." (Luke 2:19, R. V.) In this way alone can one study the Bible to the greatest profit. One pound of beef well chewed and digested and assimilated, will give more strength than tons of beef merely glanced at; and one verse of scripture chewed and digested and assimilated, will give more strength than whole chapters simply skimmed. Weigh every word we read in the Bible. Look at it. Turn it over and over. The most familiar passages get a new meaning in this way. Spend fifteen minutes on each word in Ps. 23:1, or Phil. 4:19, and see if it is not so.

Wholly Surrender to God

Jesus said, "If anyone's will is to do God's will, he will know whether the teaching is from God or whether I am speaking on my own authority." (John. 7:17, ESV) A surrendered will gives that clearness of spiritual vision, which is necessary to understand God's book. Many of the difficulties and obscurities of the Bible arise wholly from the fact that the will of the student is not surrendered to the will of the author of the book. It is remarkable how clear and straightforward and beautiful passages that once puzzled us become when we are brought to that place where we say to God, "I surrender my will unconditionally to Thine. I have no will but Thine. Teach me Thy will." A surrendered will leads to more that will make the Bible an open book than a university education.

It is just impossible to get the largest profit out of your Bible study until you do surrender your will to God. You must be very definite about this. There are many who say, "Oh, yes, my will, I think, is surrendered to God," and yet it is not. They have never gone alone with God and said intelligently and definitely to him, "O God, I here and now give myself up to Thee, for Thee to command me, and lead me, and shape me, and send me, and do with me, absolutely as Thou wilt." Such an act is a wonderful key to unlock the treasure house of God's Word. The Bible becomes a new book when a man does that. Doing that wrought a complete transformation in the author's theology and life and ministry.

Obedient to its Teachings

It was good advice James gave to early Christians, and to us, "be doers of the word, and not hearers only, deceiving yourselves." There are a good many, who consider themselves Bible students, who are deceiving themselves in this way to-day. They see what the Bible teaches, but they do not do it, and they soon lose their power to see it. Truth obeyed leads to more truth. Truth disobeyed destroys the capacity for discovering truth. There must be not only a general surrender of the will but specific practical obedience to each new word of God discovered. There is no place where the law, "For to everyone who has will more be given, and he will have an abundance. But from the one who has not, even what he has will be taken away," is more joyously certain on the one hand and more sternly inexorable on the other, than in the matter of using or refusing the truth revealed in the Bible.

Use, and we get more; refuse, and we lose all. Do not study the Bible for the mere gratification of intellectual curiosity, but to find out how to live and to please God. Whatever duty we find commanded in the Bible, do it at once. Whatever good we see in any Bible character, imitate it immediately. Whatever mistake we note in the actions of Bible men and women, scrutinize our own life to see if we are making the same mistake, and if we find that we are, correct it forthwith. James compares the Bible to a looking glass. (Jam. 1:23, 24). The chief good of a looking glass, is to show us if there is anything out of whack about us, and, if we find there is, we can set it right. Use the Bible in that way. Obeying the truth we already see, will solve the enigmas in the verses we do not as yet understand. Disobeying the truth we see, darkens the whole world of truth.

This is the secret of much of the skepticism and error of the day. Men saw the truth, but did not do it; now it is gone. I knew a bright and promising young minister. He made rapid advancement in the truth. He took very advanced ground upon one point especially, and the storm came. One day he said to his wife, "It is very nice to believe this, but we need not speak so much about it." They began, or he, at least, to hide their testimony. The wife died, and he drifted. The Bible became to him a sealed book. Faith reeled. He publicly renounced his faith in some of the fundamental truths of the Bible. He seemed to lose his grip even on the doctrine of immortality. What was the cause of it all? Truth not lived and stood for, flees. That man is much admired and applauded by some to-day, but daylight has given place to darkness in his soul.

Have a Child-Like Mind

God reveals His deepest truths to babes. No age needs more than our own to lay to heart the words of Jesus, "I thank you, Father,, Lord of heaven and earth, that you have hidden these things from the wise and understanding and revealed them to little children." (Matt. 11:25.) Wherein must we be babes if God is to reveal His truth unto us, and we are to understand His Word? A child is not full of its own wisdom. It recognizes its ignorance and is ready to be taught. It does not oppose its own notions and ideas to those of its teachers. It is in that spirit we should come to the Bible if we are to get the most profit out of our study. Do not come to the Bible full of our own ideas, and seeking from it a confirmation of them. Come rather to find out what are God's ideas as He has revealed them there. Come not to find a confirmation of our own opinion, but to be taught what God may be pleased to teach. If a man comes to the Bible just to find his notions taught there, he will find them; but if he comes, recognizing his own ignorance, just as a little child, to be taught, he will find something infinitely better than his own notions, even the mind of God.

We see why it is that many persons cannot see things, which are plainly taught in the Bible. The doctrine taught is not their notion, of which they are so full that there is no room left for that which the Bible actually teaches. We have an illustration of this in the apostles themselves at one stage in their training. In Mark 9:31 we read "he was teaching his disciples, saying to them, 'The Son of Man is going to be delivered into the hands of men, and they will kill him. And when he is killed, after three days he will rise.'" Now, that is as plain and definite as language can make it, but it was utterly contrary to the notions of the apostles as to what was to happen to the Christ. So we read in the next verse "they understood not that saying." Is not that wonderful? But is it any more wonderful than our own inability to comprehend plain statements in the Bible when they run counter to our preconceived notions? What trouble many Christians find with portions of the Sermon on the Mount, that would be plain enough, if we just came to Christ like a child to be taught what to believe and do, rather than coming as full grown men, who already know it all, and who must find some interpretations of Christ's words that will fit into our mature and infallible philosophy.

Many a man is so full of an unbiblical theology he has been taught, that it takes him a lifetime to get rid of it, and understand the clear teaching of the Bible. "Oh, what can this verse mean?" many a bewildered man cries. Why it means what it plainly says; but what we are after is not the meaning God has manifestly put into it, but the meaning we can by some ingenious trick of exegesis twist out of it and make it fit into our scheme. Do not come to the Bible to find out what we can make it mean, but to find out what God intended it to mean.

Men often miss the real truth of a verse by saying, "But that can be interpreted this way." Oh, yes, so it can, but is that the way God intended it to be interpreted? We all need to pray often, if we would get the most profit out of our Bible study, "Oh, God, make me a little child. Empty me of my own notions. Teach me thine own mind. Make me ready like a little child to receive all that thou hast to say, no matter how contrary it is to what I have thought hitherto." How the Bible opens up to one who approaches it in that way! How it closes up to the wise fool, who thinks he knows everything, and imagines he can give points to Peter and Paul, and even to Jesus Christ and to God Himself! Someone has well said the best method of Bible study is "the baby method." I was once talking with a ministerial friend about what seemed to be the clear teaching of a certain passage. "Yes," he replied, "but that doesn't agree with my philosophy." Alas! However, this man was sincere, yet he did not have the child-like spirit, which is an essential condition of the most profitable Bible study.

However, there are many who approach the Bible in the same way. It is a great point gained in Bible study when we are brought to realize that an infinite God knows more than we, that indeed our highest wisdom is less than the knowledge of the most ignorant babe compared with His, and when we come to Him as babes, just to be taught by Him, and not to argue with Him. But we so easily and so constantly forget this, that every time we open our Bibles we would do well to get down humbly before God and say, "Father, I am but a child, teach me."

Study it as the Word of God

The Apostle Paul, in writing to the Church of the Thessalonians, thanked God without ceasing that when they received the word of God they "accepted it not as the word of men, but as it is in truth the word of God." (1 Thess. 2:13, R. V.) Well, might he thank God for that, and well may we thank God when we get to the place where we receive the word of God *as the word of God.* Not that the one who does not believe the Bible is the word of God should be discouraged from studying it. Indeed, one of the best things that one who does not believe that the Bible is the word of God can do if he is honest, is to study it. The author of this book once doubted utterly that the Bible was the word of God, and the firm confidence that he has to-day that the Bible is the Word of God has come more from the study of the book itself than from anything else. Those who doubt it are more usually those who study about the book, than those who dig into the actual teachings of the book itself. But while the best book of Christian evidences is the Bible, and while the most utter skeptic should be encouraged to study it, we will not get the largest measure of profit out of that study until we reach the point where we become convinced that the Bible is God's Word, and when we study it as such. There is a great difference between believing theoretically that the Bible is God's Word and studying it as God's Word. Thousands would tell us that they believed the Bible is God's Word, who do not study it as God's Word.

Studying the Bible as the Word of God involves four things. **(1)** First, it involves the unquestioning acceptance of its teachings when definitely ascertained, even when they may appear unreasonable or impossible. Reason demands that we submit our judgment and reasoning to the statements of infinite wisdom. There is nothing more irrational than rationalism, which makes the finite wisdom the test of infinite wisdom, and submits the teachings of God's omniscience to the approval of man's judgment. It is truly the greatest self-importance that says, "This cannot be true, though God says it, for it does not approve itself to *my* reason."

Romans 9:20 Updated American Standard Version (UASV)

20 On the contrary, O man, who are you who answers back to God? Will what is molded say to the one who molded it, "Why did you make me like this"?

Real human wisdom, when it finds infinite wisdom, bows before it and says, "Speak what thou wilt and I will believe." When we have once became convinced that the Bible is God's Word, its teachings must be the end of all controversy and discussion. A "thus saith the Lord" will settle every question. Yet there are many who profess to believe that the Bible is the Word of God, and if you show them what the Bible clearly teaches on some disputed point, they will shake their heads and say, "Yes, but I *think* so and so," or "Doctor ——, or Prof. this, or our church don't teach that way."

There is little profit in that sort of Bible study. **(2)** Studying the Bible as the word of God involves, in the second place, absolute reliance upon all its promises in all their length and breadth. The man, who studies the Bible as the word of God, will not discount any one of its promises one iota. The one who studies the Bible as the word of God will say, "God who cannot lie has promised," and will not try to make God a liar by trying to make one of his promises mean less than it says. The one, who studies the Bible as the word of God, will be on the lookout for promises, and as soon as he finds one he will seek to ascertain just what it means, and, as soon as he discovers, he will step right out upon that promise, and risk everything upon its full import. That is one of the secrets of profitable Bible study. Be hunting for promises and appropriate them as fast as we find them—this is done by meeting the conditions and risking all upon them. That is the way to make our own all the fullness of blessing God has for us. This is the key to all the treasures of God's grace.

Happy is the man who has so learned to study the Bible as God's word, that he is ready to claim for himself every new promise as it appears, and to risk everything upon it. **(3)** Studying the Bible as the Word of God involves, in the third place, obedience—prompt, exact obedience, without asking any questions—to it is every precept. Obedience may seem hard, it may seem impossible, but God has bidden it and I have nothing to do but to obey, and leave the results with God. If we would get the very most profit out of our Bible study, resolve that from this time we will claim every clear promise and obey every plain command, and that as to the promises and commands whose import is not yet clear we will try to get their meaning made clear.

(4) Studying the Bible as the word of God involves, in the fourth place, studying it as in God's presence. When we read a verse of Scripture, hear the voice of the living God speaking directly to us in these written words. There is new power and attractiveness in the Bible when we have learned to hear a living, present person, God, our Father, Himself talking directly to us in these words. One of the most fascinating and inspiring statements in the Bible is "Enoch walked with God." (Gen. 5:24.) We can have God's glorious companionship any moment we please, by simply opening His Word and letting the living and ever present God speak to us through it. With what holy awe and strange and unutterable joy one studies the Bible if he studies it in this way! It is heaven come down to earth.

Prayerfulness

The Psalmist prayed, "Open my eyes, that I may behold wondrous things out of your law." (Ps. 119:18.) Everyone who desires to get the greatest profit out of his Bible study needs to offer that or a similar prayer every time he undertakes the study of the Word. Few keys open so many caskets that contain hidden treasure as prayer. Few clues unravel so many difficulties. Few microscopes will disclose so many beauties hidden from the eye of the ordinary observer. What new light often shines from an old familiar text as we bend over it in prayer! I believe in studying the Bible a good deal on our knees. When one reads an entire book through upon his knees—and this is easily done—that book has a new meaning and becomes a new book.

One ought never to open the Bible to read it without at least lifting the heart to God in silent prayer that He will interpret it, illumine its pages by the light of His Spirit. It is a rare privilege to study any book under the immediate guidance and instruction of its author, and this is the privilege of us all in studying the Bible. When one comes to a passage that is difficult to understand or difficult to interpret, instead of giving it up, or rushing to some learned friend, or to some commentary, he should lay that passage before God, and ask Him to explain it to him, pleading God's promise,

James 1:5-6 Updated American Standard Version (UASV)

5 But if any of you lacks wisdom, let him ask of God, who gives to all generously and without reproaching,[67] and it will be given to him. **6** But

---

[67] Without *criticizing*

let him ask in faith, without any doubting, for the one who doubts is like a wave of the sea that is driven and tossed by the wind.

It is simply wonderful how the seemingly most difficult passages become plain by this treatment. Harry Morehouse, one of the most remarkable Bible scholars among unlearned men, used to say, that whenever he came to a passage in the Bible which he could not understand, he would search through the Bible for some other passage that threw light upon it, and lay it before God in prayer, and that he had never found a passage that did not yield to this treatment.

CHAPTER 9 Final Suggestions

There are some suggestions that remain to be given before we close this book.

Study the Bible Daily

Regularity counts for more in Bible study than most people fancy. The spasmodic student, who at certain seasons gives lots of time to the study of the Word, and at other seasons quite neglects it, even for days at a time, does not achieve the results that he does who plods on regularly day by day. The Bereans were wise as well as "noble" in that they "searched the scriptures daily." (Acts, 17:11; see also R. V.) A man who is well known among the Christian college students of America, once remarked at a student convention, that he had been at many conventions and had received great blessings from them, but the greatest blessing he had ever received was from a convention where there were only four persons gathered together. The blessing had come to him in this way. These four had covenanted together to spend a certain portion of every day in Bible study. Since that day much of his time had been spent on the cars or in hotels and at conventions, but he had tried to keep that covenant, and the greatest blessing that had come to him in his Christian life had come through this *daily* study of the Word. No one who has not tried it realizes how much can be accomplished by setting apart a fixed portion of each day, (it may not be more than fifteen or thirty minutes, but it surely should be an hour) for Bible study, and keeping it sacredly for that purpose under all circumstances. Many will say I cannot spare the time. It will be time saved. Lord Cairnes, one of the busiest as well as most eminent men of his day, before his death testified, that the first two hours of every day were given to the study of the Bible and prayer, and he attributed the great achievements of his life to that fact. It will not do to study the Bible only when we feel like it. It will not do to study the Bible only when we have leisure. We must have fixed principles and habits in this matter if we are to study the Bible to the greatest profit. Nothing that we do will be more important than our Bible study, and it cannot give way to other less important things. What regularity in eating is to physical life, regularity in Bible study is to spiritual life. Fix upon some time, even if it is no more than fifteen minutes to start with, and hold to it until we are ready to set a longer period.

2. *Select for our Bible studies the best portion of the day that we can give to it.* Do not put our Bible study off until near bedtime, when the

mind is drowsy. It is well to take a parting verse for the day when one retires for the night, but this is not the time for study. No study demands all that there is in a man as Bible study does. Do not take the time immediately after a heavy meal. The mind is more or less torpid after a heavy meal, and it is unwise to put it on the stretch then. It is almost the unanimous opinion of those who have given this subject careful attention, which the early hours of the day are the best for Bible study if they can be secured free from interruption. It is well, wherever possible, to lock ourselves in and shut the world out when we are about to give ourselves up to the study of the Bible.

Look for Christ

We read of Jesus that "And beginning with Moses and all the Prophets, he interpreted to them in all the Scriptures the things concerning himself." (Luke 24:27.) Jesus Christ is the subject of the whole Bible, and the subject pervades the book. Some of the seemingly driest portions of the Bible became instinct with a new life when we learn to see Christ in them. I remember in my early reading of the Bible what a stupid book Leviticus seemed, but it all became different when I learned to see Jesus in the various offerings and sacrifices, in the high-priest and his garments, in the tabernacle and its furniture, indeed everywhere.

Memorize Scripture

The Psalmist said, "I have stored up your word in my heart, that I might not sin against you." (Ps. 119:11, ESV) There is nothing better to keep one from sinning than this. By the word of God laid up in His heart Jesus overcame the tempter. (Matt. 4:4, 7, 10.) But the word of God laid up in the heart is good for other purposes than victory over sin. It is good to meet and expose error; it is good to enable one "to speak a word in season to him that is weary," (Is. 1:4.) It is good for manifold uses, even "that the man of God may be complete, furnished completely unto every good work." (2 Tim. 3:17, R. V.) Memorize scripture by chapter and verse. It is quite as easy as merely memorizing the words, and it is immeasurably more useful for practical purposes. Memorize the scripture in systematic form. Do not have a chaotic heap of texts in the mind, but pigeon-hole under appropriate titles the Scripture we store in memory. Then we can bring it out when we need it, without racking our brains. There are many men who can stand up without a moment's warning, and talk coherently and cogently and Scripturally, on any vital theme; because they have a vast fund of wisdom in the form of scripture texts stored away in their mind in systematic form.

Use Spare Moments for Study of the Bible

In most men's lives, there is a vast amount of wasted time. Time spent in traveling on the public transportation; time spent in waiting for persons with whom they have engagements; time spent in waiting for meals, in the doctor's offices, etc. Most of this can be utilized in Bible study if one carries with him a pocket Bible. Or one can utilize it in meditation upon texts stored away in memory. Many of the author's sermons and addresses are worked out in that way. Then, today, we can buy an Amazon Kindle device, or a Barnes & Noble Nook, which can hold over 3,500 books, and even has a built-in dictionary a highlighter. How many books of the Bible could while we are waiting for someone or something? A friend once told me that the man who had, in some respects, the most extraordinary knowledge of the Bible of any man he knew, was a junk dealer in a Canadian city. This man had a Bible open on his shelves and in intervals of business he was pondering the Book of God. The book became very black by handling in such surroundings, but I have little doubt his soul became correspondingly white. There is no economy that pays as does economy of time, but there is no way of economizing time so thriftily as putting the moments that are going to waste into the study of or meditation upon the word of God.

PART III Biblical Interpretation

For a great conservative book on interpreting the Bible, please see INTERPRETING THE BIBLE: Introduction to Biblical Hermeneutics by Edward D. Andrews (http://tiny.cc/gulsdy) ISBN-13: 978-1-945757-07-5

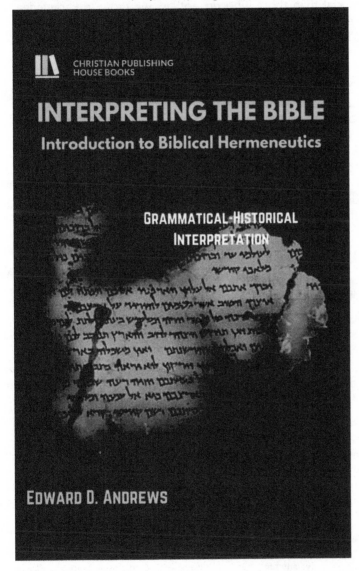

CHAPTER 10 Why Study the Bible?

The Bible is a revelation from our heavenly Father, about our heavenly Father, i.e., his will and purposes. (1 Thessalonians 2:13) If we take the things we learn, and apply them in our lives, we will live a life far more beneficial than those who do not. As we grow in knowledge, we will draw ever closer to God, the Giver of "Every good gift and every perfect gift." (James 1:17, ESV) We will discover the beauty of prayer. We will find that God is strengthening us to cope in times of trouble. If we live and walk in harmony with his Word, the opportunity of eternal life awaits us.—Romans 6:2

The Bible Gives Us Answers to Questions about Life

The Bible gives us answers to questions about this life and the one to come, which can be found nowhere else, and offers illumination to its readers. Those that take in this life-saving knowledge are freed from the misunderstandings of life that dominate billions of others. For instance, here is one that might come as a shock. We are all **Mentally Bent toward Evil**.

Psalm 51:5 Updated American Standard Version (UASV)

⁵ Behold, I was brought forth in iniquity,[68]
and in sin did my mother conceive me.

King David had his adultery with Bathsheba and the subsequent murder of her husband exposed, for which he accepted full responsibility. His words about the human condition give us one reason for the evil of man. He says, "I was brought forth in iniquity." What is iniquity? The Hebrew word *awon* essentially relates to erring, acting illegally or wrongly.

David stated that his problem was a corrupt heart, saying; **surely, I was sinful at birth**. He entered this world a sinner in nature long before he became a sinner in actions. In fact, this internal corruption predated his **birth**, actually beginning nine months earlier when he was **conceived** in the womb. It was at conception that the Adamic sin nature was

---

[68] Iniquity "signifies an offense, intentional or not, against God's law." (VCEDONTW, Volume 1, Page 122) Really, anything not in harmony with God's personality, standards, ways, and will, which mars one's relationship with God.

transmitted to him. The problem with what he did, sin, arose from what he was, a sinner.[69]

David is not here casting the blame onto his mother, as God never intended mothers to conceive and give birth children who would sin. Nevertheless, when Adam and Eve rebelled, were expelled from the Garden of Eden, they lost their ability to pass on perfection. Therefore, every child was born missing the mark of perfection. The Hebrew term translated "sin" is *chattath*; in Greek, the word is *hamartia*. Both carry the meaning of missing the mark of perfection.

The verbal forms occur in enough secular contexts to provide a basic picture of the word's meaning. In Jud 20:16 the left-handed slingers of Benjamin are said to have the skill to throw stones at targets and "not miss." In a different context, Pro. 19:2 speaks of a man in a hurry who "misses his way" (RSV, neb, KJV has "sinneth"). A similar idea of not finding a goal appears in Pro. 8:36; the concept of failure is implied.[70]

Genesis 6:5 The American Translation (AT)	**Genesis 8:21** The American Translation (AT)
5 When the LORD saw that the wickedness of man on the earth was great, and that the **whole bent of his thinking was** never anything but **evil**, the LORD regretted that he had ever made man on the earth.	21 I will never again curse the soil, though the **bent of man's mind** may be **evil from his very youth**; nor ever again will I ever again destroy all life creature as I have just done.

All of us have inherited a sinful nature, meaning that we are currently unable to live up to the mark of perfection, in which we were created. In fact, Genesis 6:5 says we all suffer from, 'our whole bent of thinking, which is nothing but evil." Genesis 8:21 says that 'our mind is evil from our very youth.' Jeremiah 17:9 says that our hearts are

---

69 Anders, Max; Lawson, Steven (2004-01-01). Holman Old Testament Commentary - Psalms: 11 (p. 266). B&H Publishing. Kindle Edition.

70 G. Herbert Livingston, "638 חטא," ed. R. Laird Harris, Gleason L. Archer Jr., and Bruce K. Waltke, *Theological Wordbook of the Old Testament* (Chicago: Moody Press, 1999), 277.

treacherous and desperately sick." What does all of this mean? It means that prior to the fall, our natural inclination; our natural leaning was toward good. However, after the fall, our natural inclination, our natural leaning was toward bad, wicked, evil.

We should never lose sight of the fact that unrighteous desires of the flesh are not to be taken lightly. (Rom. 7:19, 20) Nevertheless, if it is our desire to have a righteous relationship before God, it will be the stronger desire. Psalm 119:165 says, "Abundant peace belongs to those who love Your instruction; nothing makes them stumble." We need to cultivate our love for doing right, which will strengthen our conscience, the sense of what is right and wrong that governs somebody's thoughts and actions, urging us to do right rather than wrong. It is only through studying the Bible that we can train the conscience. Once it is trained, it will prick us like a needle in the arm, when we are thinking of doing something wrong. It will feel like a pain in our heart, sadness, nervousness, which is the voice saying, 'do not do this.' Moreover, if we ignore our voice, it will grow silent over time, and will stop telling us what is wrong.—Romans 2:14-15.

James 1:14-15 Updated American Standard Version (UASV)

14 But each one is tempted when he is carried away and enticed by his own desire.[71] 15 Then the desire when it has conceived gives birth to sin, and sin when it is fully grown brings forth death.

We have a natural desire toward wrongdoing, and Satan is the god of this world (2 Cor. 4:3-4), and he caters to the fallen flesh. James also tells us "each person is tempted when he is lured and enticed by his own desire. Then desire when it has conceived gives birth to sin, and sin, when it is fully grown, brings forth death." (James 1:14-15, ESV) We resist the devil by immediately dismissing any thought that is contrary to God's values found in his Word, which enters our mind, we do not entertain it for a moment, nor do we cultivate it, causing it to grow. We then offer rational prayers in our head, or better yet, out loud, so we can defeat irrational fleshly thinking with rational biblical thinking. The Apostle Peter, referring to the Devil wrote, "Resist him, firm in your faith, knowing that the same kinds of suffering are being experienced by your brotherhood throughout the world." (1 Pet. 5:9) While the Bible helps us better to understand the gravity of our fallen condition, this should not cause us alarm as the Bible also shows us how to control our mental bent toward evil. We can renew our mind (Rom 12:2), acquire the mind of

---

71 Or "own *lust*"

Christ (1 Cor. 2:16)), take off the old person and put on the new person (Eph. 4:20-24; Col 3:9-10), among other things.

The Bible Offers How to Get the Best out of Life Now

Another facet of benefiting from the Bible is that it shows us the way to get the best out of life now, even in imperfection.

1 Timothy 3:2 Updated American Standard Version (UASV)

2 The overseer must be above reproach, the husband of one wife, <u>temperate</u>, sober-minded, respectable, hospitable, able to teach,

2 Corinthians 7:1 Updated American Standard Version (UASV)

7 Therefore, having these promises, beloved, let us <u>cleanse ourselves from all defilement</u> of flesh and spirit, perfecting holiness in the fear of God.

1 Corinthians 6:18 Updated American Standard Version (UASV)

18 <u>Flee from sexual immorality.</u>[72] Every other sin that a man commits is outside the body, but the sexually immoral person sins against his own body.

What do we discover in these three texts? Is there any doubt that if we possess the quality of self-control that we will not have better health and better relationships. Through 'cleansing ourselves from every defilement of body and spirit,' we evade damaging our health. Finally, the marriage is on safe grounds by our 'fleeing from sexual immorality.'

The Bible Offers How to Best Live In an Imperfect World

Another aspect of the Bible is that it will help us to find true happiness in this imperfect world that we live in, with the hope of even greater happiness to come. Bible knowledge helps us to discover the innermost harmony and satisfaction that this imperfect life offers, and gives us faith and hopefulness of an even greater one to come. It assists us to develop such pleasing characteristics as empathy, love, joy, peace,

---

72 From the Greek *porneia*, "to engage in sexual immorality of any kind, often with the implication of prostitution—'to engage in illicit sex, to commit fornication, sexual immorality, fornication, prostitution.'"—GELNTBSD.

kindness, and faith. (Galatians 5:22, 23; Ephesians 4:24, 32) Such characteristics will help us to be a better spouse, father or mother, son or daughter, or friend.

The Bible helps us to See What the Future Holds

Another facet of the Bible is its prophecies, which will help us to understand where we are in the stream of time, and what is yet to unfold. Notice the conditions that are coming in the text below.

Revelation 21:3-4 Updated American Standard Version (UASV)

³ And I heard a loud voice from the throne, saying, "Behold, the tabernacle of God is among men, and he will dwell[73] among them, and they shall be his people,[74] and God himself will be among them,[75] ⁴ and he will wipe away every tear from their eyes, and death shall be no more, neither shall there be mourning, nor crying, nor pain anymore, for the former things have passed away."

The Bible helps us Share the Good News

Romans 10:13-17 Updated American Standard Version (UASV)

¹³ For "everyone who calls on the name of the Lord[76] will be saved.""

¹⁴ How then will they call on him in whom they have not believed? And how are they to believe in him of whom they have never heard? And how will they hear without someone to preach? ¹⁵ And how are they to preach unless they are sent? As it is written, "How beautiful are the feet of those who declare good news of good things!"[77]

---

[73] Lit *he will tabernacle*

[74] Some mss *peoples*

[75] One early ms and be *their God*

[76] Quotation from Joel 2:32, which reads, "everyone who calls on the name of Jehovah shall be saved." In other words, Paul was referring to the Father not the Son.

[77] Quotation from Isa 52:7; Nah 1:15

[16] But they have not all obeyed the gospel. For Isaiah says, "Lord,[78] who has believed what he has heard from us?" [17] So faith comes from hearing, and hearing through the word of Christ.

The Bible Helps Us Achieve and Maintain Our Spirituality

Matthew 4:4 Updated American Standard Version (UASV)

[4] But he answered, "It is written,[79]

"'Man shall not live by bread alone,
but by every word that proceeds out of the mouth of God.'"[80]

The Bible Helps Us Understand the Will and Purposes of the Creator

When we enter the pathway of walking with our God, we will certainly come across resistance from three different areas. **Our greatest obstacle is ourselves** because we have inherited imperfection from our first parents Adam and Eve. The Scriptures make it quite clear that we are mentally bent toward bad, not good. (Gen 6:5; 8:21, AT) In other words, our natural desire is toward wrong. Prior to sinning, Adam and Eve were perfect, and they had the natural desire of doing good, and to go against that was to go against the grain of their inner person. Scripture also tells us of our inner person, our heart.

Jeremiah 17:9 Updated American Standard Version (UASV)

[9] The heart is more deceitful than all else,
and desperately sick;
who can understand it?

---

[78] Quotation from Isaiah 53:1, which reads, "Who has believed our message? And to whom has the arm of Jehovah been revealed?"

[79] **4:4 It is written.** All three of Jesus' replies to the devil are taken from Deuteronomy. This one, from Deuteronomy 8:3, states that God allowed Israel to hunger so that He might feed them with manna and teach them to trust Him to provide for them. So the verse is directly applicable to Jesus' circumstances and a fitting reply to Satan's temptation.—MacArthur, John. The MacArthur Bible Commentary (Kindle Locations 38817-38819). Thomas Nelson. Kindle Edition.

[80] Deut. 8:3

Romans 7:21-24 Updated American Standard Version (UASV)

²¹ I find then the law in me that when I want to do right, that evil is present in me. ²² For I delight in the law of God according to the inner man, ²³ but I see a different law in my members, warring against the law of my mind and taking me captive in the law of sin which is in my members. ²⁴ Wretched man that I am! Who will deliver me from this body of death?

1 Corinthians 9:27 Updated American Standard Version (UASV)

²⁷ but I discipline my body and make it my slave, so that, after I have preached to others, I myself will not be disqualified.

Ephesians 4:1 Updated American Standard Version (UASV)

4 Therefore I, the prisoner of the Lord, implore you to walk in a manner worthy of the calling with which you have been called,

Ephesians 5:15-17 Updated American Standard Version (UASV)

¹⁵ Therefore be careful how you walk, not as unwise men but as wise, ¹⁶ buying out⁸¹ the time, because the days are evil. ¹⁷ Therefore do not be foolish, but understand what the will of the Lord is.

There are horrific dangers and deceptions that lie within the world that is under the influence of Satan. God recognizes that we are imperfect, knowing that we have human weaknesses that he originally did not intend, meaning that he is aware of how difficult it is to walk in godly wisdom. He is aware that we are all missing the mark of perfection, and that we are all mentally bent toward evil. He knows that our natural desire is to do wrong, and our heart (inner self) is treacherous, and we cannot even know it. It is for this reason that he makes allowances for our imperfection. Jesus Christ offered himself as a ransom, covering our Adamic sin and our human weaknesses when we stumble at times, but only if we demonstrate trust in him.

We need to walk not as **unwise** but as **wise**. What does Paul; mean by 'wise' and 'unwise' in this text? God has made known to us his plan of salvation, which was a mystery up until the time of Paul's writings. At that time, he had lavished upon them/us, "in all wisdom and insight making known to us the mystery of his will, according to his purpose, which he set forth in Christ." (Eph. 1:8-9) Yes, God has afforded his people wisdom, "that the God of our Lord Jesus Christ, the Father of glory, may give you

---

⁸¹ (an idiom, literally 'to redeem the time') to do something with intensity and urgency (used absolutely)—'to work urgently, to redeem the time.'—GELNTBSD

the Spirit of wisdom and of revelation in the knowledge of him, having the eyes of your hearts enlightened, that you may know what is the hope to which he has called you." (Eph. 1:17-19) It would take a wise person to understand and appreciate the mystery of salvation, and the fact that they are required to bring their life into harmony with God's magnificent plan of saving the world of mankind who are receptive to accepting Christ. To be wise also means that these ones fully grasp the will of the Father (Matt. 7:21), and are carrying that out to the best of their ability. Therefore, the wise accept, value, and see the significance of wisely walking worthily with God. On the other hand, the unwise are those of the world of humankind who are alienated from God, living their life in the moment, walking in the desires of the flesh, because they see God's Word as foolish.

Turning our attention to verse 16 of Ephesians 5, we see that the wise knows how to buy out the opportune time from the world, by living in the world, but they do not use it to the fullest extent, unlike the unwise. Why, because they know that the world of wicked mankind is passing away. The wise one buys time back from this wicked world. Some of the areas that can be bought from are watching less television, less time playing on the computer, other forms of entertainment, not always working overtime, or maybe even not taking a promotion that would cause him to miss Christian meetings, so he can focus on the better things. Some of these better things are personal family time, family Bible study, personal Bible study, religious services, sharing the Good News with others, congregational responsibilities, and so on. Notice below that we were formerly unwise, but are now the wise.

Ephesians 2:1-3 Updated American Standard Version (UASV)

2 And you being dead in the trespasses and your sins, ² in which you formerly walked according to the age of this world, according to the ruler of the authority of the air, the spirit now working in the sons of disobedience. ³ Among whom also we all formerly lived in the desires of our flesh, doing the desires of the flesh and of the thoughts, and were by nature children of wrath, even as the rest.

Help in Understanding the Bible

The irony is that hundreds of millions of Christians are humble enough to recognize that the Bible is difficult to understand, it is a deep and complex book. There are tens of millions, who believe they understand everything they read, and for them, the Bible is easy to understand. The sad part is that many of the latter do not understand it any better than the former; they are simply putting a modern-day twist on Scripture and having it say what they want it to say. Even Peter in the first century, one of the pillars of the early church, an apostle of Christ, viewed the Apostle Paul's letters as difficult to understand.

2 Peter 3:15-16 Updated American Standard Version (UASV)

[15] and regard the patience of our Lord as salvation; just as also our beloved brother Paul, according to the wisdom given him, wrote to you, [16] as also in all his letters, speaking in them of these things, in which are <u>some things hard to understand</u>, which the untaught and unstable distort, as they do also the rest of the Scriptures, to their own destruction.

If we are to appreciate and apply the Bible in our lives, we must first fully understand it. We must know what the author of a Bible book meant by the words that he used, as should have been understood by his original intended audience. Then, we will be able to attach the significance that it has in our lives. If we are unaware of the correct way of interpreting the Scriptures, grammatical-historical interpretation, then we are going to be one of those ones who Peter spoke of as, "the ignorant and unstable twist to their own destruction." Hundreds of millions of Christians unknowingly share an incorrect understanding of Scripture, because they are not aware of the principles of interpretation, and how to apply them correctly.

Our **first step** is *observation*, to get as close to the original text as possible. If we do not read Hebrew or Greek; then, two or three literal translations are preferred (ASV, NASB, UASV). The **second step** is *interpretation*, What did the author mean by the words that he used, as should have been understood by his original audience. A part of this second step would be what the differences between the biblical audience and us are? As mentioned above, the Christian today is separated from the biblical audience by differences in culture, language, situation, time, and often covenant. The **third step** is the *implications* or *principles* in this text? This is perhaps the most challenging step. In it, we are looking for the implications or principles that are reflected in the meaning of the text we identified in the second step. Part of this third step is making sure that we stay within the pattern of the original meaning when we determine any implications for us. The **fourth step** is the *application*. How should individual Christians today live out the implications and principles?

Certainly, no one would suggest that God intended such division and confusion. If each of us can give our own meaning to a text; then, it has no meaning at all, and has lost all authority over our lives.

What does the Bible really teach? For example, is the Bible completely without errors of any kind, or is it only error free on matters of faith? **(Inerrancy)** Was the universe and man created within the past 6,000 to 10,000 years, or are the days creative periods. Or rather, is there a large gap of time between Genesis 1:1 and 1:2, or the literary framework view correct that asserts that God was not having Moses address how He created the world, nor the length of time in which to do such? This view holds that this account in Genesis 1 is merely a literary outline that summarizes a theology of creation. **(Creation Account)** Is God sovereign over all things, or does God limit his control by granting freedom? **(Providence)** Is the image of God our soul, or is the image of God our God-given authority, or is it our relations? **(Divine Image)** Are we made up of a body and soul, or body, soul, and spirit, or are we the person a soul? **(Human Constitution)** Did Christ die in our place, or is it that Christ destroyed Satan and his works, or that Christ displayed God's wrath against sin? **(Atonement)** Did God from eternity in the past predestine some to salvation, and others to eternal damnation, or is it that God loves everyone, and we can choose to accept or reject that love, with God not coercing them, while they must maintain an approved standing? **(Salvation)** Is sanctification a declaration by God, or a holiness in Christ and personal conduct, or resting-faith in the sufficiency of Christ, or is it entire sanctification in perfect love? **(Sanctification)** Do we retain our security in the Power of God, or do we need to persist in faith? **(Eternal Security)** Are infants to be baptized, or are only believers to be baptized? **(Baptism)** Is speaking in tongues a true sign of faith, or did speaking in tongues die out after the first century C.E.? **(Gifts)** Is there to be a rapture before the reign of Christ, or are we working toward and waiting for a coming reign of peace, or is the thousand-year conquest of Satan symbolic? (Millennium) These sorts of questions could go on for hundreds of pages.

Help in Teaching the Bible

If we are to fulfill the great commission, that Jesus gave to every Christian, to proclaim and to teach the Good News, we must accurately understand it ourselves first. It was in the spring of 31 C.E., and Jesus was about to speak to a very large, mixed crowd on a mountainside, who were anxiously awaiting what he would teach them. He did not let them down in the least, as he was nothing short of astounding in what and how he taught them. "And when Jesus finished these sayings, the crowds were astonished at his teaching." What was special about his way of teaching, in comparison to what they had been hearing from the Jewish religious leaders? He taught with authority from the Scriptures. He quoted or referred to the Old Testament, to support what he was saying. The Jewish religious leaders referred to other Rabbis as their authority.

At the end of his ministry here on earth, he told all of his disciples that they too were to be teachers. He said, "Go therefore and make disciples of all nations ... **teaching them** to observe all that I have commanded you." (Matt. 28:19-20, ESV) The apostle Paul also exhorted Hebrew Christians of their responsibility to teach when they were trying to slide by on doing the minimum possible. "For in view of the time **you ought to be teachers**, you have need again for someone to teach you from the beginning the elementary things of the words of God, and you have come to need milk and not solid food." (Hebrews 5:12) Paul also told Timothy, "For a slave of the Lord does not need to fight, but needs to be kind to all, **qualified to teach**, showing restraint when wronged,"—2 Timothy 2:24.

What about us? Sadly, survey after survey over the last 35 years has shown that 93 percent of Christians today are in the same position as what Paul had said to the Hebrew Christians. "For in view of the time you ought to be teachers, you have need again for someone to teach you from the beginning the elementary things of the words of God, and you have come to need milk and not solid food."

Joshua 1:8-9 Updated American Standard Version (UASV)

8 This Book of the Law shall not depart from your mouth, but you shall meditate on it day and night, so that you may be careful to do according to all that is written in it; for then you will make your way prosperous, and then you will have good success. 9 Have I not commanded you? Be strong and courageous! Do not be afraid, and do not be dismayed, for Jehovah your God is with you wherever you go."

Basics in Biblical Interpretation

Step 1: What is the historical setting and background for the author of the book and his audience? Who wrote the book? When and under what circumstances was the book written? Where was the book written? Who were the recipients of the book? Was there anything noteworthy about the place of the recipients? What is the theme of the book? What was the purpose for writing the book?

Step 2a: What would this text have meant to the original audience? (The meaning of a text is what the author meant by the words that he used, as should have been understood by his readers.)

Step 2b: If there are any words in our section that we do not understand, or that stand out as interesting words that may shed some insight on the meaning, look them up in a word dictionary.

Step 2c: After reading our section from the three Bible translations, doing a word study, write down what we think the author meant. Then, pick up a trustworthy commentary, like CPH Old or New Testament commentary volume, and see if we have it correct.

Step 3: Explain the original meaning down into one or two sentences, preferably one. Then, take the sentence or two; place it in a short phrase.

Step 4: Now, consider their circumstances, the reason for it being written, what it meant to them, and consider examples from our day that would be similar to theirs, which would fit the pattern of meaning. What **implications** can be drawn from the original meaning?

Step 5: Find the pattern of meaning, i.e., the "thing like these," and consider how it could apply to our modern day life. How should individual Christians today live out the implications and principles?

We know that Scripture makes it clear that there is only one acceptable way of worshiping God, the way outlined in God's Word. Everything that we believe and do needs to be based on that Word, and our understanding of that Word needs to be accurate. There are 41,000 different Christian denominations, and clearly, not all are on the path of doing the will of the Father as outlined in the Bible, for Jesus said, in that day he will say to some, "depart from me, you workers of lawlessness." (Matt 7:23) We can either place our trust in man, who bickers and argues over what the Word of God means, or we can take the Bible's point of view itself. After all, it is the inspired Word of God, which is profitable for teaching, for reproof, for correction, and for training in righteousness, so that the man of God may be complete, equipped for every good work."—2 Timothy 3:16-17.

Proverbs 3:5-6 Updated American Standard Version (UASV)

5 Trust in Jehovah with all your heart,
and do not lean on your own understanding.
6 In all your ways acknowledge him,
and he will make straight your paths.

Milton H. Terry wrote, "It is an old and oft-repeated hermeneutical principle that words should be understood in their literal sense unless such literal interpretation involves a manifest contradiction or absurdity."[82] Robert L. Towns writes, "The Bible is the best interpreter of itself. As we study the Bible, we should learn to compare the Scriptures we are studying with other relevant passages of Scripture to interpret the Bible."[83] These are a couple of the principles, which this series of books will live by, so that we can trust that these basic Bible teachings are from the Word of God, not the Word of man. Moreover, what is offered herein will live by the rules below. Lastly, we can take advantage of the *A Basic Guide to Biblical Interpretation*, so that we are not entirely dependent on the interpretation of others. In other words, we will be able to do as the Bereans did with the Apostle Paul, and for which he commended them,

Acts 17:10-11 Updated American Standard Version (UASV)

Paul and Silas in Berea

[10] The brothers immediately sent Paul and Silas away by night to Berea, and when they arrived, they went into the synagogue of the Jews. [11] Now these were more noble-minded than those in Thessalonica, who **received the word with all eagerness,**[84] **examining the Scriptures daily** to see whether these things were so.

Note that they **(1)** "received the word with all eagerness," and then went about **(2)** "examining the Scriptures daily to see if these things were so." If the apostle Paul was to be examined to see if what he said was so, surely uninspired commentators must be examined as well.

Are We Willing to Spend Time Each Week to Understand the Bible?

Many want to understand, to be fearless, and capable of sharing Bible truth with others. However, if this is to be the case, we must be willing to buy out a small amount of time from the worldly system of things that surrounds us, and invest it into a small study program. Many people want to do many things, but they allow their time to be used on frivolous pursuits. The thought of, 'oh, if only I had started six months ago, I would be so far along now!' Do not let another six months slip by.

---

[82] Robert L. Thomas. *Evangelical Hermeneutics: The New Versus the Old* (p. 280). Kindle Edition.

[83] Towns, *AMG Concise Bible Doctrines* (AMG Concise Series) (Kindle Locations 1011-1012). AMG Publishers. Kindle Edition.

[84] Or with all *readiness of mind*. The Greek word *prothumias* means that one is eager, ready, mentally prepared to engage in some activity.

Colossians 4:5-6 Updated American Standard Version (UASV)

⁵ Walk in wisdom toward outsiders, buying out for yourselves the time. ⁶ Let your speech always be gracious, seasoned with salt, so that you may know **how you ought to answer each person.**

The recommendation once more is to set aside one hour each day for God. If we are able to spend more time, this is entirely up to us. What must be realized is just how much time we give to the world around us, a world that lies in the hands of Satan. Is it too much to ask that we give one hour a day to the Creator of life? We can simply get up one hour earlier than we normally do, and we will have our study in before the day even gets started. The beautiful thing about that plan is; it will start our day on a spiritual track, meaning a better day from the beginning.

Digging Deeper

Psalm 92:5 Updated American Standard Version (UASV)

⁵ How great are your works, O Jehovah!
　Your thoughts are very deep!

1 Corinthians 2:10 Updated American Standard Version (UASV)

¹⁰ For to us God revealed them through the Spirit; for the Spirit searches all things, even **the depths of God.**

There is no doubt that God's thoughts are deep, these deeper things of God are very complex at times, and as Peter tells us, they are not easy to understand. Therefore, we must dig deeper by the use of the many wonderful tools on the market, along with prayerful reflection as we carry on in our studies. However, even before we begin that, we need to know that our way of interpreting the Scriptures is correct.

Psalm 139:17-18 Updated American Standard Version (UASV)

¹⁷ How precious to me are **your thoughts, O God!**
　How vast is the sum of them!
¹⁸ If I should count them, they would outnumber the sand.
　When I awake, I am still with you.

Psalm 119:160 Updated American Standard Version (UASV)

¹⁶⁰ The sum of **your word is truth,**
　and every one of your righteous judgments endures forever.

As was true of the Psalmist, we should view God's sharing His thoughts as very precious. We should be very thankful and appreciative that we have access to 'the sum of God's Word' as being truths that He has revealed to us, and therefore, we must dig deeper in the sum of God's Word.

Holy Spirit and Biblical Interpretation

2 Corinthians 4:3-4 Updated American Standard Version (UASV)

3 And even if our gospel is **veiled**, it is veiled to those who are perishing. **4** In their case the god of this world has **blinded the minds of the unbelievers,**[85] to keep them from seeing the light of the gospel of the glory of Christ, who is the image of God.

2 Corinthians 3:12-18 Updated American Standard Version (UASV)

12 Therefore having such a hope, we use great boldness in our speech, **13** and are not like Moses, who used to put a veil over his face so that the sons of Israel would not look intently at the end of what was fading away. **14** But their **minds were hardened**; for until this very day at the reading of the old covenant the same veil remains unlifted, because **it is taken away only by means of Christ**. **15** But to this day whenever Moses is read, a veil lies over their hearts; **16** but whenever one **turns to the Lord, the veil is taken away**. **17** Now the Lord is the Spirit, and where the Spirit of the Lord is, there is freedom. **18** But we all, with unveiled face, beholding as in a mirror the glory of the Lord, are being transformed into the same image from glory to glory, just as from the Lord, the Spirit.

Let us start by looking at an example of blind minds within Scripture. This was not a case of physical blindness, but mental blindness. There was a Syrian military force coming after Elisha, and God **blinded them mentally**. If it had been physical blindness, then each of them would have to have been led by the hand. However, what does the account say?

---

[85] By **unbelievers** Paul has in view non-Christians (1 Cor. 6:6; 7:12–15; 10:27; 14:22–24). First, the unbelievers of verse 4 are a subset of those who are perishing in verse 3. In other words, the two are the same. Second, the unbelievers are not persons, who have never heard the truth. No, rather, they are persons who have heard the truth, and have rejected it as foolish rubble. This is how this writer is using the term "unbeliever" as well. Technically, how could one ever truly be an unbeliever if they had never heard and understood the truth, to say they did not believe the truth? Therefore, to be an unbeliever, one needs to hear the truth, understand the truth, and reject that truth (i.e., not believing the truth is just that, the truth).

2 Kings 6:18-20 Updated American Standard Version (UASV)

¹⁸ And when the Syrians came down against him, Elisha prayed to Jehovah and said, "Please strike this nation[86] with blindness." So he struck them with blindness in accordance with the prayer of Elisha. ¹⁹ Then Elisha said to them, "This is not the way, nor is this the city; follow me and I will bring you to the man whom you seek." And he brought them to Samaria.

²⁰ When they had come into Samaria, Elisha said, "O Jehovah, open the eyes of these men, that they may see." So Jehovah opened their eyes and they saw; and behold, they were in the midst of Samaria.

Are we to believe that one man led the entire Syrian military force to Samaria? If they were physically blind, they would have to have all held hands. Were the Syrian military forces not able physically to see the images that were before them? No, rather, it was more of an inability to understand them. This must have been some form of mental blindness, where we see everything that everyone else sees, but something just does not register. Another example can be found in the account about the men of Sodom. When they were blinded, they did not become distressed, running into each other.

Definitely, Paul is speaking of people, who are not receptive to truth, because their heart is hardened to it, callused, unfeeling. They are not responding because their figurative heart is opposed. It is as though, God handed them over to Satan, to be mentally blinded from the truth, not because he disliked them per se, but because they had closed their hearts and minds to the Gospel. Thus, no manner of argumentation is likely to bring them back to their senses.

However, at one time Saul (Paul) was one of these. Until he met the risen Jesus on the road to Damascus, he was mentally blind to the truth. He was well aware of what the coming Messiah was to do, but Jesus did none of these things because it was not time. Thus, Paul was blinded by his love for the Law, Jewish tradition, and history. So much so, he was unable to grasp the Gospel. Not to mention, he lived during the days of Jesus ministry, studied under Gamaliel, who was likely there in the area. He could have even been there when Jesus impressed the Jewish religious leaders, at the age of twelve. Therefore, Saul (Paul) needed a real wake-up call, to get through the veil that blinded him.

---

[86] Or *people*

Hence, a mentally blind person sees the same information as another, but the truth cannot or will not get down into their heart. I have had the privilege of talking to dozens of small groups of unbelievers, ranging from four people to ten people in my life. I saw this in action. As I spoke to these groups, inevitably, I would see the light going off in the eyes of some (they would be shaking their heads in agreement as I spoke). However, others having a cynical look, a doubting look (they would be shaking their heads in disgust or disapproval), and they eventually walked away. This is not saying that the unbeliever cannot understand the Bible; it is simply that they see no significance in it, as it is foolishness to them.

1 Corinthians 2:14 Updated American Standard Version (UASV)

¹⁴ But the natural man <u>does not accept</u> the things of the Spirit of God, for <u>they are foolishness</u> to him, and <u>he is **not able to understand**[87]</u> them, because they are examined spiritually.

Hundreds of millions of Christians use this verse as support that without the "Holy Spirit," we can fully understand God's Word. They would argue that without the "Spirit" the Bible is nothing more than foolish nonsense to the reader. What we need to do before, arriving at the correct meaning of what Paul meant, is grasp what he meant by his use of the word "understand," as to what is 'foolish.' In short, "the things of the Spirit of God" are the "Spirit" inspired Word of God. The natural man sees the inspired Word of God as foolish, and "he is not able to understand them."

Paul wrote, "But the natural man does not accept the things of the Spirit of God, for they are foolishness to him." What did Paul mean by this statement? Did he mean that if the Bible reader did not have the "Spirit" helping him, he would not be able to grasp the correct meaning of the text? Are we to understand Paul as saying that without the "Spirit," the Bible and its teachings are beyond our understanding?

We can gain a measure of understanding as to what Paul meant, by observing how he uses the term "foolishness" elsewhere in the very same letter. At 1 Corinthians 3:19, it is used in the following way, "For the wisdom of this world is foolishness with God." This verse helps us to arrive at the use in two stages: (1) the verse states that human wisdom is foolishness with God, (2) and we know that the use of foolishness here

---

[87] "The Greek word *ginosko* ("to understand") does not mean comprehend intellectually; it means know by experience. The unsaved obviously do not experience God's Word because they do not welcome it. Only the regenerate have the capacity to welcome and experience the Scriptures, by means of the Holy Spirit."— (Zuck 1991, 23)

does not mean that God cannot understand (or grasp) human wisdom. The use is that He sees human wisdom as 'foolish' and rejects it as such.

Therefore, the term "foolishness" of 1 Corinthians 3:19 is not in reference to not "understanding," but as to one's view of the text, its significance, or better yet, lack of significance, or lack of value. We certainly know that God can understand the wisdom of the world, but condemns it as being 'foolish.' The same holds true of 1 Corinthians 1:20, where the verbal form of foolishness is used, "Has not God made foolish the wisdom of the world?" Thus, we have the term "foolishness" being used before and after 1 Corinthians 2:14, (1:20; 3:19). In all three cases, we are dealing with the significance, the value being attributed to something.

Thus, it seems obvious that we should attribute the same meaning to our text in question, 1 Corinthians 2:14. In other words, the Apostle Paul, by his use of the term "foolishness," is not saying that the unbeliever is unable to understand, to grasp the Word of God. If this were the case, why would we ever share the Word of God, the gospel message with an unbeliever? Unbelievers can understand the Word of God; however, unbelievers see it as foolish, having no value or significance. The resultant meaning of chapters 1-3 of 1 Corinthians is that unbelieving world of mankind can understand the Word of God. However, they view it as foolish (missing value or significance). God, on the other hand, understands the wisdom of the world of mankind, but views it foolish (missing value or significance). Therefore, in both cases, the information is understood or grasped; however, it is rejected because to the party considering it, believes it lacks value or significance.

We pray for the guidance of the Holy Spirit, and our spirit, or mental disposition, needs to be attuned to God and His Spirit through study and application. Now, if our mental disposition is not in tune with the Spirit, we will not come away with the right answer. As Ephesians shows, we can grieve the Spirit.

Ephesians 4:30 Updated American Standard Version (UASV)

30 And do not **grieve the Holy Spirit** of God, by[88] whom you were sealed for the day of redemption.

How do we grieve the Holy Spirit? We do that by acting contrary to its leading through deception, human weaknesses, imperfections, setting our figurative heart on something other than the leading.

---

[88] Lit *in*

Ephesians 1:18 Updated American Standard Version (UASV)

[18] having the **eyes of your heart** enlightened, that you may know what is the hope to which he has called you, what are the riches of the glory of his inheritance in the holy ones,

"Eyes of your heart" is a Hebrew Scripture expression, meaning spiritual insight, to grasp the truth of God's Word. So we could pray for the guidance of God's Spirit, and at the same time, we can explain why there are so many different understandings (many wrong answers), some of which contradict each other. This is because of human imperfection that is diluting some of those interpreters, causing them to lose the Spirit's guidance.

A person sits down to study and prays earnestly for the guidance of Holy Spirit, that his mental disposition be in harmony with God's Word [or simply that his heart be in harmony with . . .], and sets out to study a chapter, an article, something biblical. In the process of that study, he allows himself to be moved, not by a mental disposition in harmony with the Spirit, but by human imperfection, by way of his wrong worldview, his biases, his preunderstanding.[89] A fundamental of grammatical-historical interpretation is that that we are to look for the simple meaning, the essential meaning, the obvious meaning. However, when this one comes to a text that does not say what he wants it to say, he rationalizes until he has the text in harmony with his preunderstanding. In other words, he reads his presuppositions into the text,[90] as opposed to discovering the meaning that was in the text. Even though his Christian conscience was tweaked at the correct meaning, he ignored it, as well as his mental disposition that could have been in harmony with the Spirit, to get the outcome he wanted.

In another example, it may be that the text does mean what he wants, but this is only because the translation he is using is full of theological bias, which is **violating** grammar and syntax, or maybe textual criticism rules and principles that arrive at the correct reading. Therefore, when this student takes a deeper look, he discovers that it could very well read another way, and likely should because of the context. He buries that evidence beneath his conscience, and never

---

[89] Preunderstanding is all of the knowledge and understanding that we possess before we begin the study of the text.

[90] Presupposition is to believe that a particular thing is so before there is any proof of it

mentions it when this text comes up in a Bible discussion. In other words, he is grieving the Holy Spirit and loses it on this particular occasion.

Human imperfection, human weakness, theological bias, preunderstanding, and many other things could dilute the Spirit, or even grieve the Spirit. So that while one may be praying for assistance, he is not getting it or has lost it, because one, some, or all of these things he is doing has grieved the Spirit.

Again, it is not that an unbeliever cannot understand what the Bible means; otherwise, there would be no need to witness to him. Rather, he does not have the spiritual awareness to see the significance of studying Scripture. An unbeliever can look at "the setting in which the Bible books were written and the circumstances involved in the writing," as well as "studying the words and sentences of Scripture in their normal, plain sense," to arrive the meaning of a text. However, without having any spiritual awareness about themselves, they would not see the significance of applying it in their lives. 1 Corinthians 2:14 says, "The natural person does not **accept** [Gr., dechomai] the things of the Spirit of God." Dechomai means, "to welcome, accept or receive." Thus, the unbeliever may very well understand the meaning of a text, but just does not *accept, receive* or *welcome* it as truth.

Acts 17:10-11 Updated American Standard Version (UASV)

¹⁰ The brothers immediately sent Paul and Silas away by night to Berea, and when they arrived, they went into the synagogue of the Jews. ¹¹ Now these were more noble-minded than those in Thessalonica, who received the word with all readiness of mind,[91] examining the Scriptures daily to see whether these things were so.

Unlike the natural person, the Bereans accepted, received, or welcomed the Word of God eagerly. Paul said the Thessalonians "received [*dechomai*] the word in much affliction, with the joy of the Holy Spirit." (1 Thess. 1:6) At the beginning of a person's introduction to the good news, he will take in the knowledge of the Scriptures (1 Tim. 2:3-4), which if his heart is receptive, he will begin to apply them in his life, taking off the old person and putting on the new person. (Eph. 4:22-24) Seeing how the Scriptures have begun to alter his life, he will start to have a genuine faith in the things he has learned (Heb. 11:6), repenting of his sins. (Acts 17:30-31) He will turn around his life, and his sins will be blotted out. (Acts 3:19) At some point, he will go to God in prayer, telling

---

[91] Or with all *eager readiness of mind*. The Greek word *prothumias* means that one is eager, ready, mentally prepared to engage in some activity.

the Father that he is dedicating his life to him, to carry out his will and purposes. (Matt. 16:24; 22:37) This regeneration is the Holy Spirit working in his life, giving him a new nature, placing him on the path to salvation.—2 Corinthians 5:17.

A new believer will become "acquainted with the sacred writings, which are able to make [him] wise for salvation through faith in Christ Jesus." (2 Tim. 3:15) As the Bible informs us, the Scriptures are holy and are to be viewed as such. If we are to acquire an accurate or full knowledge, to have the correct mental grasp of the things that we carried out an exegetical analysis on, it must be done with a prayerful and humble heart. It is as Dr. Norman L. Geisler said, "the role of the Holy Spirit, at least in His special work on believers related to Scripture, is in illuminating our understanding of the significance (not the meaning) of the text. The meaning is clear apart from any special work of the Holy Spirit." What level of understanding that we are able to acquire is based on the degree to which we are **not** grieving the Holy Spirit with our worldview, our preunderstanding, our presuppositions, our theological biases? In addition, anyone living in sin will struggle to grasp God's Word as well.

No interpreter is infallible. The only infallibility or inerrancy belonged to the original manuscripts. Each Christian has the right to interpret God's Word, to discover what it means, but this does not guarantee that they will come away with the correct meaning. The Holy Spirit will guide us into and through the truth, by way of our working on behalf of our prayers to have the correct understanding. Our working in harmony with the Holy Spirit means that we buy out the time for a personal study program, not to mention the time to prepare properly and carefully for our Christian meetings. In these studies, do not expect that the Holy Spirit is going to give us miraculously some flash of understanding, but rather understanding will come to us as we set aside our personal biases, worldviews, human imperfections, presuppositions, preunderstanding, opening our mental disposition to the Spirit's leading as we study.

The Work of the Holy Spirit

The following is adopted and adapted from Douglas A. Foster of Abilene Christian University.

Christian Publishing House's understanding of the Holy Spirit is **not** that of the Charismatic groups (the ecstatic and irrational), but rather the calm and rational. The work of the Holy Spirit is inseparably and uniquely linked to the words and ideas of God's inspired and inerrant Word. We see the indwelling of the Holy Spirit as Christians taking the words and ideas of Scripture into our mind and drawing spiritual strength from them. The Spirit moves persons toward salvation, but the Spirit does that, in the same way, any person moves another—by persuasion with words and ideas:

> Now we cannot separate the Spirit and the Word of God, and ascribe so much power to the one and so much to the other; for so did not the Apostles. Whatever the word does, the Spirit does, and whatever the Spirit does in the work of converting, the word does. We neither believe nor teach abstract Spirit nor abstract word, but word and Spirit, Spirit and word. But the Spirit is not promised to any persons outside of Christ. It is promised only to them who believe and obey him.[92]

The Holy Spirit works only through the word in the conversion of sinners. In other words, the Spirit acting through the Word of God can accomplish everything claimed to be affected by a personal indwelling of the Spirit.

Longtime preacher Z. T. (Zachary Taylor) Sweeney, in His book *The Spirit and the Word: A Treatise on the Holy Spirit in the Light of a Rational Interpretation of the Word of God*, writes after examining every Scripture that might be used by advocates of a literal personal indwelling of the Holy Spirit,

> In the above cases, we have covered all the conceivable things a direct indwelling Spirit could do for one, and have also shown that all these things the Spirit does through the word of God. It is not claimed that a direct indwelling of the Spirit makes any new revelations, adds any new reasons or offers any new motives than are found in the word of God. Of what use, then, would a direct indwelling Spirit be? God makes nothing in vain. We are necessarily, therefore, led to the conclusion that, in dealing with his children today, God deals with them in the same psychological way that he deals with men in inducing them to become children. This conclusion is strengthened by the utter absence of any test by which we could know the Spirit dwells in us, if such were the case.[93]

---

92 Alexander Campbell, The Christian System (6th ed.; Cincinnati: Standard, 1850), 64.

93 Z. T. Sweeney, The Spirit and the Word (Nashville: Gospel Advocate, n.d.), 121–26.

This author and Christian Publishing House is defined by our rejection of Holiness and Pentecostal understandings of the Holy Spirit. The Holy Spirit transforms a person, empowering him through the Word of God, to put on the "new person" required of true Christians, "So, as those who have been chosen of God, holy and beloved, put on a heart of compassion, kindness, humility, gentleness and patience." – Colossians 3:12.

Ephesians 4:20-24 Updated American Standard Version (UASV)

20 But you did not learn Christ in this way, **21** if indeed you have heard him and have been taught in him, just as truth is in Jesus, **22** that you take off, according to your former way of life, the old man, who is being destroyed according to deceitful desires, **23** and to be renewed in the spirit of your minds, **24** and put on the new man,[94] the one created according to the likeness of God in righteousness and loyalty of the truth.

Colossians 3:9-10 Updated American Standard Version (UASV)

9 Do not lie to one another, seeing that you have put off the old man[95] with its practices **10** and have put on the new man[96] who is being renewed through accurate knowledge[97] according to the image of the one who created him,

How Are We to Understand the Indwelling of the Holy Spirit?

1 Corinthians 3:16 Updated American Standard Version (UASV)

16 Do you not know that you are a temple of God and that the Spirit of God dwells in you?

Before delving into the phrase, "indwelling of the Holy Spirit, let us consider the **mistaken view** of New Testament scholars Simon J. Kistemaker and William Hendriksen, who wrote,

> The Spirit of God lives within you." The church is holy because God's Spirit dwells in the hearts and lives of the

---

[94] An interpretive translation would have, "put on the new person," because it does mean male or female.

[95] Or *old person*

[96] Or *new person*

[97] See Romans 3:20 ftn.

believers. In 6:19 Paul indicates that the Holy Spirit lives in the physical bodies of the believers. But now he tells the Corinthians that the presence of the Spirit is within them, and they are the temple of God.

The Corinthians should know that they have received the gift of God's Spirit. Paul had already called attention to the fact that they had not received the spirit of the world but the Spirit of God (2:12). He teaches that Christians are controlled not by sinful human nature but by the Spirit of God, who is dwelling within them (Rom. 8:9).

The behavior—strife, jealousy, immorality, and permissiveness—of the Christians in Corinth was reprehensible. By their conduct the Corinthians were desecrating God's temple and, as Paul writes in another epistle, were grieving the Holy Spirit (Eph. 4:30; compare 1 Thess. 5:19).[98]

First, it must be told that I am almost amazed at how so many Bible scholars say nonsensical things, contradictory things when it comes to the Holy Spirit. Bible Commentators use many verses to say that the Holy Spirit literally,

(5) **dwells in** the individual Christian believers,

(6) having **control over** them,

(7) **enabling them** to live a righteous and faithful life,[99]

(8) with the believer **still being able to sin**, even to the point of grieving the Holy Spirit (Eph. 4:30).

Let us walk through this again, and please take it slow, ponder whether it makes sense, is reasonable, logical, even Scriptural. The Holy Spirit literally dwells in individual believers, controlling them so they can live a righteous and faithful life, yet they can still freely sin, even to the point of grieving the Holy Spirit. Does this mean that the Holy Spirit is not powerful enough to prevent their sinful nature from affecting them? The commentators say the Holy Spirit now controls the Christian, not their sinful nature. If that were true, it must mean the Holy Spirit is

---

[98] Simon J. Kistemaker and William Hendriksen, *Exposition of the First Epistle to the Corinthians*, vol. 18, New Testament Commentary (Grand Rapids: Baker Book House, 1953–2001), 117

[99] Millard J. Erickson, *Introducing Christian Doctrine* (Grand Rapids: Baker Book House, 1992), 265–270

ineffectual and less powerful than their sinful nature of the Christian, because the Christian can still reject the Holy Spirit and sin to the point of grieving the Holy Spirit. If the Holy Spirit is controlling the individual Christian, how is it possible that he still possesses free will?

Let us return to the phrase of "indwelling of the Holy Spirit." Just how often do we find "indwelling" in the Bible? I have looked at over fifty English translations and found it once in the King James Version ad two in an earlier version of the New American Standard Bible. One reference is to sin dwelling within us, and the other reference is to the Holy Spirit dwelling within us.

The Updated American Standard Version removed such usage. We may be asking ourselves since "indwelling" is almost nonexistent in the Scriptures, why the commentaries, Bible encyclopedias, Hebrew and Greek word dictionaries, Bible dictionaries, pastors and Christians using it to such an extent, especially in reference to the Holy Spirit? I say in reference to the Holy Spirit because some scholars refer to the indwelling of Christ and the Word of God.

Before addressing those questions, we must take a look at the Greek word behind 1 Corinthians 3:16 "the Spirit of God **dwells [οἰκέω]** in you." The transliteration of our Greek word is *oikeo*. It means "'to dwell' (from *oikos*, 'a house'), 'to inhabit as one's abode,' is derived from the Sanskrit, *vic*, 'a dwelling place' (the Eng. termination —'wick' is connected). It is used (a) of God as 'dwelling' in light, 1 Tim. 6:16; (b) of the 'indwelling' of the Spirit of God in the believer, Rom. 8:9, 11, or in a church, 1 Cor. 3:16; (c) of the 'indwelling' of sin, Rom. 7:20; (d) of the absence of any good thing in the flesh of the believer, Rom. 7:18; (e) of the 'dwelling' together of those who are married, 1 Cor. 7:12-13."[100]

Thus, for our text, means the Holy Spirit dwelling in true Christians. The TDNT tells us, "Jn.'s μένειν [*menein*] corresponds to Paul's οἰκεῖν [*oikein*], cf. Jn. 1:33: καταβαῖνον καὶ μένον ἐπ' αὐτόν [descending and remaining upon him]. The new possession of the Spirit is more than ecstatic."[101] What does TDNT mean? It means that John is using *meno* ("to remain," "to stay" or "to abide") in the same way that Paul is using *oikeo* ('to dwell').

---

[100] W. E. Vine, Merrill F. Unger, and William White Jr., *Vine's Complete Expository Dictionary of Old and New Testament Words* (Nashville, TN: T. Nelson, 1996), 180.

[101] Gerhard Kittel, Geoffrey W. Bromiley, and Gerhard Friedrich, eds., *Theological Dictionary of the New Testament* (Grand Rapids, MI: Eerdmans, 1964–)

When we are considering the Father or the Son alone, and even the Father and the Son together, we are able to have a straightforward conversation. However, when we get to the Holy Spirit we tend to get off into mysterious and mystical thinking. When we think of humans and the words *dwell* and *abide*, both have the sense of where we 'live or reside in a place.'

However, there is another sense of 'where we might stand on something,' 'our position on something.' Thus, in English dwell and abide can be used interchangeably, similarly, just as Paul and John use *meno* "abide" or "remain" and *oikeo* "dwell" similarly. Let us look at the apostle John's use of meno,

1 John 4:16 Updated American Standard Version (UASV)

[16] We have come to know and have believed the love which God has for us. God is love, and the one who remains [*meno*] in love remains in God, and God remains [*meno*] in him.

Here we notice that God is the embodiment of "love" and if we **abide in** or **remain in** that love, God then **abides in** or **remain in** us. We do not attach any mysterious or mystical sense to this verse, such as God literally being in us and us being in God. If we suggest that this verse, i.e., God being in us, means his taking control of our lives, does our being in God, also mean we control his life? We would think to suggest such a thing is unreasonable, illogical, nonsensical, and such. Commentator Max Anders in the *Holman New Testament Commentary* says, "This is the test of true Christianity in the letters of John. We must recognize the basic character of God, rooted in love. We must experience that love in our own relationship with God. Others must experience this God kind of love in their relationships with us." (Walls and Anders 1999, 211) Our love for God and man is the motivating factor in what we do and not do as Christians. John is saying that we need to remain in that love if we are to remain in God and God is to remain in us. We may be thinking, well, is it not true that God guides and direct us? Yes, however, this is because we have given our lives over to him.

1 John 2:14 Updated American Standard Version (UASV)

[14] I have written to you, fathers, because you know Him who has been from the beginning. I have written to you, young men, because you are strong, and the word of God remains [*meno*] in you, and you have overcome the evil one.

Here we see that the Word of God abides or remains in us. Does this mean that the Word of God is literally within our body, controlling us? No, this means that our love for God and our love for his Word is a motivating factor in our walk with God. We are one with the Father as Jesus was and is one with the Father and he is one with us. Listen to the words of Paul in the book of Hebrews,

Hebrews 4:12 Updated American Standard Version (UASV)

¹² For the word of God is living and active and sharper than any two-edged sword, and piercing as far as the division of soul and spirit, of both joints and marrow, and able to judge the thoughts and intentions of the heart.

Is the Word of God literally living, and an animate thing? No, it is an inanimate object. Is our Bible literally sharper than a two-edged sword? No, if we decide to stab someone with it, it would look quite silly. Is the Word of God literally able to pierce our joints and marrow? No, again, this would seem ridiculous. If we literally hold the Bible up to our head, is it able to discern our thinking, what we intend to do? What did Paul mean? The Word of God does these things by our being able to evaluate ourselves by looking into the light of the Scriptures, which helps us to identify the intentions of our heart, i.e., inner person. When we meditatively read God's Word daily and ponder what the author meant, we are taking into our mind, God's thoughts and intentions. When we accept the Bible as the inspired, inerrant Word of God, take its counsel and apply its principles in our lives, it will have an impact on our conscience. The conscience is the moral code that God gave Adam and Eve, our mental power or ability that enables us to reason between what is good and what is bad. (Rom. 9:1) Then, the inner voice within us is not entirely ours, but is also God's Word, empowering us to avoid choosing the wrong path.

1 John 2:24 Updated American Standard Version (UASV)

²⁴ As for you, let that remain [*meno*] in you which you heard from the beginning. If what you heard from the beginning remains [*meno*] in you, you also will remain [*meno*] in the Son and in the Father.

Those who had followed Jesus **from the beginning** of his three and half ministry cleaved to what they had heard about the Father and the Son. Therefore, if the same truths are within our heart, inner person, our mental power or ability, we too can **abide** or **remain [*meno*]** in the Son and the Father. (John 17:3) It is as James said, if we draw close to God, through his Word the Bible, he will draw close to us. (Jam. 4:8) In other words, God becomes a part of us and we a part of him through the Word of God that is "living and active, sharper than any two-edged sword, piercing to the division of soul and of spirit, of joints and of marrow, and discerning the thoughts and intentions of the heart."

In John chapter 14, we see this two-way relationship more closely. Jesus said, "Believe me that I am in the Father and the Father is in me, or else believe on account of the works themselves." **(14:11)** He also said, "In that day you will know that I am in my Father, and you in me, and I in you." **(14:20)** We see that the Father and Son have a close relationship, a relationship that we are invited to join.

All through the above discussion of the Father and the Son, we likely had no problem following the line of thought. However, once we interject the Holy Spirit, it is as though our common sense is thrown out. Christians know that the Father and the Son reside in heaven. They also understand that when we speak of the Word of God, the Father and the Son dwelling in us, it is in reference to our being one with them, our unified relationship, by way of the Word of God. However, when we contemplate the Holy Spirit, it is as though our mental powers shut down, and we enter the realms of the mysterious and mysticism. However, we just understood John **14:11** and **14:20**, i.e., how Jesus is in the Father, the Father in Jesus, and their being in us. So, let us now consider the verses that lie between verse **11** and **20**.

Jesus Promises the Holy Spirit

John 14:16-17 English Standard Version (ESV)

16 And I will ask the Father, and he will give you another Helper, to be with you forever, 17 even the Spirit of truth, whom the world cannot receive, because it neither sees him nor knows him. You know him, for he dwells [*meno*] with you and will be in you.

John 14:16-17 Updated American Standard Version (UASV)

16 And I will ask the Father, and he will give you another Helper, that he may be with you forever; 17 the Spirit of truth, whom the world cannot receive, because it does not see him or know him, but you know him because he remains [*meno*] with you and will be in you.

Do we not find it a bit disconcerting that, all along when looking at John's writings as to the Son and the Father abiding [*meno*] in one another, in us, and us in them. In those places, the translation rendered *meno* as abiding, but now that the Holy Spirit is mentioned, they render *meno* as "dwell."

Do these verses call for us to drive off the path of reason, into the realms of mysteriousness and mysticism talk? No, these verses are very similar to our 1 John 2:24 that we dealt with above, but will quote again, "Let what you heard from the beginning **abide [meno]** in you. If what you heard from the beginning **abides [meno]** in you, then you too will **abide [meno]** in the Son and in the Father." In 1 John 2:24, we are told that if the Word of God that we heard from the beginning of being a Christian, **abides [meno]** in us, we will **abide [meno]** in the Son and the Father. In John 14:15-17, if we keep Jesus' commands, the Holy Spirit will **dwell**, actually **abide [meno]** in us. In all of this, the common denominator has been the spirit inspired, fully inerrant Word of God. It is what we are to take into our mind and heart, which will affect change in our person, and enable us to abide or remain in the Father and the Son, and they in us, as well as the Holy Spirit, abiding or remaining in us.

The Holy Spirit, through the Spirit-inspired, inerrant Word of God is the motivating factor for our taking off the old person and putting on the new person. (Eph. 4:20-24; Col. 3:8-9) It is also the tool used by God so that we can "be transformed by the renewal of your mind so that you may approve what is the good and well-pleasing and perfect will of God." (Rom. 12:2; See 8:9) *The Theological Dictionary of the New Testament* compares this line of thinking with Paul's reference, at Romans 7:20, to the "sin that dwells within me."

The dwelling of sin in man denotes its dominion over him, its lasting connection with his flesh, and yet also a certain distinction from it. The sin which dwells in me (ἡ οἰκοῦσα ἐν ἐμοὶ ἁμαρτία) is no passing guest, but by its continuous presence becomes the master of the house (cf. Str.-B., III, 239).[102] Paul can speak in just the same way, however, of the lordship of the Spirit. The community knows (οὐκ οἴδατε, a reference to catechetical instruction, 1 C. 3:16) that the Spirit of God dwells in the new man (ἐν ὑμῖν οἰκεῖ, 1 C. 3:16; R. 8:9, 11). This "dwelling" is more than ecstatic rapture or impulsion by a superior power.[103]

How does the Holy Spirit control a Christian? Certainly, some mysterious or mystical feeling does not control him.

---

[102] Str.-B. H. L. Strack and P. Billerbeck, *Kommentar zum NT aus Talmud und Midrasch*, 1922 ff.

[103] Gerhard Kittel, Geoffrey W. Bromiley, and Gerhard Friedrich, eds., *Theological Dictionary of the New Testament* (Grand Rapids, MI: Eerdmans, 1964–), 135

Paul told the Christians in Rome,

Romans 12:2 Updated American Standard Version (UASV)

2 And do not be conformed to this world, but be transformed by the **renewing of your mind**, so that you may prove what the will of God is, that which is good and acceptable and perfect.

Just how do we **renew our mind**? This is done by taking in an accurate knowledge of Biblical truth, which enables us to meet God's current standards of righteousness. (Titus 1:1) This Bible knowledge, if applied, will allow us to move our mind in a different direction, by filling the void, after having removed our former sinful practices, with the principles of God's Word, principles that guide our actions, especially ones that guide moral behavior.

Psalm 119:105 Updated American Standard Version (UASV)

105 Your word is a lamp to my feet
and a light to my path.

The Biblical truths that lay in between Genesis 1:1 and Revelation 22:21 will transform our way of thinking, which will in return affect our mood and actions and our inner person. It will be as the apostle Paul said to the Ephesians. We need to "to put off your old self, which belongs to your former manner of life and is corrupt through deceitful desires, and to be renewed in the spirit of your minds, and to put on the new self, created after the likeness of God in true righteousness and holiness ..." (Eph. 4:22-24) This force that contributes to our acting or behaving in a certain way, for our best interest is internal.

Paul told the Christians in Colossae,

Colossians 3:9-11 Updated American Standard Version (UASV)

9 Do not lie to one another, seeing that you have put off the old man[104] with its practices 10 and have put on the new man[105] who is being **renewed through accurate knowledge**[106] according to the image of the one who created him, 11 where there is not Greek and Jew,

---

104 Or old person

105 Or new person

106 See Romans 3:20 ftn.

circumcised and uncircumcised, barbarian, Scythian, slave, free; but Christ is all, and in all.

Science has indeed taken us a long way in our understanding of how the mind works, but it is only a grain of sand on the beach of sand in comparison to what we do not know. We have enough in these basics to understand some fundamental processes. When we open our eyes to the light of a new morning, it is altered into and electrical charge by the time it arrives at the gray matter of our brain's cerebral cortex. As the sound of the morning birds reaches our gray matter, it comes as electrical impulses. The rest of our senses (smell, taste, and touch) arrive as electrical currents in the brain's cortex as well. The white matter of our brain lies within the cortex of gray matter, used as a tool to send electrical messages to other cells in other parts of the gray matter. Thus, when anyone of our five senses detects danger, at the speed of light, a message is sent to the motor section, to prepare us for the needed action of either fight or flight.

Here lies the key to altering our way of thinking. Every single thought, whether it is conscious or subconscious makes an electrical path through the white matter of our brain, with a record of the thought and event. This holds true with our actions as well. If it is a repeated way of thinking or acting, it has no need to form a new path; it only digs a deeper, ingrained, established path.

This would explain how a factory worker who has been on the job for some time, gives little thought as he performs his repetitive functions each day; it becomes unthinking, automatic, mechanical. These repeated actions become habitual. There is yet another facet to be considered; the habits, repeated thoughts, and actions become simple and effortless to repeat. Any new thoughts and actions are harder to perform, as there need to be new pathways opened up.

The human baby starts with a blank slate, with a minimal amount of stable paths built in to survive those first few crucial years. As the boy grows into childhood, there is a flood of pathways established, more than all of the internet connections worldwide.

Our five senses are continuously adding to the maze. Ps. 139:14: "I will give thanks to you, for I am fearfully and wonderfully made. . . ." (NASB) So, it could never be overstated as to the importance of the foundational thinking and behavior that should be established in our children from infancy forward.

Paul told the Christians in Ephesus,

Ephesians 4:20-24 Updated American Standard Version (UASV)

20 But you did not learn Christ in this way, **21** if indeed you have heard him and have been taught in him, just as truth is in Jesus, **22** that you take off, according to your former way of life, the old man, who is being destroyed according to deceitful desires, **23** and to be **renewed in the spirit of your minds**, **24** and put on the new man,[107] the one created according to the likeness of God in righteousness and loyalty of the truth.

How are we to understand being **renewed in the spirit of our minds**? Christian living is carried out through the study and application of God's Word, in which, our spirit (mental disposition), is in harmony with God's Spirit. Our day-to-day decisions are made with a biblical mind, a biblically guided conscience, and a heart that is motivated by love of God and neighbor. Because we have,

- Received the Word of God,
- treasured up the Word of God,
- have been attentive to the Word of God,
- inclining our heart to understand the Word of God,
- calling out for insight into the Word of God,
- raising our voice for an understanding of the Word of God,
- sought the Word of God like silver,
- have searched for the Word of God like gold,
- we have come to understand the fear of God and have
- found the very knowledge of God, which now
- leads and directs us daily in our Christian walk.

Proverbs 23:7 New King James Version (NKJV)

7 For as he thinks in his heart, so is he. "Eat and drink!" he says to you, But his heart is not with you. [Our thinking affects our emotions, which in turn affects our behavior.]

Irrational thinking produces irrational feelings, which will produce wrong moods, leading to wrong behavior. It may be difficult for each of us to wrap our mind around it, but we are very good at telling ourselves outright lies and half-truths, repeatedly throughout each day. In fact,

---

107 An interpretive translation would have, "put on the new person," because it does mean male or female.

some of us are so good at it that it has become our reality and leads to mental distress and bad behaviors.

When we couple our leaning toward wrongdoing with the fact that Satan the devil, who is "the god of this world," (2 Co 4:4) has worked to entice these leanings, the desires of the fallen flesh; we are even further removed from our relationship with our loving heavenly Father. During these 'last days, grievous times' has fallen on us as Satan is working all the more to prevent God's once perfect creation to achieve a righteous standing with God and entertaining the hope of eternal life. – 2 Timothy 3:1-5.

When we enter the pathway of walking with our God, we will certainly come across resistance from three different areas (Our sinful nature, Satan and demons, and the world that caters to our flesh). **Our greatest obstacle** is **ourselves** because we have inherited imperfection from our first parents Adam and Eve. The Scriptures make it quite clear that we are **mentally bent toward bad**, not good. (Gen 6:5; 8:21, AT) In other words, our natural desire is toward wrong. Prior to sinning, Adam and Eve were perfect, and they had the natural desire of doing good, and to go against that was to go against the grain of their inner person. Scripture also tells us of our inner person, our heart.

Jeremiah 17:9 Updated American Standard Version (UASV)

⁹ The **heart is more deceitful** than all else,
and desperately sick;
who can understand it?

Jeremiah's words should serve as a wake-up call, if we are to be pleasing in the eyes of our heavenly Father, we must focus on our inner person. Maybe we have been a Christian for many years; maybe we have a deep knowledge of Scripture, perhaps we feel that we are spiritually strong, and nothing will stumble us. Nevertheless, our heart can be enticed by secret desires, where he fails to dismiss them; he eventually commits a serious sin.

Our conscious thinking (aware) and subconscious thinking (present in our mind without our being aware of it) originates in the mind. For good, or for bad, our mind follows certain rules of action, which if entertained one will move even further in that direction until they are eventually consumed for good or for bad. In our imperfect state, our bent thinking will lean toward wrong, especially with Satan using his world, with so many forms of entertainment that simply feeds the flesh.

James 1:14-15 Updated American Standard Version (UASV)

¹⁴ But each one is tempted when he is carried away and enticed by his own desire.[108] ¹⁵ Then the desire when it has conceived gives birth to sin, and sin when it is fully grown brings forth death.

1 John 2:16 Updated American Standard Version (UASV)

¹⁶ For all that is in the world, the lust of the flesh and the lust of the eyes and the boastful pride of life, is not from the Father, but is from the world.

Matthew 5:28 Updated American Standard Version (UASV)

²⁸ but I say to you that everyone who looks at a woman with lust[109] for her has already committed adultery with her in his heart.

1 Peter 1:14 Updated American Standard Version (UASV)

¹⁴ As children of obedience,[110] do not be conformed according to the desires you formerly had in your ignorance,

If we do not want to be affected by the world of humankind around us, which is alienated from God, we must again consider the words of the Apostle Paul's. He writes (Rom 12:2) "Do not be conformed to this world, but be transformed by the renewal of your mind that by testing you may discern what is the will of God, what is good and acceptable and perfect." Just how do we do that? This is done by taking in an accurate knowledge of the Biblical truth, which enables us to meet God's current standards of righteousness. (Titus 1:1) This Bible knowledge, if applied, will enable us to move our mind in a different direction, by filling the void with the principles of God's Word, principles that guide our actions, especially ones that guide moral behavior.

Psalm 119:105 Updated American Standard Version (UASV)

¹⁰⁵ Your word is a lamp to my feet
and a light to my path.

We have said this before but it bears repeating. The Biblical truths that lay in between Genesis 1:1 and Revelation 22:21 will transform our

---

[108] Or "own *lust*"

[109] ἐπιθυμία [*Epithumia*] to strongly desire to have what belongs to someone else and/or to engage in an activity which is morally wrong—'to covet, to lust, evil desires, lust, desire.'– GELNTBSD

[110] I.e., *obedient children*

way of thinking, which will in return affect our mood and actions and our inner person. It will be as the apostle Paul set it out to the Ephesians. We need to "to put off your old self, which belongs to your former manner of life and is corrupt through deceitful desires, and to be renewed in the spirit of your minds, and to put on the new self, created after the likeness of God in true righteousness and holiness ..." (Eph. 4:22-24) This force that contributes to our acting or behaving in a certain way, for our best interest is internal.

Bringing This Transformation About

The mind is the mental ability that we use in a conscious way to garner information and to consider ideas and come to conclusions. Therefore, if we perceive our realities based on the information, which surrounds us, generally speaking, most are inundated in a world that reeks of Satan's influence. This means that our perception, our attitude, thoughts, speech, and conduct are in opposition to God and his Word. Most are in true ignorance to the changing power of God's Word. The apostle Paul helps us to appreciate the depths of those who reflect this world's disposition. He writes,

Ephesians 4:17-19 Updated American Standard Version (UASV)

17 This, therefore, I say and bear witness to in the Lord, that you no longer walk as the Gentiles [unbelievers] also walk, in the futility of their mind [emptiness, idleness, sluggishness, vanity, foolishness, purposelessness], **18** being darkened in their understanding [mind being the center of human perception], alienated from the life of God, because of the ignorance that is in them, because of the hardness of their heart [hardening as if by calluses, unfeeling]; **19** who being past feeling gave themselves up to shameless conduct,[111] for the practice of every uncleanness with greediness.

Hebrews 4:12 Updated American Standard Version (UASV)

12 For the word of God is living and active and sharper than any two-edged sword, and piercing as far as the division of soul and spirit, of both joints and marrow, and able to judge the thoughts and intentions of the heart.

By taking in this knowledge of God's Word, we will be altering our way of thinking, which will affect our emotions and behavior, as well as

---

[111] Or "loose conduct," "sensuality," "licentiousness" "promiscuity" Greek, *aselgeia*. This phrase refers to acts of conduct that are serious sins. It reveals a shameless condescending arrogance; i.e., disregard or even disdain for authority, laws, and standards.

our lives now and for eternity. This Word will influence our minds, making corrections in the way we think. If we are to have the Holy Spirit controlling our lives, we must 'renew our mind' (Rom. 12:2) "which is being renewed in knowledge" (Col. 3:10) of God and his will and purposes. (Matt 7:21-23; See Pro 2:1-6) All of this boils down to each individual Christian digging into the Scriptures in a meditative way, so he can 'discover the knowledge of God, receiving wisdom; from God's mouth, as well as knowledge and understanding.' (Pro. 2:5-6) As he acquires the mind that is inundated with the Word of God, he must also,

James 1:22-25 Updated American Standard Version (UASV)

[22] But be doers of the word, and not hearers only, deceiving yourselves. [23] For if anyone is a hearer of the word and not a doer, he is like a man who looks intently at his natural face[112] in a mirror.

[24] for he looks at himself and goes away, and immediately forgets what sort of man he was. [25] But he that looks into the perfect law, the law of liberty, and abides by it, being no hearer who forgets but a doer of a work, he will be blessed in his doing.

The Spirit and Christians

By Z. T. Sweeney

Updated[113] By Edward D. Andrews

It has been aptly and truthfully said, "No importance can be attached to a religion that is not begun, carried on and completed by the Spirit of God." That the Christian is led, guided and strengthened by the Spirit cannot be denied by any Bible reader. To deny the fact that the Spirit dwells in us is to deny the Bible. However, it is asserted with equal clearness in the inspired, inerrant Word that *the Father dwells in us*. The apostle Paul wrote, "And what agreement has the temple of God with idols? For we are the temple of the living God; just as God said, '**I will dwell in them** and I will walk among them, and I will be their God, and they shall be my people.'" (2 Cor. 6:16; Lev 26:12; also similar to Jer. 32:38, Eze. 37:27) This not only says that God will dwell in us, but that he *walks in us*. It is also clearly taught that *Christ dwells in us*. Paul wrote,

---

[112] Lit *the face of his birth*

[113] What do we mean by updated? The chapter's by Sween are from almost one hundred years ago. We update his archaic language and his translation to a modern day translation, such as the UASV, NASB, ESV, HCSB, etc. Nevertheless, what he has to say is very biblical and quite clear.

"So that Christ may dwell in your hearts through faith; that you, being rooted and grounded in love." – Ephesians 3:17.

Thus, we see that Scripture clearly teaches that the Father, the Son and the Holy Spirit dwell in us. The question before us is this, is there anything within Scripture that says the Holy Spirit dwells in us in a different sense from that in which the Father and the Son dwell in us? The apostle quoted from Leviticus 26:12 in our Scripture above at 2 Corinthians 6:16, where he explained what the Father meant by his words in Leviticus,

2 Corinthians 6:16	Leviticus 26:12
Updated American Standard Version (UASV)	Updated American Standard Version (UASV)
¹⁶ And what agreement has the temple of God with idols? For we are the temple of the living God; just as God said,	¹² And I will also walk among you and be your God, and you shall be my people.
"I will dwell in them and I will walk among them, and I will be their God, and they shall be my people.	

The Greek word *enoikeso* literally means, "I shall indwell" *en autois* "in them." We learn from Paul's quote of Leviticus 26:12 that God had promised to be in communion with Israel. However, there is nothing in Leviticus 26:12 to show God's personal "indwelling" in any one person.

How does Christ dwell in us? Ephesians 3:17 quoted above says, "Christ may dwell in your hearts through faith;" the Greek literally reading *ho pisteos*, "the faith" or *the gospel*. How does the Spirit dwell in us? Paul asks the Galatians, "Did you receive the Spirit by works of the law or by the hearing of faith?" In other words, 'Did you receive the Spirit by works of the law or by the hearing of the gospel?' The above Scriptures clearly teach that when the words, thoughts, and Spirit of God are controlling in our lives, *God dwells in us*; that when the gospel controls us, *Christ dwells in us*; that when we receive the gospel by the hearing of faith, *the Spirit dwells in us*.

Now, what reason has any man for declaring that the Spirit dwells in us in any other way unless he can point to an explicit declaration of God's word defining and explaining that other way? This cannot be done, for there is no such passage. However, some might argue, "I do not have to depend on the Word. I know it by my own consciousness." It is a principle as old as metaphysics that consciousness does not take cognizance of causes, but of effects. We may be conscious of an effect on us, but we cannot be aware of the cause that produced the effect.

Suppose we are lying asleep on the ground; a severe pain suddenly awakens us in our lower limb; consciousness tells us that we are suffering pain, but it does not tell us what produced that pain. This must be decided by *reason* or *faith*. If we find a thorn in the grass where our limb was resting, *reason* says the thorn *stuck us*. On the other hand, if we find a bumblebee mashed in the grass, *reason* will say the insect *stung us*; or, if someone near us says, a boy with a pin in his hand ran away from us, *faith* will say the boy *stuck us*.

However, in either case, reason or faith decided the cause of our pain. Now, when a man says, "I am conscious of the presence of the Holy Spirit within me," he simply means, "I am conscious of a *feeling* within me which I *have been taught* was caused by the Holy Spirit." If the man has been taught wrong, he assigns a *wrong cause* for the feeling. What is the feeling usually assigned for the presence of the Holy Spirit's personal indwelling? It is a feeling of joy, peace, and love. However, cannot such feeling be excited by other causes?

We know there are dozens of causes that will produce such feelings. In the absence of clear testimony, what right has anyone to attribute such feeling to the personal presence of the Holy Spirit? A man is found murdered. The testimony shows that any one of a dozen men could have killed him. Is there an intelligent jury in the land that would convict anyone of the men of being the murderer? What would we think of a jury that would render such a verdict?

"Well," says one, "what of the great numbers who pray for a 'Pentecostal revival'? Are they all wrong?" Not wrong in what they *want*, but wrong in *what they call it*. All that those people desire is to be filled with a *genuine revival of religious enthusiasm*. Their mistake is in calling it a "Pentecostal shower." A Pentecostal shower would lead every preacher under its influence to say, with the apostle Peter, to inquiring sinners, "Repent and be baptized every one of you in the name of Jesus Christ for the forgiveness of your sins ..." This is what they are careful *not to say*. It is clear evidence that the Spirit, which guided Peter, is not guiding them. I assert it to be a fact that the Spirit acting through the word of God as clearly accomplishes everything that is claimed to be affected by a personal indwelling of the Spirit.

I do not wish to rest content with asserting that statement, but I wish to prove it. What are the things that might be accomplished by a direct personal indwelling of the Spirit in us?

1. The Holy Spirit might give us faith.

This is accomplished through the Word of God.

Romans 10:17 Updated American Standard Version (UASV)

[17] So faith comes from hearing, and hearing through the word of Christ.

2. The Holy Spirit might enable us to enjoy a new birth.

This is accomplished through the Word of God.

1 Peter 1:23 Updated American Standard Version (UASV)

[23] having been born again, not of perishable seed but of imperishable, through the living and enduring word of God.

3. The Holy Spirit might give us light.

This is accomplished through the Word of God.

Psalm 119:130 Updated American Standard Version (UASV)

[130] The unfolding of your words gives light;
it gives understanding to the simple.

4. The Holy Spirit might give us wisdom.

This is accomplished through the Word of God.

2 Timothy 3:14-15 Updated American Standard Version (UASV)

[14] You, however, continue in the things you have learned and were persuaded to believe, knowing from whom you have learned them, [15] and that from infancy[114] you have known the sacred writings, which are able to make you wise for salvation through trust[115] in Christ Jesus.

This is accomplished through the Word of God.

---

[114] *Brephos* is "the period of time when one is very young—'childhood (probably implying a time when a child is still nursing), infancy." – GELNTBSD

[115] *Pisteuo* is "to believe to the extent of complete trust and reliance—'to believe in, to have confidence in, to have faith in, to trust, faith, trust.' – GELNTBSD

Psalm 19:7 Updated American Standard Version (UASV)

⁷ The law of Jehovah is perfect,
restoring the soul;
the testimony of Jehovah is sure,
making wise the simple

5. The Holy Spirit might convert us.

This is accomplished through the Word of God.

Psalm 19:7 Updated American Standard Version (UASV)

⁷ The law of Jehovah is perfect,
restoring the soul ...

6. The Holy Spirit might open our eyes.

This is accomplished through the Word of God.

Psalm 19:8 Updated American Standard Version (UASV)

⁸ The precepts of Jehovah are right,
rejoicing the heart;
the commandment of Jehovah is pure,
enlightening the eyes.

7. The Holy Spirit might give us understanding.

This is accomplished through the Word of God.

Psalm 119:104 Updated American Standard Version (UASV)

¹⁰⁴ From your precepts I get understanding;
therefore I hate every false way.

8. The Holy Spirit might preserve or give us life, i.e., quicken us.

This is accomplished through the Word of God.

Psalm 119:50 Updated American Standard Version (UASV)

⁵⁰ This is my comfort in my affliction,
that your word has preserved me alive.[116]

9. The Holy Spirit might save us.

---

[116] Older translations read, *quickened me*

This is accomplished through the Word of God.

James 1:21 Updated American Standard Version (UASV)

²¹ Therefore, putting aside all filthiness and abundance of wickedness, and receive with meekness the implanted word, which is able to save your souls.[117]

10. The Holy Spirit might sanctify us.

This is accomplished through the Word of God.

John 17:17 Updated American Standard Version (UASV)

¹⁷ Sanctify them in the truth; your word is truth.

11. The Holy Spirit might purify us.

This is accomplished through the Word of God.

"Seeing ye have purified your souls in your obedience to *the truth*

1 Peter 1:22 Updated American Standard Version (UASV)

²² The souls of you having been purified by obedience to the truth, for an unhypocritical love of the brothers, intensely love one another from the heart,[118]

12. The Holy Spirit might cleanse us.

This is accomplished through the Word of God.

John 15:3 Updated American Standard Version (UASV)

³ Already ye are clean because of the word which I have spoken unto you.

13. The Holy Spirit might make us free from sin.

This is accomplished through the Word of God.

Romans 6:17-18 Updated American Standard Version (ASV)

¹⁷ But thanks be to God that you were slaves of sin, but you became obedient from the heart to that form of teaching to which you were committed, ¹⁸ and having been freed from sin, you became slaves of righteousness.

---

[117] Or "is able to save *you*"

[118] Two early mss read *a clean heart*

14. The Holy Spirit might impart a divine nature.

This is accomplished through the Word of God.

2 Peter 1:4 Updated American Standard Version (UASV)

4 By which he has granted to us his precious and very great promises, so that through them you may become partakers of the divine nature, having escaped from the corruption that is in the world because of sinful desire.

15. The Holy Spirit might fit us for glory.

This is accomplished through the Word of God.

Acts 20:32 Updated American Standard Version (UASV)

32 And now I commend you to God and to the word of his grace, which is able to build you up and to give you the inheritance among all those who are sanctified.

16. The Holy Spirit might strengthen us.

This is accomplished through the Word of God.

Psalm 119:28 Updated American Standard Version (ASV)

28 My soul weeps[119] because of grief;
strengthen me according to your word!

In the above cases, we have covered all the possible things a direct indwelling Spirit could do for one, and have shown that all these things the Spirit does through the word of God. It is not claimed that a direct indwelling of the Spirit makes any new revelations, adds any new reasons or offers any new motives than are found in the word of God. Of what use, then, would a direct indwelling Spirit be? God makes nothing in vain. We are, therefore, necessarily, led to the conclusion that, in dealing with his children today, God deals with them in the same psychological way that he deals with men in inducing them to become children. This conclusion is strengthened by the utter absence of any test by which we could know the Spirit dwells in us if such were the case.

What the Spirit Does for the Christian

1. The Holy Spirit is active in our birth.

---

[119] Lit *drops*

John 3:5 Updated American Standard Version (ASV)

⁵ Jesus answered, "Truly, truly I say to you, unless someone is born from water and spirit, he is not able to enter into the kingdom of God.

Here is a distinct statement of radical change, so radical as to be likened to a new birth in order that we may enter the kingdom of God. What is it that is born? Christ says, "A man." However, what is a man? We regard a man as having a mind, heart and a body. There is no perfect man where any of these elements is lacking. If therefore, a man is born again, he must be born in mind, in heart, and in body. How is this birth accomplished? Let us see what the Word says,

John 1:12-13 Updated American Standard Version (ASV)

¹² On the other hand, as many as received him, he gave authority to them to become children of God, to the *ones* trusting in his name; ¹³ who were born, not of blood,[120] nor of the will of the flesh, nor of the will of man, but of God.

God gives all things—sometimes directly, sometimes through an agent. The Holy Spirit is the agent, i.e., "Born of water and the Spirit." However, an agent often works through an instrument. What is the instrument? It is the Word of God. "The souls of you having been purified by obedience to the truth, for an unhypocritical love of the brothers, intensely love one another from the heart, having been born again, not of perishable seed but of imperishable, **through the living and enduring word of God.**"—1 Peter 1:22-23.

How can the word of God accomplish the new birth?

Paul tells us, "**All Scripture is inspired by God** and profitable for teaching, for reproof, for correction, for training in righteousness; so that the man of God may be fully competent, equipped for every good work." (2 Tim. 3:16-17) The apostle Peter tells us, "For no prophecy was ever produced by the will of man, but **men carried along by the Holy Spirit** spoke from God." (2 Pet 1:21) The apostle Paul tells us, "For **the word of God is living and active** and sharper than any two-edged sword, and piercing as far as the division of soul and spirit, of both joints and marrow, and able to judge the thoughts and intentions of the heart." (Hebrews 4:12) The Word of God is inspired, literally God-breathed; as

---

[120] Literally "bloods." This is the only place in the NT that we will find the plural form of blood. It possible that it could refer either to hereditary (that is, blood from one's father and mother) or to the OT blood sacrifice. Neither is necessary for birth into the family of God.

the Bible authors were carried along by Holy Spirit, meaning the words are is living and active. Let us listen in as New Testament Bible scholar Thomas D. Lea writes about Hebrews 4:12,

> This vivid expression of the power of God's message provides the explanation for the strong warning of verse 11. Because God's message is alive, active, sharp, and discerning, those who listen to God's message can enter his rest. Two questions are important in this verse. First, what is **the word of God?** Second, what does this passage say about it?
>
> Although the Bible sometimes refers to Christ as God's Word (John 1:14), the reference here is not speaking of Jesus Christ. Here we have a general reference to God's message to human beings. In the past God had spoken to human beings through dreams, angelic appearances, and miracles. He still can use those methods today, but our primary contact with God is through his written Word, the Bible. God's Word will include any method God uses to communicate with human beings.
>
> This verse contains four statements about God's Word. First, it is **living.** God is a **living** God (Heb. 3:12). His message is dynamic and productive. It causes things to happen. It drives home warnings to the disobedient and promises to the believer. Second, God's Word is **active,** an emphasis virtually identical in meaning with the term **living.** God's Word is not something you passively hear and then ignore. It actively works in our lives, changes us, and sends us into action for God.
>
> Third, God's Word penetrates the **soul and spirit.** To the Hebrew people, the body was a unity. We should not think of dividing the soul from the spirit. God's message is capable of penetrating the impenetrable. It can divide what is indivisible. Fourth, God's message is discerning. **It judges the thoughts and attitudes of the heart.** It passes judgment on our feelings and our thoughts. What we regard as secret and hidden, God brought out for inspection by the discerning power of his Word. (Lea, Holman New Testament Commentary: Vol. 10, Hebrews, James 1999, 72)

George Washington put his spirit into the sentence, "United we stand, divided we fall." As long as the American people are faithful to the above words, the spirit of George Washington will live in them. However, make the same words read, "Divided we stand, united we fall," and the spirit of Washington is removed from them. The only way to take the Spirit of God from the word of God is to add to, take from or transpose the Word so it will not say what the Spirit *said in it*.

"Well," says one, "if we are born of the Spirit operating through the Word, must we not understand all the Word in order that we may be born again?" No, the apostle limits the part of the Word we must understand in verse 25 of this same chapter, "This word is the good news that was preached to you." Let us now endeavor to learn how the gospel, good news produces this change. How is the mind born again! In order to learn this, we must understand what is the normal condition of the mind of those who are not reborn spiritually and not repentant (unregenerate). In general, we may say it is in a state of *unbelief*. Now, the proclamation of the great facts of the death, burial and resurrection of Christ according to the Scriptures will break up that condition of unbelief and produce a conviction of the truth of the gospel. When the mind is changed from a state of unbelief to one of hearty belief, the birth of the mind is complete.

However, the mind is only a part of man. The heart must be born again. What is the normal state of the unregenerate heart? It is one of either *indifference* or *hatred*. The latter is the former fully ripened. It is said that Voltaire carried a seal ring upon which were engraved the words, "Crush the wretch," and every time he sealed a letter he impressed his spirit of hatred upon that letter. Now, the gospel sets forth the love of God in Christ and the loveliness of Christ's sacrifice for us in such a manner as to change the indifferent or malignant heart into one of supreme love to Christ. When the heart has thus been changed from hatred to love, it is born again.

However, man has also a body, and upon this spirit cannot act. If the body is to be born again, some element must be used that can act upon the body. Hence, our Savior says, "born of water and the Spirit," because water can act upon the body. Now, the only use of water in the new birth is in the act of baptism. All scholars of note in the religious world agree that Christ's use of water in the new birth has reference to baptism. Paul also speaks of "having our hearts sprinkled clean from an evil conscience and our bodies washed with pure water." (Heb. 10:22) Thus, with mind and heart changed by the Spirit through the gospel, and the body solemnly consecrated to God in baptism, the entire man is born again. This is all accomplished by the Spirit of God working *in and through the gospel*.

2.   Another work of the Spirit is to "*bear witness with our spirit that we are children of God, and if children, then heirs.*" (Rom. 8:16) It does not say, "bear witness *to* our spirit," but "*with* our spirit." Many people

gauge the witness of the Spirit by feelings within themselves. If they feel good, it is evidence to them of the Spirit's testimony, but they frequently feel bad also; whose testimony is that? The testimony of the Spirit should be clear testimony, and not fluctuating; it should be in words, and not in feelings. Feelings, impressions, and emotions come and go like the waves of the sea, but words remain forever the same. "Heaven and earth shall pass away, but my word shall not pass away," said the Lord. The idea of the conscious testimony of the Spirit is not sustained by either the Word of God or a correct psychology. It is the testimony of metaphysicians, from Sir William Hamilton down to the writer, that consciousness does not take cognizance of causes, but effects. Feelings are effects and not causes. Consciousness tells us when we feel good or bad, but it does not tell us what makes us feel good or bad. When a man has been taught that a certain feeling in the heart is produced by a certain agency, his faith and reason may decide that that agency produced the feeling, but consciousness has nothing whatever to do with *the cause* of the feeling. Likewise, a certain feeling in the heart may be attributed to the Spirit because one has been taught that the Spirit will produce such a feeling, but consciousness cannot trace that feeling to the Spirit himself. A man should feel right because he knows he is right, and not know he is right because he feels right.

In deciding whether we be children of God, we have two witnesses: first, the Spirit himself, and, second, our spirit. The Spirit testifies as to who is a child of God; our spirits testify as to what we are. If our spirits testify that we are the character, which the Spirit says belongs to a child of God, then we have the testimony of the Spirit himself bearing witness with our spirits that we are children of God. The testimony of the Spirit, in the nature of the case, must be general. He testifies that whosoever believes in Christ, repents of his sins, and is baptized into him, is a child of God. This is the whole of his testimony. Our spirit, likewise, must bear witness to our position on all of these points.

No one but our own spirit can testify that we believe in Christ; we may profess to, and the whole world may believe that we do, but our own spirit knows that we are a hypocrite in making the profession. Likewise, no one can testify but our own spirit that we have repented; we may make professions of repentance, and the world may believe we thoroughly sincere, but our own spirit may tell us that our profession is false. In a similar manner, no one but our own spirit can testify that we have been baptized; our father and mother may say so, the church record may so testify, and yet it is possible for them to be mistaken. To be certain we are a child of God we must have the testimony of our own spirit that we believe, that we have repented and that we have been baptized. If, in the judgment day, God should ask such people, "Have you obeyed me in the act of Christian baptism?" they would not have the testimony of their spirit that they had so obeyed; they would have to fall back upon the church record or that of their father and mother. Others may be satisfied with such testimony, but, as for myself, if I did not have the testimony of my own spirit that I had obeyed the Lord in Christian baptism, I would obtain that testimony before the going down of the sun.

"Well," says one "is that all the witness of the Spirit mentioned by the apostle?" Yes, that is all, absolutely and unqualifiedly all. What more can you desire? "Well," says another, "I want something more than the mere word; I want to be saved like the thief on the cross." How do we know that the thief on the cross was saved? "Oh, the Bible says he was." True, but that is the testimony of the "mere word;" so we have as much testimony to our own salvation as we have for the salvation of the thief on the cross, and it would be impossible for us to have anymore. Suppose the Lord were to come down and take us up bodily and set us down before his throne in heaven, and, in the presence of all the angels and the archangel, say to us: "My child, your sins are all forgiven." "Now," says one, "that would be testimony indeed." Yes, it would be testimony, but no more testimony than we have in the word of God now; we would then have only the testimony of the "mere word" of God that we were forgiven. All such criticisms arise out of infidelity as to the truthfulness of God's word.

3.   *The Spirit make intercession for us*. This is not a work done neither in us nor upon us, but is something done for us before the throne of God. We cannot dogmatize as to *how* the Spirit maketh intercession, but Paul says he does it "*according to the will of God*." This is a fact that appeals to *our faith* and not to our Christian *experience*. It "cannot be uttered." We can rest upon it and draw comfort from it as a child draws strength from its mother's breast. We can also draw comfort from the fact that Christ "always lives to make intercession" us, though we have no knowledge as to *how* he does it.

4.   Another work of the Spirit is to "*change us from glory to glory*." "But we all, with unveiled face, reflecting as a mirror the glory of the Lord, are transformed into the same image from glory to glory, even as from the Lord the Spirit." (2 Cor. 3:18) The figure used here by the apostle is taken from the process of mirror-making among the ancients. They had not the glass mirrors of our day, but a mirror of highly polished metal. A piece of coarse metal would be placed upon

168

a stone, and the workmen would begin to polish it. At first, it made no reflection at all, but when polished for a while would give a distorted and perverted reflection; but in the process of polishing, that reflection would grow clearer and clearer, when finally a man could behold his face in it perfectly reflected. And so, the same holds true for us. When taken into the great spiritual laboratory of Christianity we are blocks in the rough, but in the polishing process of the church and spiritual surroundings we begin to reflect the image of our Master, and when we have completed the work, we reflect him as perfectly as an imperfect human being can. Take, for illustration, the brothers Peter and John. At first they were called Boanerges, sons of thunder; they wanted to call down fire from heaven to destroy men who differed from them; but in the great laboratory of the Christian life they grew more and more Christlike, transformed by the Spirit of God, until at last we see the old apostle John at Ephesus, beautified and ennobled, sitting in his chair and lifting up trembling hands, and saying to the young disciples: "Little children, love one another, for love is of God." We see the transforming power of the spiritual atmosphere of the church and the Christian life upon human nature. Christian, with this illustration before you, how can you excuse yourself for keeping out of the spiritual atmosphere of God, for staying away from the communion and the spiritual convocation of God's people? Is it a burden and a duty to attend the house of God, or is it a pleasure gladly and joyfully anticipated? When you rise on the Lord's Day morning, do you say, "Must I go to church today?" or do you say,

"You may sing of the beauty of mountain and dale, The water of streamlet and the flowers of the Vale, But the place most delightful this earth can afford, Is the place of devotion, the house of the Lord"?

The last work of the Spirit, which the Word of God mentions, is "*giving life to our mortal bodies.*" "If the Spirit of him who raised Jesus from the dead dwells in you, he who raised Christ Jesus from the dead will also give life to your mortal bodies through his Spirit who dwells in you." (Rom. 8:11) This Spirit, which has ever been with us, watching over us, will never leave us until he raises our bodies from the dead and fashions our vile bodies like unto the glorious body of our Lord. It matters much where we now live; it matters little where and how we die. Our bodies may be buried in the unfathomed caves of ocean; they may lie upon some mountain-peak or be placed in a crowded cemetery of some great city. No stone may mark our resting-place, no friend may be able to find the spot and place a flower of love upon it; but the infinite Spirit of

God knows that abiding-place, and from our ashes, he will give life to our bodies and present us faultless before the throne of God.

CHAPTER 11 Interpreting with the Grammatical-Historical Method

We have already been talking about the grammatical-historical method of interpretation, which is to be distinguished from the historical-critical method of interpretation, allegorical, mythical, as well as many other methods of interpretation.

Brief History of Biblical Interpretation

Old Hermeneutics refers to (grammatical-historical-interpretation), which[121] has given way to the New Hermeneutics of the 19th and 20th centuries (grammatical-critical-historical interpretation).[122] The former preserves objectivity in interpretation, the latter subjectivity.[123] The former preserved the integrity and trustworthiness of the Bible writers and the text; the latter made both the Bible writer and the text untrustworthy. In other words, New Hermeneutics, with its pseudo-scholarship has done nothing more than weaken and demoralize people's assurance in the Bible being the inspired and fully inerrant Word of God.

Early Jewish Method of Interpretation

In the days of Ezra and beyond, there would have been an increasing need of copying the Old Testament manuscripts. As we may recall from our personal Bible study, the Babylonians took the Jews into captivity for seventy years. Most of the Jews did not return upon their release in 537 B.C.E., and after that. Tens of thousands stayed in Babylon, while others migrated throughout the ancient world, settling in the commercial centers. However, the Jews would pilgrimage back to Jerusalem several times each year, for religious festivals. Once there, they would be reading from the Hebrew Old Testament, and sharing in the worship of God. Over a

---

121 By "historical" is a reference to the setting in which the Bible books were written and the circumstances involved in the writing. By "grammatical" we mean determining the meaning of the Bible by studying the words and sentences of Scripture in their normal, plain sense. Roy B. Zuck.

122 Higher Criticism or Historical Criticism Methodology with its sub-criticisms: Source Criticism, Tradition Criticism, Form Criticism, Redaction Criticism, and so on, has undermined God's Word.

123 Subjective means that something is based on somebody's opinions or feelings rather than on facts or evidence. Objective means that something is free of any bias or prejudice caused by personal feelings, based on facts rather than thoughts or opinions.

century later in Ezra's day, the need to travel back to Jerusalem was no longer a concern, as they carried on their studies in places of worship known as synagogues,[124] where they read aloud from the Hebrew Scriptures, and discussed their meaning. As one might imagine, the scattered Jewish populations throughout the ancient world would have been in need of their own personal copies of the Hebrew Scriptures.

Within the synagogues, there was a storage room, known as the Genizah.[125] Over time, a manuscript would have been worn to the point of tearing. Thus, it would have been placed in the Genizah and replaced with new copies. Over time, after the old manuscripts were built up in the Genizah, they would eventually need to be buried in the earth. They performed this duty, as opposed to just burning them, so the holy name of God, Jehovah, would not be desecrated. Throughout many centuries, many thousands of Hebrew manuscripts were disposed of in this way. Gratefully, the well-stocked Genizah of the synagogue in Old Cairo was saved from this handling of their manuscripts, perhaps because it was enclosed and overlooked until the middle of the 19th century. In 1890, as soon as the synagogue was being restored, the contents of the Genizah were checked, and its materials were gradually either sold or donated. From this source, manuscripts that were almost complete and thousands of fragments (some said to be of the sixth century C.E.) have found their way to Cambridge University Library and other libraries in Europe and America.

Hebrew is the language in which the sixty-six inspired books of the Old Testament were penned, apart from the Aramaic sections in Ezra 4:8–6:18; 7:12–26; Dan. 2:4b–7:28; Jer. 10:11, as well as a few other words and phrases from Aramaic and other languages. The language is not called "Hebrew" in the Old Testament. At Isaiah 19:18 it is spoken of as "the language [Literally "lip"] of Canaan." The language that became known as "Hebrew" is first shown in the introduction to Ecclesiasticus, an Apocrypha[126] book. Moses, being raised in the household of Pharaoh,

---

[124] Synagogue (Greek, "place of assembly"; Hebrew bet knesset), in Judaism, an assembly house for communal prayer, study, and meeting; a central communal institution. Central and Eastern European Jews called their synagogues shuls (Yiddish, "schools"); Reform Jews sometimes use the word temple.—Microsoft ® Encarta ® 2006. © 1993-2005 Microsoft Corporation. All rights reserved.

[125] The Genizah was storehouse for Hebrew books: a repository for Hebrew documents and sacred books that were no longer in use, e.g. because they are old and worn, but must not be destroyed.

[126] The Old Testament Apocrypha are unauthentic writings: writings or reports that are not regarded as authentic.

would have been given the wisdom of Egypt, as well as the Hebrew language of his ancestors. This would have made him the perfect person to look through any ancient Hebrew documents that may have been handed down to him, giving him the foundation for the book of Genesis.

Later, in the days of the Jewish kings, Hebrew came to be known as "Judean" (LEB), that is to say, the language of Judah (Neh. 13:24; Isa. 36:11; 2 Ki. 18:26, 28). As we enter the time of Jesus, the Jewish people spoke an expanded form of Hebrew, which would become Rabbinic Hebrew. Nevertheless, in the Greek New Testament, the language is referred to as the "Hebrew" language, not the Aramaic. (John 5:2; 19:13, 17; Acts 22:2; Rev. 9:11) Therefore, for more that 2,000 years, Biblical Hebrew served God's chosen people, as a means of communication.

However, once God chose to use a new spiritual Israel, made up of Jew and Gentile, there would be a difficulty within the line of communication, as not all would be able to understand the Hebrew language. It became obvious, 300 years before the rise of Christianity; there was a need for the Hebrew Scriptures to be translated into the Greek language of the day, because of the Jewish diaspora who lived in Egypt. Down to our day, all or portions of the Bible have been translated into about 2,287 languages.

Even the Bible itself expresses the need of translating it into all languages. Paul, quoting Deuteronomy 32:43, refers to "rejoice, O Gentiles [people of the nations], with his people." And again, 'Praise the Lord, all you Gentiles, and let all the peoples extol him.'" (Rom 15:10) Moreover, all Christians are given what is known as the Great Commission, to "go therefore and make disciples of all nations." (Matt 28:19-20) In addition, Jesus stated that "this gospel of the kingdom will be proclaimed throughout the whole world as a testimony to all nations." (Matt 24:14) All of the above could never take place without translating the original language into the languages of the nations. What is more, ancient translations of the Bible that extant (still in existence) in manuscript form have likewise aided in confirming the high degree of textual faithfulness of the Hebrew manuscripts.

When a history of biblical interpretation is undertaken, it generally begins in the days of Ezra and Nehemiah (537 B.C.E. – 440 B.C.E.) Almost 100-years after the Israelites had returned from Babylonian exile, Jerusalem's walls were rebuilt in about 455 B.C.E. (Neh. 6:15) Thereafter, Nehemiah assigns his brother Hanani as govern over Jerusalem (Neh. 7:1-3), and then takes a census of the first exiles (7:4–73).

Ezra stands in front of the Water Gate and reads the book of the Law of Moses that Jehovah had commanded Israel. We read,

Nehemiah 8:7-8

7 Also Jeshua, Bani, Sherebiah, Jamin, Akkub, Shabbethai, Hodiah, Maaseiah, Kelita, Azariah, Jozabad, Hanan, Pelaiah, the Levites, helped the people to understand the Law, while the people remained in their places. **8** They read from the book, from the Law of God, clearly, and they gave the sense, so that the people understood the reading.

Most Bible scholars suggest that the Jews were no longer proficient in Hebrew after 70 years of exile in Babylon, where Aramaic was spoken. Therefore, the belief is that Ezra and the other Levites were paraphrasing the reading from Hebrew into Aramaic. However, while this may be true in part, such as their having clarified some linguistic terms, the Hebrew *mephorash*, "interpreting," also involved expounding on the text, so that the Israelites could understand its meaning and apply it in their lives. Exactly what rules and principles of biblical interpretation were applied is not known. However, as Virkler and Ayayo wrote, "thus began the science and art of biblical interpretation." (Virkler and Ayayo 1981, 2007, 44)

The Sopherim Method of Interpretation

The Sopherim (scribes) were copyist from the days of Ezra down to the time of Jesus, and into the second century C.E. While they were very serious about their task as copyist, they did take liberties in making textual changes at times. These ones believed that the Hebrew Scriptures, from the figures of speech, the parallelisms, to even the shape of letters, carried meaning, which was too difficult to understand, requiring a high degree of scholarship or specialist knowledge to be understood (Rabbi Akiba 50 C.E. – 135 C.E.). Akiba taught that "as a hammer divides fire into many sparks, so every verse of Scripture has many explanations."[127] Rabbi Akiba believed that every verse of Scripture could have multiple meanings,

If there is a superfluous "and" or "also," or sign of case, these are always to be specially interpreted. If in 2 Kings 2:14, it said of Elisha that "he also had smitten the waters" [KJV] it means that Elisha did more wonders at the Jordan than Elijah. If David says "Thy servant slew also the lion, also the bear," the meaning (by the rule of inclusion after

---

[127] Frederic W. Farrar, History of Interpretation (1886 reprint, Grand Rapids Baker Book House, 1961),

inclusion), is that he slew three animals besides. If it is written that God visited Sarah, it means that with her He [also] visited other barren women.'

However, Aqiba [ben Joseph (40 C.E. – 137 C.E.)] went still farther. He not only explained every particle and copula, but said that there was a mystic meaning in every letter of Scripture, and in ever horn and letter flourish of every letter, "just as in every fibre of an ant's foot or a gnat's wing." The Rabbis delighted to tell how "many rules unknown to Moses were declared by Aqiba."[128]

There was a strong trend within rabbinic Judaism, which moved the Jewish people away from a literal interpretation of Scripture. Allegories and legends involving Biblical words and verses flourished. These ample comments and stories were written down over time, which became known as Midrash, meaning, "to inquire, study, investigate," and additionally "to preach."

The apostle Paul studied under the renowned Pharisee Gamaliel, who was the grandson of Hillel the Elder (110 B.C.E.[129] – 10 C.E.), the founder of one of the two schools within Judaism. After the destruction of Jerusalem in 70 C.E., the house of Hillel became the official form of Judaism, as opposed the rival House of Shammai. Hillel had seven rules of interpretation,

The first has to do with inferences from the less to the more important and vice versa. The second is inference by analogy. The third is "constructing a family," that is, where a group of passages has a resemblance in contents, the group is regarded as having a common character derived from the meaning of the principal passage of the group. Thus, what is not explicit in any one of the passages may be interpreted in the light of the principal passage. The fourth is the same as the third but is limited to two passages. The fifth rule was based on a relation between the General and the Particular. The sixth was exposition by means of another similar passage. The seventh was a deduction from the context.[130]

---

[128] Ibid., 73-75

[129] B.C.E. years ran down toward zero, although the Romans had no zero, and C.E. years ran up from zero. (100, 10, 3, 2, 1 ◀B.C.E. | C.E.▶ 1, 2, 3, 10, and 100)

[130] James D. Wood, The Interpretation of the Bible (London, Gerald Duckworth and Co., 1958), 14

Jewish Method of Interpretation

Allegory is when Bible characters and events are to be understood as representing other things and symbolically expressing a deeper, often spiritual, moral meaning. Philo of Alexandria (20 B.C.E – 50 C. E.) was a Hellenistic Jewish philosopher, whose first language was Greek, which was the case with many Jews in Alexandria. Therefore, the Greek Septuagint version of the Hebrew Old Testament was what he used in his study of the Scriptures. As Philo studied the Septuagint text, he concluded that it encompassed the fundamentals of philosophy and for him Moses possessed "the genius of the philosopher." Bernard Ramm observes,

However, most of it led to the fantastic and the absurd. For example, Abraham's trek to Palestine is really the story of a Stoic philosopher who leaves Chaldea (sensual understanding) and stops at Haran, which means "holes," and signifies the emptiness of knowing things by the holes; that is the senses. When he becomes Abraham, he becomes a truly enlightened philosopher. To marry Sarah is to marry abstract wisdom.[131]

More on Philo and allegory later, but suffice it to say, any interpretation method that allows an interpreter to go beyond the literal meaning, the plain sense of the text, outside of the context, the historical setting, the norms of language, is absolutely worthless. Moreover, any interpretation principles that are applied out of balance, to arrive at some random meaning are to be set aside as well. In addition, the use of allegory to clear up perceived "tension" within Scripture is no justification for such subjective exegetical analysis. (Virkler and Ayayo 1981, 2007, 47) While it may be true that Bible writers used allegory, they have a license for such subjective behavior, as they were inspired, moved along by Holy Spirit. Readers of God's word are not inspired, nor moved along by Holy Spirit, and are to remain within the objective method of biblical interpretation, grammatical-historical.

Patristic Method of Interpretation

The patristic period covers several centuries after the death of the last apostle, John (100 C.E.). Throughout the next five hundred years, there were different methods of interpreting the Scriptures. One of the earliest

---

[131] Ramm, Bernard (1999-08-01). *Protestant Biblical Interpretation: A Textbook of Hermeneutics* (Kindle Locations 575-578). Baker Publishing Group. Kindle Edition.

schools that gave religious instruction was the **School of Alexandria**.[132] "Christianity spread to Egypt and North Africa at an early date. In fact, it became a prominent religious center, with a noted scholar named Pantaenus, who founded a catechetical school in Alexandria, Egypt, about 160 C.E. In about 180 C.E. another prominent scholar, Clement of Alexandria, took over his position. Clement really put this religious, educational institution on the map as the possible center for the whole of the Christian congregation throughout the Roman Empire. The persecution that came about the year 202 C.E. forced Clement to flee Alexandria, but one of the most noted scholars of early Christian history, Origen, replaced him. In addition, Origen took this scholarly environment to Caesarea in 231 C.E. and started yet another prominent school and scriptorium."[133] **School of Alexandria** leaned heavily toward the allegorical method of interpretation. Another one of the earliest schools that gave religious instruction was the **School of Antioch**, which stressed the literal interpretation method of Scripture, which was founded in Syria about 200 C.E.

Medieval Method of Interpretation

The Medieval period ran from 600 C.E. – 1500 C.E., which corresponds with what became known as the Dark Ages. The Bible became a closed book during this time, with no real new scholarship. It was merely a regurgitation of past church father's traditions and the continuation of allegory.

The Roman Catholic theologians of the Middle Ages developed their doctrine of hermeneutics into the so-called Four-Fold Method. A given passage of Scripture may have four meanings: (i) a literal or historical; (ii) a moral or ethical; (iii) a prophetic, or allegorical, or typological and (iv) an anagogical. "Anagogical" means, "to lead up" and refers to the possible future or eschatological element in the text. It was step number three, the allegorical, which has caused so much trouble in the history of hermeneutics. (Ramm 1999, 242)

Reformation and Post-Reformation Method of Interpretation

---

[132] http://www.britannica.com/EBchecked/topic/14441/School-of-Alexandria

[133] Edward D. Andrews, *The Text of the New Testament: A Beginner's Guide to New Testament Textual Criticism* (Cambridge, OH: Christian Publishing House, 2012), 92.

The Dark Ages is the period of European history between the fall of the Roman Empire in ad 476 and about 1000 C.E., for which there are few historical records and during which life was comparatively uncivilized. This was followed by the Middle Ages, the period in European history between antiquity and the Italian Renaissance, often considered to be between the end of the Roman Empire in the fifth century and the early fifteenth century C.E. Throughout this period, the Bible was locked up in the Latin language, and the church was under the control of Roman Catholic Church, with scholarship and learning at a low ebb. However, all of that was to change at the inception of printing in 1455, combined with the Reformation of the 16th-century C.E.

Additional self-determination overcame, and there was a reawakening of awareness in the Greek language. It was throughout this initial revival of learning that the famous Dutch scholar Desiderius Erasmus produced his first edition of a Greek text of the New Testament. This first edition was printed in Basel, Switzerland, in 1516, one year prior to the start of the Reformation in Germany. The first edition had many errors, with minor improved texts presented in succeeding editions in 1519, 1522, 1527, and 1535. Erasmus had only a few late cursive manuscripts accessible to him for comparing and preparing his Greek Text.[134]

The Reformation (16th century) brought the Bible to the fore, a rejection of allegory, tradition of men, and return to the literal approach to biblical interpretation. "The tradition of the Syrian school was reflected among the Victorines and became the essential hermeneutical theory of the Reformers. Although historians admit that the West was ripe for the Reformation due to several forces at work in European culture, nevertheless there was a hermeneutical Reformation, which preceded the ecclesiastical Reformation." (Ramm 1999, 51-2)

The post-Reformation of the 17th and 18th centuries was "noted for several influential movements and activities. These include the confirming and spread of Calvinism, reactions to Calvinism, textual and linguistic studies, and rationalism." (Zuck 1991, 49) The greatest accomplishment of the three major paths of the Reformation: Lutheran, Calvinist, and Anglican, was the Bible accessible to the people, the plowboy as William Tyndale had put it, would have the Word of God in their own language. "A clergyman hopelessly entrenched in Roman Catholic dogma once taunted William Tyndale with the statement, 'We are better to be without

---

[134] Edward D. Andrews, *The Complete Guide to Bible Translation: Bible Translation Choices and Translation Principles* (Cambridge, OH: Christian Publishing House, 2012), 46–47.

God's laws than the Pope's.' Tyndale was infuriated by such Roman Catholic heresies, and he replied, '*I defy the Pope and all his laws. If God spare my life ere many years, I will cause the boy that drives the plow to know more of the scriptures than you!'"*[135]

Modern Method of Interpretation

Several strands of biblical interpretation have been present in the 20th century. Liberalism has continued much of the rationalistic and higher critical approach of the 19th century. Orthodoxy has taken a literal as well as a devotional approach to the Bible. Neo-orthodoxy has said the Bible becomes the Word of God in man's existential encounters. Bultmannism has taken a mythological approach to the Bible.

Liberalism, strong in influence in the 19th century, has continued into the 20th century. It views the Bible as a human book not given by divine inspiration, and it teaches that supernatural elements in the Bible can be explained rationally. (Zuck 1991, 53)

Would any Christian living in 1700 C.E. have ever doubted the writership of Moses? Hardly! So how did the Documentary Hypothesis[136] become Documentary Fact? All it took was for some leading professors at major universities to plant seeds of doubt within their students. Being at the entrance of the era of higher criticism and skepticism of the nineteenth century, this Documentary Hypothesis had a well-cultivated field in which to grow. It created a domino effect as a few scholars produced a generation of students, who would then be the next generation of scholars, and so on.

As we moved into the twentieth century, these questions had become "facts" in the eyes of many; in fact, it became in vogue to challenge the Bible. Leading schools and leading scholars of higher criticism were the norm, and soon the conservative Christian was isolated. The twentieth-century student received a lean diet from those few scholars who still accepted God's Word as just that, the Word of God, fully inerrant, with 40 writers of 66 books over a period of about 1,600 years. No, these students would now be fed mostly liberal theology, and any who disagreed were portrayed as ignorant and naïve. This planting of

---

[135] http://www.william-tyndale.com/tyndale-bible-history.html

[136] The suggestion that Genesis through Deuteronomy is actually a compilation of the works of four different anonymous authors (usually called J, E, D, P), centuries after the life of Moses, represents the famous "documentary hypothesis," which has dominated the last century of Pentateuchal criticism. (Kaiser and Silva 1994, 2007).

uncertainty or mistrust, with question after question bringing Moses' writership into doubt, with most literature focusing on this type of propaganda, would create the latest generation of scholars, and today they dominate the world of scholarship.

How did this progressive takeover come off without a hitch? The conservative scholarship of the early twentieth century saw these liberal naysayers as nothing more than a fly at a picnic. Most did not even deem it necessary to address their questions, so by 1950–1970, the Documentary Hypothesis machine was in full throttle. It was about this same time that the sleeping giant finally woke to find that conservative scholarship had taken a backseat to this new creature, liberal scholarship. It is only within the last 30–40 years that some very influential conservative scholars have started to publish books in a move to dislodge this liberal movement.[137] Is it too little, too late?

It is possible to displace higher criticism, but many factors stand in the way. For one, any opposition is painted as uninformed and inexperienced regarding the subject matter. Moreover, the books that tear down the Bible with all their alleged critical analysis sell far better than those do that encourage putting faith in God's Word. In addition, many conservative scholars tend to sit on the sideline and watch as a few leading scholars attempt to do the work of the many. In addition, there are liberal scholars continually putting out numerous articles and books, dominating the market. Unlike the conservative scholars in the first part of the twentieth century, these liberal scholars in the first part of the twenty-first century are not slowing down. Moreover, they have become more aggressive.

Historical-Critical Method

The historical-critical method is also known as higher criticism. It is used in most universities throughout the United States. It should be differentiated from lower criticism. Lower criticism is also known as textual criticism, and is the study of families of original language manuscripts, as well as patristic writings, versions, and lectionaries, in order to determine which is the original reading. Since the job of lower criticism is to restore the text to the original; it is constructive, not destructive. As was stated above, higher criticism is pseudo-scholarship and has done nothing more than weaken and demoralize people's

---

[137] This is not to say that the 19th and early 20th century did not have any apologist defending against biblical criticism. There were some giants in this field, like R. A. Torrey.

assurance in the Bible being the inspired and fully inerrant Word of God, and is destructive in its very nature. Higher criticism or historical-critical method is made up of many forms of biblical criticism that is harmful to the authoritative, inspired and inerrant Word of God: historical criticism, source criticism, form criticism, redaction criticism, social-science criticism, canonical criticism, rhetorical criticism, structural criticism, narrative criticism, reader-response criticism, poststructuralist criticism, feminist criticism, and socioeconomic criticism.[138] While we cannot cover each of these in the space allotted, the ones we do will evidence their destructive nature.

Source Criticism

Source Criticism, a sub-discipline of Higher Criticism, is an attempt by liberal Bible scholars to discover the original sources that the Bible writer(s) [not Moses as our example] used to pen these five books. It should be noted that most scholars who engage in higher criticism start with liberal presuppositions. Bible scholar, theologian, and educator Gleason L. Archer, Jr., identifies many flaws in the reasoning of those who support the Documentary Hypothesis; however, this one flaw being quoted herein is indeed the most grievous and lays the foundation for other irrational reasoning in their thinking. Identifying their problem, Archer writes: "The Wellhausen school started with the pure assumption (which they have hardly bothered to demonstrate) that Israel's religion was of merely human origin like any other and that it was to be explained as a mere product of evolution." In other words, Wellhausen and those who followed him begin with the presupposition that God's Word is not that at all, the Word of God, but is the word of mere man, and then they reason beyond this based on that premise. As to the effect, this has on God's Word and those who hold it as such; it is comparable to having a natural disaster wash the foundation right out from under our home.

The first five books of the Bible came to be called the Pentateuch (Greek for "five rolls"), which both Jewish and Christian conservatives view as being penned by the one writer, Moses. Originally, the Pentateuch made up one book; later this was divided into five rolls or scrolls, making it much easier to handle. In our English Bibles, these five books came to be called Genesis, Exodus, Leviticus, Numbers, and

---

138 BASICS OF BIBLICAL CRITICISM: Helpful or Harmful? [Second Edition] F. David Farnell, Thomas Howe, Thomas Marshall, Benjamin Cocar, Edward D. Andrews, and Dianna Newman (http://www.christianpublishers.org/apps/webstore/products/show/5346435)

Deuteronomy. From the beginning, these writings were accepted by the nation of Israel as a canon. Moses' successor, Joshua, said: "Be very strong and continue obeying all that is written in the book of the law of Moses so that you do not turn from it to the right or left. So be very diligent to love the LORD your God for your own well-being." (Joshua 23:6, 11, HCSB) The Jews accept the Pentateuch with Moses as its writer; this has been the case since 1,500 years before the birth of Jesus Christ. Later, Jesus Christ and the writers of the New Testament accepted the Pentateuch as entirely trustworthy, with Moses as its writer who was inspired by God.

For about 3,500 years, Moses' first five books have been the foundation of the Old Testament, which itself had paved the way for the writing of the New Testament. These five books were actually the first mini-canon by which all other Bible books could be compared. Many scholars have claimed, however, that Moses was not the writer of the first five books of the Bible. Their claim is known as the Documentary Hypothesis. Moreover, this hypothesis also calls into question the writership of the books of Joshua, Judges, 1 and 2 Samuel, and 1 and 2 Kings.

It was in the latter half of the nineteenth century that higher criticism began to be taken seriously. These critics rejected Moses as the writer of the Pentateuch, arguing instead that the accounts in Genesis, Exodus, Leviticus, Numbers, and Deuteronomy were based on four other sources [writers] written between the tenth and the sixth centuries B.C.E. To differentiate these sources one from the other, they are simply known as the "J," "E," "D," and "P" sources. The letters are an initial to the name of these alleged sources, as we will soon see.

The capital letter "J" is used to represent an alleged writer. In this case, it stands for any place God's personal name, Jehovah, is used. It is argued that this author is perhaps a woman as it is the only one of their presented authors who is not a priest. (Harold Bloom, *The Book of "J"*) They date the portion set out to "J" to c.850 B.C.E.[139] Some scholars place this author in the southern portion of the Promised Land, Judah.[140]

Another writer is put forth as "E," for it stands for the portion that has Jehovah's title Elohim, God. Most higher critics place this author c.750–700 B.C.E. Unlike "J," this author "E" is said to reside in the northern kingdom of Israel. As stated earlier, this author is reckoned to be

---

[139] Symbols: a. for "after"; b. for "before"; c. for "circa," or "about."

140. Mark F. Rooker, *Leviticus: The New American Commentary* (Nashville: Broadman & Holman, 2001), 23.

a priest, with his lineage going back to Moses. It is has also been said that he bought this office. In addition, it is argued that an editor combined "J" and "E" after the destruction of Israel by the Assyrians but before the destruction of Jerusalem by the Babylonians, which they date to about 722 BC.E.[141]

These same critics hold out that the language and theological content of "D," Deuteronomy, is different from Genesis, Exodus, Leviticus, and Numbers. Thus they have another author. They argue that "D" was gathered over several hundred years by the priests living in the northern kingdom of Israel; however, it wasn't until much later that "D" was combined with the earlier works. It is also said that the "D" writer (source) was also behind Joshua, Judges, 1 and 2 Samuel and 1 and 2 Kings (Dtr). It is suggested strongly that, in fact, this is the book found in the temple by Hilkiah the high priest and given to King Josiah. (2 Kings 22:8) It is further put forth that J/E/D were fused together as one document in about 586 B.C.E.[142]

The source critics use the capital letter "P" for Priestly. This is because this portion of the Pentateuch usually relates to the priesthood. For instance, things like the sacrifices would be tagged as belonging to this author. Many scholars suggest that "P" was written before the destruction of Jerusalem, which they date at 586 B.C.E. Others put forth that it was written during the exile of seventy years, the Priest(s) composing this holy portion for the people who would return from exile, while others say it was written after the exile, about 450 B.C.E. These liberal scholars find no consensus on when this supposed author "P" wrote this portion of the first five books. The critics tell us that the final form of J/E/D/P was composed into one document about 400 B.C.E.[143]

The capital "R" represents the editor(s) who put it together and may have altered some portions to facilitate their social circumstances of their day. The "R" comes from the German word *Redakteur* (Redactor), which is an editor or reviser of a work.

---

141. Ibid., 23.

142. Ibid., 23.

143. Ibid., 23–24.

Redaction Criticism

As stated above in our alphabet soup of alleged authors ("J," "E," "D," "P," and "R"), a redactor is an editor or reviser of a work. Redaction Criticism is another form of Biblical criticism that intends to investigate the Scriptures and draw conclusions concerning their authorship, historicity, and time of writing. This form of criticism, as well as the others, has really done nothing more than tear down God's Word. R. E. Friedman, the Documentary Hypothesis' biggest advocate, asserts that the "J" document was composed between 922–722 B.C.E. in the southern kingdom of Judah, while the northern kingdom of Israel was composing the "E" document during these same years. Friedman contends that sometime thereafter a compiler of history put these two sources together, resulting in "J/E," with the compiler being known as "RJE." Friedman states that shortly thereafter, the priesthood in Jerusalem put out yet another document, known today as "P," this being another story to be added to the above "J/E." Going back to their authors for the first five books of the Bible, Friedman and these critics claim a redactor or editor put the whole Pentateuch together using "D," "P," and the combination of "J/E." For them, this editor (Deuteronomist) used the written sources he had available to make his additions for the purpose of dealing with the social conditions of his day. They claim this editor's express purpose was to alter Scripture to bring comfort and hope to those who were in exile in Babylon. Wellhausen's theories, with some adjustments, have spread like a contagious disease, until they have consumed the body of Christendom. However, the real question is, Do these higher critics have any serious evidence to overturn thousands of years of belief by three major religious groups (Jews, Christians, and Muslims) that the Pentateuch was written by Moses?

What these critics have are pebbles, each representing minute inferences and implications [circumstantial evidence at best] that they place on one side of a scale. These are weighed out against the conservative evidence of Moses' authorship of the Pentateuch. As unsuspecting readers work their way through the books and articles written by these critics, the scales seem to be tilted all to one side, as if there were no evidence for the other side. Thus, like a jury, many uninformed readers; conclude that there is no alternative but to accept the idea that there are multiple authors for the Pentateuch instead of Moses, who is traditionally held to be the sole author.

Reader-Response Criticism

The idea that the reader is the one who determines the meaning is known as the "reader response." For those who hold to this position, all meaning is equal to another, and all are correct. We can have a set of verses, and 20 people may give us different interpretations, and many may seem the opposite of others. Those believing in the "reader "response" will say that all are correct. Under this position, the text allows each reader the right to derive his or her own meaning from the text. Again, this is where we hear "I think this means," "I believe this means," "this means to me," and "I feel this means to me." The problem with this is that the text loses its authority; God and his author lose their authority over the intended meaning of the text. When God inspired the writer, to express his will and purposes, there was the intention of one meaning, i.e., what the author under inspiration meant by the words he used. If anyone can come along and give it whatever meaning pleases them, then God's authority over the meaning is lost, and there is no real meaning at all.

Grammatical-Historical Interpretation

The grammatical-historical method is a method, which attempts to ascertain what the author meant by the words that he used, which should have been understood by his original readers. (Stein 1994, 38-9) It was the primary method of interpretation when higher criticism's Historical-Critical Method was in its infancy back in the 19th century (Milton Terry), and remains the only method of interpretation for true conservative scholarship in the later 20th century into the 21st century.

Grammatical Aspect

When we speak of interpreting the Bible grammatically, we are referring to the process of seeking to determine its meaning by ascertaining four things: (a) the meaning of words (lexicology), (b) the form of words (morphology), (c) the function of words (parts of speech), and (d) the relationships of words (syntax). In the meaning of words (lexicology), we are concerned with (a) etymology- how words are derived and developed, (b) usage how words are used by the same and other authors, (c) synonyms and antonyms -how similar and opposite words are used, and (d) context-how words are used in various contexts.

In discussing the form of words (morphology), we are looking at how words are structured and how that affects their meaning. For example, the word eat means something different from ate, though the same letters are used. The word part changes meaning when the letter "s" is added to it to make the word parts. The function of words (parts of speech) considers what the various forms do. These include attention to subjects, verbs, objects, nouns, and others, as will be discussed later. The relationships of words (syntax) are the way words are related or put together to form phrases, clauses, and sentences. (Zuck 1991, 100-101)

Historical Aspect

By "historical" they meant the setting in which the Bible books were written and the circumstances involved in the writing. ... taking into consideration the circumstances of the writings and the cultural environment.

The context in which a given Scripture passage is written influences how that passage is to be understood. Context includes several things:

- the verse(s) immediately before and after a passage

- the paragraph and book in which the verses occur

- the dispensation in which it was written

- the message of the entire Bible

- the historical-cultural environment of that time when it was written. (Zuck 1991, 77)

Some of the truly conservative scholars who have remained faithful to the grammatical-historical method of interpretation are Bernard Ramm, Harold Lindsell, Gleason L. Archer, Robert I. Thomas, Norman L. Geisler, Thomas Howe, Roy, B. Zuck, David F. Farnell, among other select ones. Such ones are referred to as "fundamentalist Protestants," as though fundamentalism is now a dirty word. Some modern day scholar believes that they can dip their feet in the pool of higher criticism, suggesting that they can use certain aspects of these forms of criticisms, without ending up doing any harm to the trustworthiness of the text, to inerrancy. This is very naïve, as some of them end up swimming in the deep end of higher criticism, while others walk along the edges of the deep end.

Here is just ten of the "tip-of-the-iceberg" of the things that these scholars would agree with:

- Matthew, not Jesus, Created the Sermon on the Mount.

186

- The commissioning of the Twelve in Matthew 10 is a group of instructions compiled and organized by Matthew, not spoken by Jesus on a single occasion.

- The parable accounts of Matthew 13 and Mark 4 are anthologies of parables that Jesus uttered on separate occasions.

- Jesus did not preach the Olivet Discourse in its entirety, as found in the of the gospel accounts.

- Jesus gave his teaching on divorce and remarriage without the exception clauses found in Matthew 5:32 and 19:9.

- In Matthew 19:16-17, Matthew changed the words of Jesus and the rich man to obtain a different emphasis or to avoid a theological problem involved in the wording of Mark's and Luke's accounts of the same event.

- The scribes and the Pharisees were in reality decent people whom Matthew painted in an entirely negative light because of his personal bias against them.

- The genealogies of Jesus in Matthew 1 and Luke 3 are figures of speech and not accurate records of Jesus' physical/and or legal lineage.

- The magi who, according to Matthew 2, visited the child Jesus after his birth are fictional, not real characters.

- Jesus uttered only three or four of the eight or nine beatitudes in Matthew 5:3-12[144]

The Original Meaning

The objective of the exegete in his use of the grammatical-historical method of interpretation is to discover what the author meant by the words that he used, as should have been understood by his originally intended audience. Each and every text has one single meaning. Milton S. Terry wrote, "A fundamental principle in grammatico-historical exposition is that the words and sentences can have but one significance in one and the same connection. The moment we neglect this principle we drift out upon a sea of uncertainty and conjecture." (Terry, Biblical Hermeneutics: A Treatise on the Interpretation of the Old and New Testaments 1883, 205)

---

[144] (Thomas and Farnell 1998)

Other Methods of Interpretation

Proof-Text Method

Another misapplication of the text is what is known as *proof texting*. **Proof texting** is stringing along a series of verses that one has found throughout the Bible, using a sentence or two from each, to find support for what he wants the Bible to say. The problem with this process is that they are taking the texts out of their context. There is nothing wrong with listing verses that support what we believe, but they need to be within the context of their actual meaning. Let us look at one Scriptural example:

Acts 2:38

[38]And Peter said to them, "Repent and be baptized every one of you in the name of Jesus Christ for the forgiveness of your sins, and you will receive the gift of the Holy Spirit.

Immediately, there are several doctrinal points that this text could be used for: **(1)** One must be baptized to be saved, **(2)** baptism takes ones sins away, and **(3)** one must be baptized only in Jesus' name. The interpreter has forgotten the first word uttered by Peter in verse 38, "repent." To repent means to turn one's life *around* and live in another direction. This is what initiates the forgiveness of sins, not baptism. Baptism is an outward display of this repentance, a life course that is now made known to others by the ceremony of baptism. Everyone offers texts, as proof of a position they hold, so proof texting in and of itself is not wrong, it is using several verses out of cotext and context, which makes it wrong.

Allegorical Method

Allegorical Interpretation is an approach in which the characters and events are viewed as being beyond the literal plain sense of a text, to be understood as representing other things and symbolically expressing a deeper, often spiritual or moral meaning. For example, Genesis 3:22 in Bagster's Greek Septuagint of the Old Testament, which says, "The Lord God made for Adam and his wife garments of skin, and clothed them." Philo[145] found symbolism in that verse and stated, "The real meaning,

---

[145] PHILO JUDAEUS: Early Jewish interpreter of Scripture known for use of allegory. Also known as Philo of Alexandria, he lived about the same time as Jesus (about 20 B.C. to A.D. 50). A member of a wealthy Jewish family in Alexandria, Egypt, He was well educated in Greek schools and used the Greek OT, the Septuagint, as his Bible. Philo's writings,

then the garment of skins is a figurative expression for the natural skin, that is to say, our body; for God, when first of all he made the intellect, called it Adam; after that he created the outward sense, to which he gave the name of Life. In the third place, he of necessity also made a body, calling that by a figurative expression, a garment of skins."[146] Thus, Philo endeavored to make the historical act of God clothing Adam and Eve an allegory. Consider also the historical and geographical account of Genesis 2:10-14.

Genesis 2:10-14

[10] A river flowed out of Eden to water the garden, and there it divided and became four rivers. [11] The name of the first is the Pishon. It is the one that flowed around the whole land of Havilah, where there is gold.[12] And the gold of that land is good; bdellium and onyx stone are there. [13] The name of the second river is the Gihon. It is the one that flowed around the whole land of Cush. [14] And the name of the third river is the Tigris, which flows east of Assyria. And the fourth river is the Euphrates.

Philo made an effort to go beyond the words and look to a so-called deeper meaning. "Perhaps this passage also contains an allegorical meaning; for the four rivers are the signs of four virtues: Phison being the sign of prudence, as deriving its name from parsimony; and Gihon being the sign of sobriety, as having its employment in the regulation of meat and drink, and as restraining the appetites of the belly, and of those parts which are blow the belly, as being earthly; the Tigris again is the sign of fortitude, for this it is which regulates the raging commotion of anger within us; and the Euphrates is the sign of justice, since there is nothing in which the thoughts of men exult more than in justice."[147]

Certainly, one can see the danger of allegorical interpretation, because the interpreter can align it with whatever he wants it to mean. If we could talk with many of the liberal Bible scholars today, they would say things like, "the book of Genesis, including Adam and Eve, are

---

particularly his commentaries on the Scriptures, influenced the early church. A literal interpretation was all right for the average scholar, but for the enlightened ones such as himself, he advocated an allegorical interpretation.—James Taulman, "Philo Judaeus", in Holman Illustrated Bible Dictionary, ed. Chad Brand, Charles Draper, Archie England et al., 1293-94 (Nashville, TN: Holman Bible Publishers, 2003).

[146] Philo of Alexandria and Charles Duke Yonge, The Works of Philo: Complete and Unabridged, 802 (Peabody, MA: Hendrickson, 1995).

[147] Philo of Alexandria and Charles Duke Yonge, The Works of Philo: Complete and Unabridged, 793 (Peabody, MA: Hendrickson, 1995).

allegorical." In other words, Adam and Even are fictional characters, not real persons. This is why the reformers of the Reformation of the 16th century abandoned allegorical interpretation. However, it has hung on through the writings of some religious groups, as well as some Bible scholars. Did any of the New Testament writers use allegorical interpretation in their writings? Moreover, should we mimic them if they did use allegorical interpretation? Please see what Paul wrote to the Galatians below, which is one of the few places that are viewed as allegorical.

Galatians 4:24-26

24 Now this may be interpreted allegorically: these women are two covenants. One is from Mount Sinai, bearing children for slavery; she is Hagar. 25 Now Hagar is Mount Sinai in Arabia; she corresponds to the present Jerusalem, for she is in slavery with her children. 26 But the Jerusalem above is free, and she is our mother.

The first part of verse 24 could be rendered differently. Such as, "these things are illustrations" or "these things are symbolic." Regardless, Paul sounds pretty much like what Philo sounded like, correct? Thus, for the sake of making our point, we will say Paul is interpreting allegorically here. What is the difference between Philo and Paul? Yes, Paul is an inspired Bible writer, who is penning his book under inspiration, and it is subjective. **Subjective** means that something is based on somebody's opinions or feelings rather than on facts or evidence. **Objective** means that something is free of any bias or prejudice caused by personal feelings, based on facts rather than thoughts or opinions.[148]

Allegorical interpretation is subjective, based on opinion. Paul's opinion just so happens to be under the inspiration of God, as Holy Spirit moved him along. In other words, it is God's opinion. This is perfectly acceptable. Philo's allegorical interpretation is subjective too, meaning it is not based on any facts, but rather based on his personal feelings, and is his opinion. This is absolutely not acceptable. Thus, we do no interpret Scripture allegorically. If the New Testament writer has done it for us; then, we accept it as the Word of God. We also arrive at our

---

[148] We are faced then with the fact that we possess two separate and distinct methods of interpretation. One is defined by hermeneutical guidelines and is objective in nature. The other is subjective in nature but finds its authority not in the science that drives it, but in its source—inspiration from God. If you have inspiration, you do not need historical-grammatical hermeneutics. If you do not have inspiration, you must proceed by the acknowledged guidelines of hermeneutics.—Page(s): 6, Inspired Subjectivity and Hermeneutical Objectivity by John H. Walton Master's Seminary Journal March 01, 2002.pdf

understanding based on historical-grammatical interpretation, which is primarily objective. The New Testament writer did not need to use historical-grammatical hermeneutics because Holy Spirit led him. We on the other hand, are not lead by Holy Spirit.[149]

Finally, if a New Testament writer uses allegory for an Old Testament people, object, institution or event, this does not mean that the New Testament writer's allegorical interpretation is to be carried back to the Old Testament, as though that is what the Old Testament writer meant to convey. That allegorical meaning would be a different meaning, belonging to the New Testament writer alone. Finally, we are not inspired, so we do not use allegorical interpretation unless it is what the New Testament writer penned.

Typological Method

Typological Interpretation is the study of religious texts for identifying entities (people, objects, institutions and events) in them that appear to prefigure subsequent corresponding entities. For example, King David is viewed as a type of Christ.

A biblical "type" is an illustration, an example, or a pattern of God's activity in the history of his people Israel and the church through persons, events, or institutions. Typology is not the same thing as an exegetical analysis of a passage, for a biblical text has only one meaning, its natural or normal meaning as determined by means of grammatical-historical study. If the typical sense is not indicated by the original author or his text, then it probably is not consistent with the normal or natural (some read: literal) meaning of the text.[150]

Like allegory, typological interpretation is subjective, meaning one's opinion. Therefore, it is fine that a New Testament writer used typological interpretation, because they were inspired, and the result was

---

[149] NT authors never claim to have engaged in a hermeneutical process, nor do they claim that they can support their findings from the text; instead, they claim inspiration.—Page(s): 6, Inspired Subjectivity and Hermeneutical Objectivity by John H. Walton Master's Seminary Journal March 01, 2002.pdf

[150] Kaiser Jr., Walter C.; Silva, Moises (2009-08-12). Introduction to Biblical Hermeneutics: The Search for Meaning (Kindle Locations 2100-2104). Zondervan. Kindle Edition.

the Word of God.[151] However, we are not inspired, so like allegory, we do not use typological interpretation, unless we are using what the New Testament writer already established as typological. Again, the New Testament writer did not need to use historical-grammatical hermeneutics, because Holy Spirit led him.

---

[151] The NT typologists did not get their typological correspondence from their exegetical analysis of the context of the OT. Hermeneutics is incapable of extracting a typological meaning from the OT context because hermeneutics operates objectively while the typological identification can only be made subjectively.—Page(s): 6, Inspired Subjectivity and Hermeneutical Objectivity by John H. Walton Master's Seminary Journal March 01, 2002.pdf

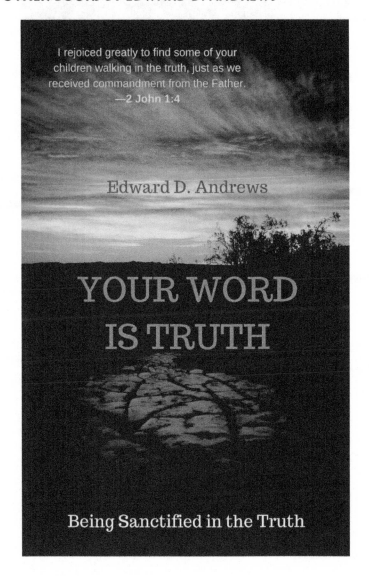

No greater joy do I have than this, to hear of my
children walking in the truth.
—3 John 1:4

WALK HUMBLY WITH YOUR GOD

Putting God's Purpose First in Your Life

Second Edition

EDWARD D. ANDREWS

"SAVING Those Who DOUBT"

CRISIS OF FAITH

EDWARD D. ANDREWS

EVIDENCE THAT YOU ARE TRULY CHRISTIAN

Keep Testing Yourselves to See If You Are In the Faith—Keep Examining Yourselves

EDWARD D. ANDREWS

"Excellent info on regaining scriptural thinking and taking thoughts captive!"
– "very informative and useful."
Book Rev

FOR AS I THINK I AM

IN MY HEART

SO I AM

Combining Biblical Counseling with
Cognitive Behavioral Therapy

EDWARD D. ANDREWS

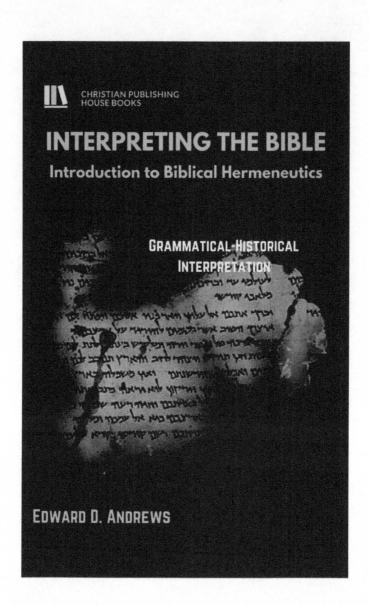

CHRISTIAN PUBLISHING
HOUSE BOOKS

INTERPRETING THE BIBLE

Introduction to Biblical Hermeneutics

GRAMMATICAL-HISTORICAL INTERPRETATION

EDWARD D. ANDREWS

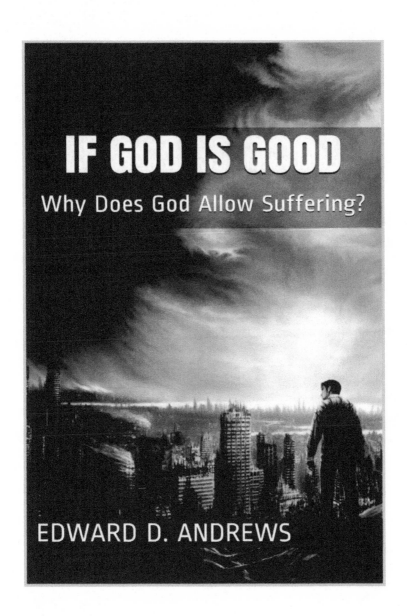

IF GOD IS GOOD

Why Does God Allow Suffering?

EDWARD D. ANDREWS

MIRACLES—DO THEY STILL HAPPEN TODAY?

God Miraculously Saving People's Lives, Apparitions, Speaking In Tongues, Faith Healing

EDWARD D. ANDREWS

OVERCOMING BIBLE DIFFICULTIES

Answers to the So-Called Errors and Contradictions

EDWARD D. ANDREWS

Edward D. Andrews

PUT OFF THE OLD PERSON WITH ITS PRACTICES

And Put On the New Person

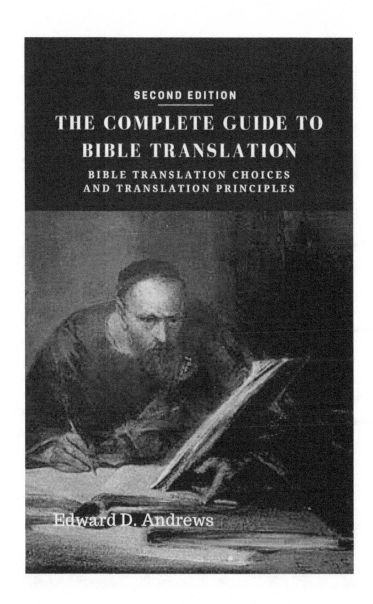

SECOND EDITION

THE COMPLETE GUIDE TO BIBLE TRANSLATION

BIBLE TRANSLATION CHOICES
AND TRANSLATION PRINCIPLES

Edward D. Andrews

Edward D. Andrews

THE TEXT OF THE NEW TESTAMENT

A Beginner's Guide to New Testament Textual Criticism

SECOND EDITION
REVISED & EXPANDED

BASIC BIBLE
DOCTRINES

OF THE
CHRISTIAN FAITH

UNDERSTANDING THE
CREATION ACCOUNT

Edward D. Andrews

GENESIS 1-4

EDWARD D. ANDREWS

THE CHRISTIAN APOLOGIST

Always Being Prepared
to Make a Defense

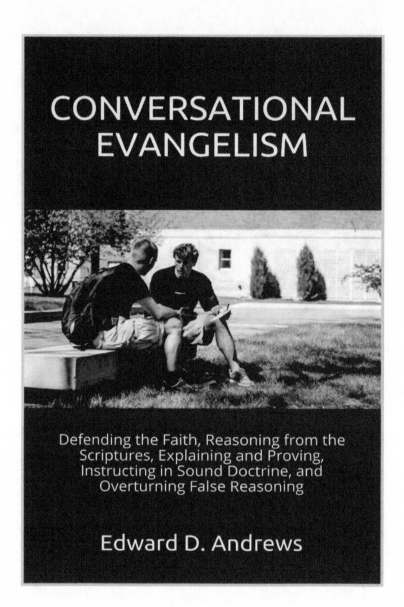

CONVERSATIONAL EVANGELISM

Defending the Faith, Reasoning from the Scriptures, Explaining and Proving, Instructing in Sound Doctrine, and Overturning False Reasoning

Edward D. Andrews

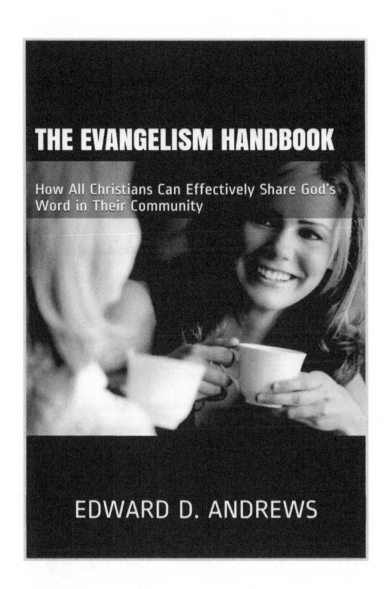

THE EVANGELISM HANDBOOK

How All Christians Can Effectively Share God's Word in Their Community

EDWARD D. ANDREWS

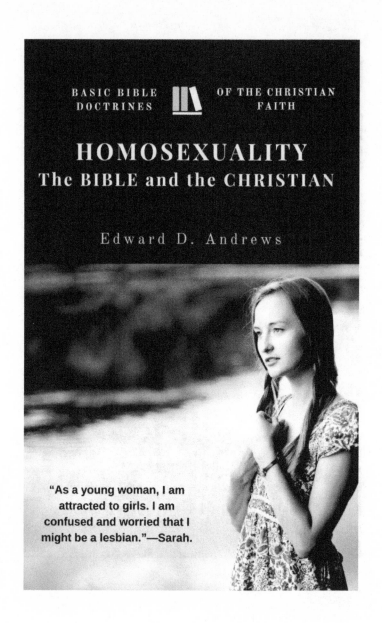

BASIC BIBLE
DOCTRINES

OF THE CHRISTIAN
FAITH

HOMOSEXUALITY
The BIBLE and the CHRISTIAN

Edward D. Andrews

"As a young woman, I am
attracted to girls. I am
confused and worried that I
might be a lesbian."—Sarah.

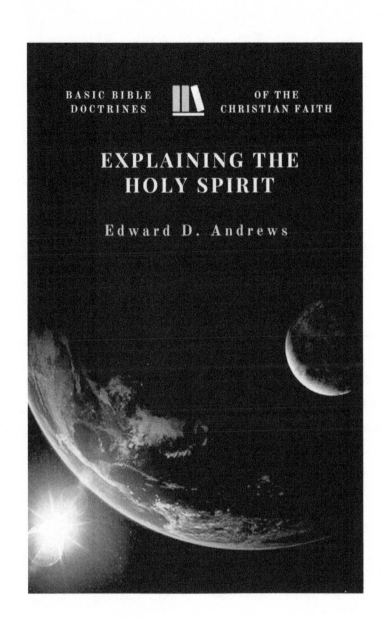

BASIC BIBLE
DOCTRINES

OF THE
CHRISTIAN FAITH

EXPLAINING THE
HOLY SPIRIT

Edward D. Andrews

IDENTIFYING THE ANTICHRIST AND THE MAN OF LAWLESSNESS

Edward D. Andrews

Mark of the Beast Also Revealed

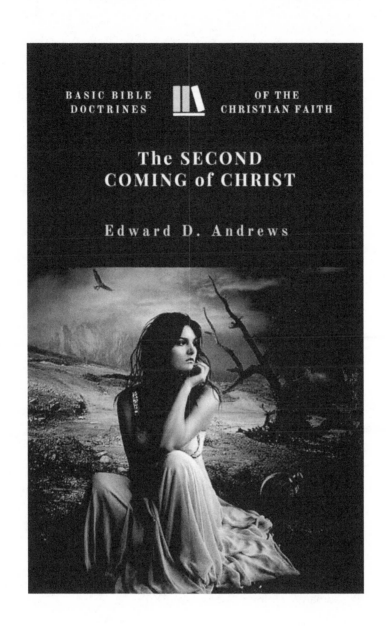

BASIC BIBLE
DOCTRINES

OF THE
CHRISTIAN FAITH

The SECOND
COMING of CHRIST

Edward D. Andrews

Bibliography

Akin, Daniel L. *The New American Commentary: 1, 2, 3 John*. Nashville, TN: Broadman & Holman , 2001.

Alden, Robert L. *Job, The New American Commentary, vol. 11* . Nashville: Broadman & Holman Publishers, 2001.

Anders, Max. *Holman New Testament Commentary: vol. 8, Galatians, Ephesians, Philippians, Colossians*. Nashville, TN: Broadman & Holman Publishers, 1999.

—. *Holman Old Testament Commentary - Proverbs* . Nashville: B&H Publishing, 2005.

Anders, Max, and Doug McIntosh. *Holman Old Testament Commentary - Deuteronomy*. Nashville: B&H Publishing, 2009.

Anders, Max, and Steven Lawson. *Holman Old Testament Commentary - Psalms: 11*. Grand Rapids: B&H Publishing, 2004.

Anders, Max, and Trent Butler. *Holman Old Testament Commentary: Isaiah*. Nashville, TN: B&H Publishing, 2002.

Andrews, Edward D. *INTERPRETING THE BIBLE: Introduction to Biblical Hermeneutics [Second Edition]*. Cambridge: Christian Publishing House, 2016.

Andrews, Stephen J, and Robert D Bergen. *Holman Old Testament Commentary: 1-2 Samuel*. Nashville: Broadman & Holman, 2009.

Archer, Gleason L. *Encyclopedia of Bible Difficulties*. Grand Rapids: Zondervan, 1982.

Balz, Horst, and Gerhard Schneider. *Exegetical Dictionary of the New Testament*. Edinburgh: T & T Clark Ltd, 1978.

Barker, Kenneth L., and Waylon Bailey. *The New American Commentary: vol. 20, Micah, Nahum, Habakkuk, Zephaniah*. Nashville, TN: Broadman & Holman Publishers, 2001.

Bercot, David W. *A Dictionary of Early Christian Beliefs*. Peabody: Hendrickson, 1998.

Bergen, Robert D. *The New American Commentary: 1-2 Samuel*. Nashville: Broadman & Holman, 1996.

Blomberg, Craig. *The New American Commentary: Matthew*. Nashville, TN: Broadman & Holman Publishers, 1992.

Boa, Kenneth, and William Kruidenier. *Holman New Testament Commentary: Romans.* Nashville: Broadman & Holman, 2000.

Borchert, Gerald L. *The New American Commentary: John 1-11* . Nashville, TN: Broadman & Holman Publishers, 2001.

Borchert, Gerald L. *The New American Commentary vol. 25B, John 12– 21.* Nashville: Broadman & Holman Publishers, 2002.

Brand, Chad, Charles Draper, and England Archie. *Holman Illustrated Bible Dictionary: Revised, Updated and Expanded.* Nashville, TN: Holman, 2003.

Breneman, Mervin. *The New American Commentary, vol. 10, Ezra, Nehemiah, Esther.* Nashville: Broadman & Holman Publishers, 1993.

Bromiley, Geoffrey W. *The International Standard Bible Encyclopedia (Vol. 1-4).* Grand Rapids, MI: William B. Eerdmans Publishing Co., 1986.

Bromiley, Geoffry W., and Gerhard Friedrich. *Theological Dictionary of the New Testament, ed. Gerhard Kittel, vol. 4.* Grand Rapids, MI: Eerdmans, 1964-.

Brooks, James A. *The New American Commentary: Mark (Volume 23).* Nashville: Broadman & Holman Publishers, 1992.

Butler, Trent C. *Holman New Testament Commentary: Luke.* Nashville, TN: Broadman & Holman Publishers, 2000.

Butler, Trent C. *Holman Old Testament Commentary - Hosea, Joel, Amos, Obadiah, Jonah, Micah* . Nashville: Broadman & Holman Publishers, 2005.

Cole, R. Dennis. *THE NEW AMERICAN COMMENTARY: Volume 3b Numbers.* Nashville: Broadman & Holman Publishers, 2000.

Cooper, Lamar Eugene. *The New American Commentary, Ezekiel, vol. 17.* Nashville, TN: Broadman & Holman Publishers, 1994.

Cooper, Rodney. *Holman New Testament Commentary: Mark.* Nashville: Broadman & Holman Publishers, 2000.

Easley, Kendell H. *Holman New Testament Commentary, vol. 12, Revelation.* (Nashville, TN: Broadman & Holman Publishers, 1998.

Elwell, Walter A. *Baker Encyclopedia of the Bible*. Grand Rapids: Baker Book House, 1988.

—. *Evangelical Dictionary of Theology (Second Edition)*. Grand Rapids: Baker Academic, 2001.

Elwell, Walter A, and Philip Wesley Comfort. *Tyndale Bible Dictionary*. Wheaton, Ill: Tyndale House Publishers, 2001.

Fahlbusch, Erwin, and Geoffrey William Bromiley. *The Encyclopedia of Christianity*. Grand Rapids: Wm. B. Eerdmans, 1999-2003.

Freedman, David Noel, Allen C. Myers, and Astrid B. Beck. *Eerdmans Dictionary of the Bible* . Grand Rapids, Mich.: W.B. Eerdmans , 2000.

Gangel, Kenneth O. *Holman New Testament Commentary: Acts*. Nashville, TN: Broadman & Holman Publishers, 1998.

Gangel, Kenneth O. *Holman New Testament Commentary, vol. 4, John* . Nashville, TN: Broadman & Holman Publishers, 2000.

—. *Holman Old Testament Commentary: Daniel*. Nashville: Broadman & Holman Publishers, 2001.

Garrett, Duane A. *Proverbs, Ecclesiastes, Song of Songs, The New American Commentary, vol. 14*. Nashville: Broadman & Holman Publishers, 1993.

—. *The New American Commentary: Vol. 14 (Proverbs, Ecclesiastes, Song of Songs)*. Nashville: Broadman & Holman Publishers, 1993.

Geisler, Norman L. *A Popular Survey of the New Testament*. Grand Rapids: Baker Books, 2007.

Geisler, Norman L. *Baker Encyclopedia of Christian Apologetics*. Grand Rapids: Baker Books, 1999.

Geisler, Norman L., and Thomas Howe. *The Big Book of Bible Difficulties*. Grand Rapids: Baker Books, 1992.

George, Timothy. *The New American Commentary: Galatians* . Nashville, TN: Broadman & Holman Publishers, 2001.

Green, Joel B, Scot McKnight, and Howard Marshall. *Dictionary of Jesus and the Gospels*. Downers Grove, IL: InterVarsity Press, 1992.

Guralnik, David B. *Webster's New World Dictionary, 2d college ed*. New York, NY: Simon and Schuster, 1984.

Hindson, Ed, and Ergun Caner. *The Popular Encyclopedia of Apologetics: Surveying the Evidence for the Truth of Christianity.* Eugene: Harvest House, 2008.

House, Paul R. *The New American Commentary: Vol. 8., 2 Kings.* Nashville: Broadman & Holman Publishers, 2001.

Kaiser, Walter C, and Moises Silva. *Introduction to Biblical Hermeneutics: The Search for Meaning.* Grand Rapids: Zondervan, 1994, 2007.

Kittel, Gerhard, Gerhard Friedrich, and Geoffrey William Bromiley. *Theological Dictionary of the New Testament.* Grand Rapids: Eerdmans, 1995, c1985.

Lantz, Charles Craig. *Hermeneutics: The Art and Science of Biblical Interpretation.* Seattle, WA: Create Space, 2012.

Larson, Knute. *Holman New Testament Commentary, vol. 9, I & II Thessalonians, I & II Timothy, Titus, Philemon.* Nashville, TN: Broadman & Holman Publishers, 2000.

Lea, Thomas D. *Holman New Testament Commentary: Vol. 10, Hebrews, James.* Nashville, TN: Broadman & Holman Publishers, 1999.

—. *Holman New Testament Commentary: Vol. 10, Hebrews, James.* Nashville, TN: Broadman & Holman Publishers, 1999.

Lea, Thomas D., and Hayne P. Griffin. *The New American Commentary, vol. 34, 1, 2 Timothy, Titus.* Nashville: Broadman & Holman Publishers, 1992.

Martin, D Michael. *The New American Commentary 33 1, 2 Thessalonians* . Nashville, TN: Broadman & Holman, 2001, c1995 .

Martin, Glen S. *Holman Old Testament Commentary: Numbers.* Nashville: Broadman & Holman Publishers, 2002.

Mathews, K. A. *The New American Commentary vol. 1A, Genesis 1-11:26* . Nashville: Broadman & Holman Publishers, 2001.

Matthews, K. A. *The New American Commentary Vol. 1B, Genesis 11:27-50:26.* Nashville: Broadman and Holman Publishers, 2001.

Melick, Richard R. *The New American Commentary: vol. 32, Philippians, Colissians, Philemon.* Nashville, TN : Broadman & Holman Publishers, 2001.

Miller, Stephen R. *The New American Commentary: Volume 18 Daniel.* Nashville: Broadman & Holman Publishers, 1994.

Mirriam-Webster, Inc. *Mirriam-Webster's Collegiate Dictionary. Eleventh Edition.* Springfield: Mirriam-Webster, Inc., 2003.

Mounce, Robert H. *Romans: The New American Commentary 27.* Nashville: Broadman & Holman, 2001, c1995.

Mounce, Robert H. *The New American Commentary: Vol. 27 Romans.* Nashville, TN: Broadman & Holman Publishers, 2001.

Mounce, William D. *Mounce's Complete Expository Dictionary of Old & New Testament Words.* Grand Rapids, MI: Zondervan, 2006.

Polhill, John B. *The New American Commentary 26: Acts.* Nashville: Broadman & Holman Publishers, 2001.

Pratt Jr, Richard L. *Holman New Testament Commentary: I & II Corinthians, vol. 7.* Nashville: Broadman & Holman Publishers, 2000.

Ramm, Bernard. *Protestant Biblical Interpretation: A Textbook of Hermeneutics, 3rd rev. ed.* Grand Rapids, MI: Baker, 1999.

Richardson, Kurt. *The New American Commentary Vol. 36 James.* Nashville: Broadman & Holman Publishers, 1997.

Robinson, G. L., and R. K. Harrison. *The International Standard Bible Encyclopedia, vol. 2.* Grand Rapids: Eerdmans, 1982.

Rooker, Mark F. *The New American Commentary, vol. 3A, Leviticus.* Nashville: Broadman & Holman Publishers, 2000.

—. *Holman Old Testament Commentary: Ezekiel.* Nashville: Broadman & Holman Publishers, 2005.

Schreiner, Thomas R. *The New American Commentary: 1, 2 Peter, Jude.* Nashville: Broadman & Holman, 2003.

Smith, Gary. *The New American Commentary: Isaiah 1-39, Vol. 15a.* Nashville, TN: B & H Publishing Group, 2007.

—. *The New American Commentary: Isaiah 40-66, Vol. 15b.* Nashville, TN: B&H Publishing, 2009.

Stein, Robert H. *A Basic Guide to Interpreting the Bible: Playing by the Rules.* Grand Rapids: Baker Books, 1994.

—. *The New American Commentary: Luke.* Nashville, TN: Broadman & Holman , 2001, c1992.

Stuart, Douglas K. *The New American Commentary: An Exegetical Theological Exposition of Holy Scripture EXODUS.* Nashville: Broadman & Holman, 2006.

Taylor, Richard A, and Ray E Clendenen. *The New American Commentary: Haggai, Malachi, , vol. 21A .* Nashville, TN: Broadman & Holman Publishers, 2007.

Tenney, Merrill C. et. al. *Zondervan Pictorial Encyclopedia of the Bible.* Grand Rapids: Zondervan, 1975.

Terry, Milton S. *Biblical Hermeneutics: A Treatise on the Interpretation of the Old and New Testaments.* Grand Rapids: Zondervan, 1974.

—. *Biblical Hermeneutics: A Treatise on the Interpretation of the Old and New Testaments.* Grand Rapids: Zondervan, 1883.

Thomas, Robert L. *Evangelical Hermeneutics.* Grand Rapids: Kregel Publications, 2002.

Vine, W E. *Vine's Expository Dictionary of Old and New Testament Words.* Nashville: Thomas Nelson, 1996.

Virkler, Henry A, and Karelynne Gerber Ayayo. *Hermeneutics: Principles and Processes of Biblical Interpretation.* Grand Rapids, MI: Baker Academic, 1981, 2007.

Walls, David, and Max Anders. *Holman New Testament Commentary: I & II Peter, I, II & III John, Jude.* Nashville: Broadman & Holman Publishers, 1996.

Watson, Richard. *A Biblical and Theological Dictionary: Explanatory of the History, Manners and Customs of the Jews.* New York: Waugh and T. Mason, 1832.

Weber, Stuart K. *Holman New Testament Commentary, vol. 1, Matthew.* Nashville, TN: Broadman & Holman Publishers, 2000.

Wood, D R W. *New Bible Dictionary (Third Edition).* Downers Grove: InterVarsity Press, 1996.

Zuck, Roy B. *Basic Bible Interpretation: A Prafctical Guide to Discovering Biblical Truth.* Colorado Springs: David C. Cook, 1991.

Made in the USA
Las Vegas, NV
02 May 2021